IMAGES
of America

WEEHAWKEN

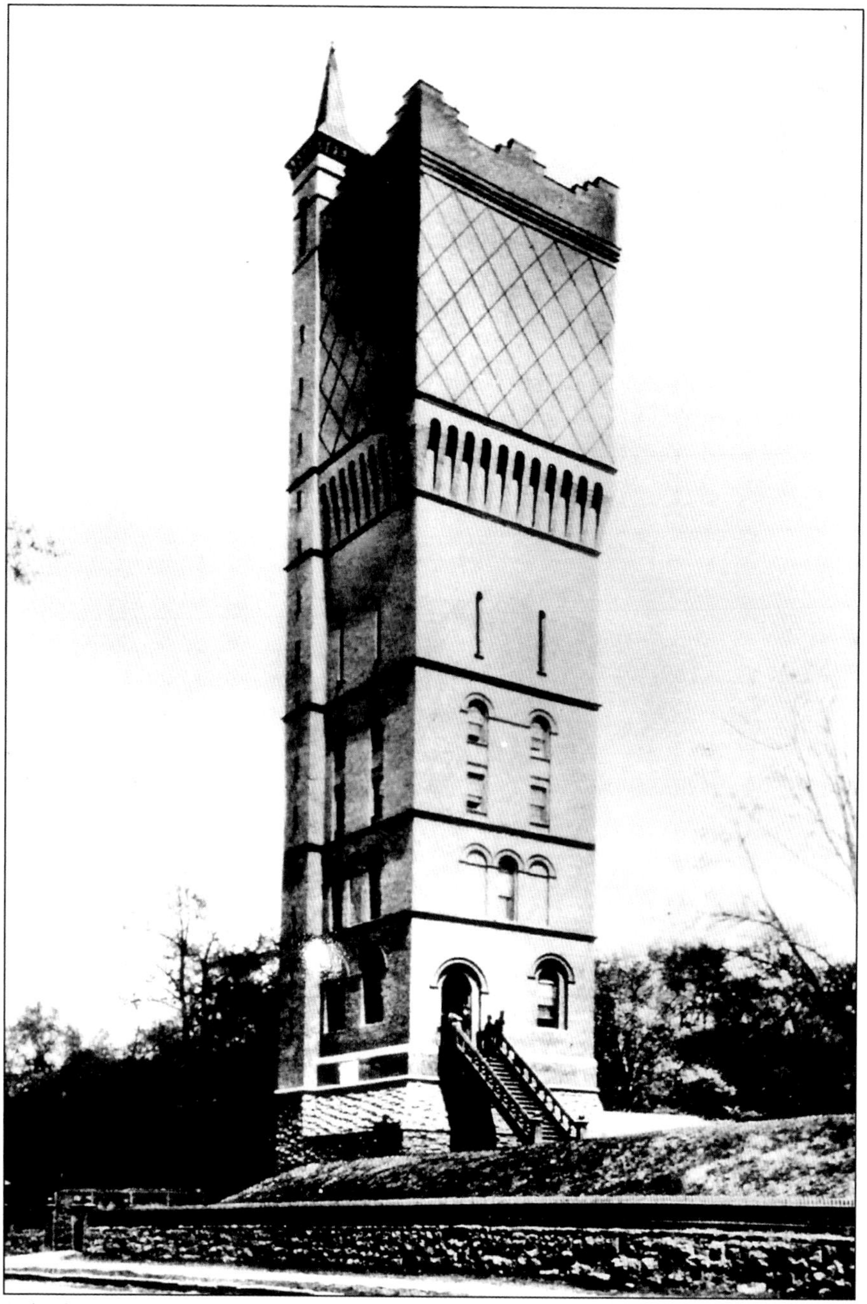

In 1885, the free-standing Hackensack Water Company's water tower rose above Bulls Ferry Road in a countrified setting. After a century and a quarter, the Weehawken Water Tower, its exterior handsomely restored, still stands tall amidst the bustle of a main commercial thoroughfare and remains an iconic symbol of the township of Weehawken. (United Water.)

On the cover: The Palisade Hose Company No. 2, organized in 1896, is posed in full regalia at the dawn of the 20th century near its Jane Street headquarters on the Weehawken heights. (Weehawken Historical Commission.)

IMAGES
of America

WEEHAWKEN

Lauren Sherman and Ellen Robb Gaulkin
for the Weehawken Historical Commission

ARCADIA
PUBLISHING

Copyright © 2009 by Lauren Sherman and Ellen Robb Gaulkin for the Weehawken Historical Commission
ISBN 978-0-7385-6268-1

Published by Arcadia Publishing
Charleston, South Carolina

Printed in the United States of America

Library of Congress Catalog Card Number: 2008933017

For all general information contact Arcadia Publishing at:
Telephone 843-853-2070
Fax 843-853-0044
E-mail sales@arcadiapublishing.com
For customer service and orders:
Toll-Free 1-888-313-2665

Visit us on the Internet at www.arcadiapublishing.com

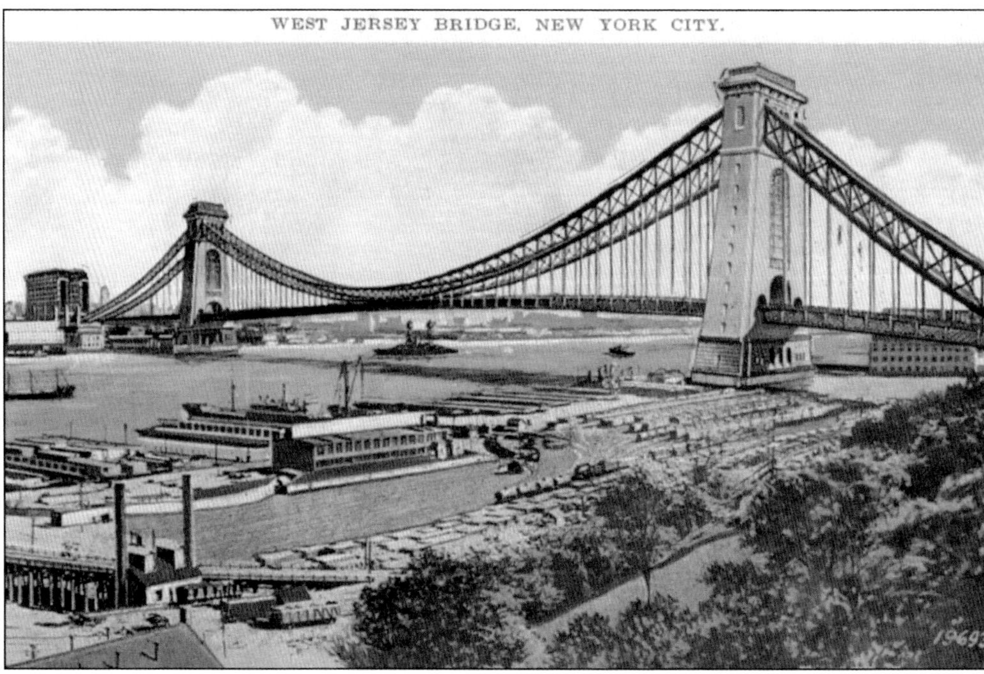

If civil engineer and bridge designer Gustav Lindenthal had his way, Weehawken would have been the New Jersey terminus of a suspension bridge linking 57th Street in Manhattan and the northern border of Weehawken. His original 1920s proposal called for a double-deck bridge, with the upper deck carrying 20 lanes of traffic and two pedestrian walkways. The lower level was to have 12 lanes of rapid transit. The width of the bridge was a mere 235 feet. (Willie Demontreux.)

Contents

ACKNOWLEDGMENTS

The authors and the Weehawken Historical Commission thank all of our friends and neighbors for sharing their photographs, postcards, and stories. We are particularly grateful to our colleagues, Al Berg and Willie Demontreux. Al's extraordinary and extensive collection of Weehawken memorabilia and Willie's broad-based personal knowledge of the community's history and ability to track down many significant images have been invaluable to this effort.

Special mention is offered to Patricia Hannan and the Hannan family for an outstanding historical donation to the commission, Donna Testa of United Water, Virginia Hessner, Barbara Hansen, Cindy Dally Cimino, Jim and Evelyn Dette, Steve Dorio, Ruth Elsasser, Mark Gould, Bill Applegate of Elks Lodge No. 1456, Marlene Brandt Riley, Michael Weber of the Nuertingen Town Council, Dr. Peter Oliveri, Billy Rapacki, Cheryl Burns Mansfield, the Charlesworth family, Joe Bradley, Pat Sullivan, Donna Jandik, Rev. L. W. Guilfoyle Jr. of the Park United Methodist Church, Jean Kiralfy Kent, Jean Meister Pierson, Alane Finnerty, Thomas Flagg, the Weehawken Public Library, and Mayor Richard F. Turner and the Weehawken Township Council in appreciation of their assistance and support. Our good wishes go to former Weehawken Historical Commission chair Edward Fleckenstein and special thanks to Marie Alberian for her many years of support to our historical endeavors.

We would also like to thank our Arcadia editor Erin Rocha.

We are beholden to the patience of Bruce and Geoff.

Finally, in the name of the Weehawken Historical Commission, we remember and honor two remarkable people, Lillie M. Stokes (1893–1996) and Edward J. Kirk (1892–1961). We are indebted to these preservers of Weehawken's past.

This volume follows Weehawken's history through 1959, just after the completion of the third Lincoln Tunnel tube and its centennial celebration. Of course its history continues, but we leave the next 50 years and beyond to a new generation of historians.

Images used in this book, unless otherwise noted, are from the collection of the Weehawken Historical Commission.

INTRODUCTION

The recorded history of Weehawken traces back to October 2, 1609, when Henry Hudson, in search of a more direct trade route to the far eastern trading posts of the Dutch East India Company, anchored the *Half Moon* in Weehawken cove below a great promontory of 200-foot rock cliffs. An entry that day in the ship's log registered the imposing geography of the river's western shore.

Hudson's exploration did not yield a new passage to the East, but by 1621, the Dutch laid claim to a trading colony covering the mid-Atlantic section of the North American continent with its principal trading post of New Amsterdam on the island of Manhattan. On the west bank of the Hudson River, the Dutch settlement of Bergen developed over the area that is now Hudson and Bergen Counties. While national territorial claims changed from Dutch to English to American, that local governmental entity lasted into the 19th century.

The first Weehawken settlement is registered in a 1647 deed for 50 Dutch morgens (100 acres) of land in "Awiehaken," granted to Maryn Andriaesen, considered the township's first settler. Within a generation, a small encampment of houses, barns, and a gristmill had grown around a creek in the lowlands below the Palisades about where the Lincoln Tunnel helix now stands. As early as 1690, a ferry service began between "Wiehacken" and Manhattan to transport produce to New York from the farms that were developing in Bergen. In 1718, the Hackensack Plank Road was built over the rugged cliffs to further facilitate movement to and from the hinterlands of New Jersey and beyond. Those were the beginnings of Weehawken's importance as a transit connection.

The meaning of the name Weehawken is uncertain. It is generally believed to be derived from Native American language, probably of the Leni Lenape, but decoding of the indigenous word is confused by the various spellings recorded by 17th century Europeans including Whehockan, Weehacken, and Wehauk. Linguistic theories generally relate the name to the visual landscape: rocks that look like trees, open land without trees, open tract between streams, the end of the Palisades, perhaps even a man-made gristmill. No definitive explanation is agreed upon nor is it known when the present spelling was generally accepted.

In the 18th and early 19th centuries, the cliffs of the Palisades remained wild, a perfect locale for the clandestine dueling proclivities of men of honor from the city of New York, where such illegal activity was stringently prosecuted. Of the 18 documented duels, the most famous was the Hamilton-Burr debacle of July 11, 1804, in which the sitting vice president of the United States, Aaron Burr, mortally wounded his political nemesis of many years, Gen. Alexander Hamilton, constitutional statesman and first secretary of the treasury of the new republic. This singular piece of dueling history has fascinated inhabitants and visitors alike since that day. The event has been memorialized in Weehawken on its 100th and 150th and on its 200th anniversary in 2004 with a duel re-enactment by descendants of the protagonists before more than 1,000 spectators.

The pastoral landscape also attracted 19th-century New Yorkers seeking escape from the urban tumult across the river. Day excursions for genteel city dwellers to the Weehawken shore were popular, and more robust climbs into the wooded cliffs offered the romantic spirit, fresh air, and splendid views. Notable families of wealth established comfortable estates on the uplands. Early engravings offer a glimpse of this idyllic lifestyle as does an 1830 poem by the poet and essayist Fitz-Greene Halleck: "Weehawken, in the mountain scenery set, / All we adore of nature in her wild."

The political entity of Bergen evolved over the course of time. In 1840, Hudson County was formed, separated from Bergen County, and began to split into individual towns. The township of Weehawken, barely a square mile in area, was incorporated on March 15, 1859, with a meager population of 269, but from that time on through the remainder of the 19th century, the town was drawn into the inexorable growth of an industrializing nation and an expanding metropolitan port.

In the 1880s, Weehawken was still sparsely populated, with about 1,100 inhabitants, while Hoboken on its southern border had already grown to 30,000. A plan to provide clean water to Hoboken brought the technologically remarkable and aesthetically unique Hackensack Water Company's 175-foot water tower, designed by renowned architect Frederick Clarke Withers.

In the early 1890s, there was still enough vacant acreage in Weehawken for the development of Eldorado, a grand pleasure garden atop the Palisades, described in an 1891 advertising handbill as overlooking the "noble Hudson" and the great "metropolis of the new world" and offering "shady walks, Moorish pavilions, mammoth fountains and a vast amphitheatre" where theatrical extravaganzas with casts of thousands were produced. The Eldorado was a hugely popular summer entertainment destination. New Yorkers arrived by ferry and were carried up the Palisades on an enormous passenger elevator, another engineering wonder of the time.

The Eldorado lasted only four seasons, but its demise opened up an extremely lucrative real estate opportunity. A development brochure of the Eldorado Realty Company shows large, fashionable homes laid out in an elegant parklike setting beckoning city dwellers to a suburban lifestyle in proximity to the commercial and cultural benefits of Manhattan. Many of these homes are still in existence and attract New Yorkers for the breathtaking skyline views.

However, by virtue of its location on the Hudson River opposite New York City, a growing population demanded more than stately homesteads for the affluent. As development surged in Manhattan so too did it flourish on the Jersey side. Railroads and shipping dominated the waterfront, streets were laid out, factories and houses were built, schools, churches and hospitals were established, and police and fire departments were organized. In the 50 years following its 1859 incorporation, Weehawken's population grew more than 40-fold to over 11,000 residents in 1910.

In its 400-year history, Weehawken has moved from rural outpost to full integration into the most densely populated region of the country. Its adjacence to midtown Manhattan brought the construction of the Lincoln Tunnel to accommodate the vast increase in traffic in and out of New York City. Yet today despite intense urbanization and its unique position as a gateway to a great metropolis, Weehawken has maintained much of its small-town character. The population has remained level at about 13,500, the residential neighborhoods of the early 20th century are intact, and the community is closely knit. Still, change and renewal will continue with redevelopment of the waterfront from abandoned railroad yards to luxury condominiums and offices and with restoration of ferry service to New York.

One

The Early Days

Weehawken's celebrity began in the late 1700s as its terrain was reckoned ideal for the fine art of the duel. Hidden glades below the Palisades provided verdant cover for this clandestine activity.

The events that defined the ultimate character of this little town on the Palisades began when New York banking magnate James Gore King moved his family to Weehawken in 1832. He was one of the first to realize the locale's benefits of peace, quiet, fresh air, and breathtaking scenery within commuting distance of the hurly-burly of New York City. King built his beloved home, Highwood, on 50 wooded acres encompassing all of the Weehawken bluff and set the tone for a lifestyle that would be enjoyed by only a handful of wealthy and notable families through the balance of the 19th century. The homes are gone or greatly altered, but many of their names have survived in the neighborhoods and streets.

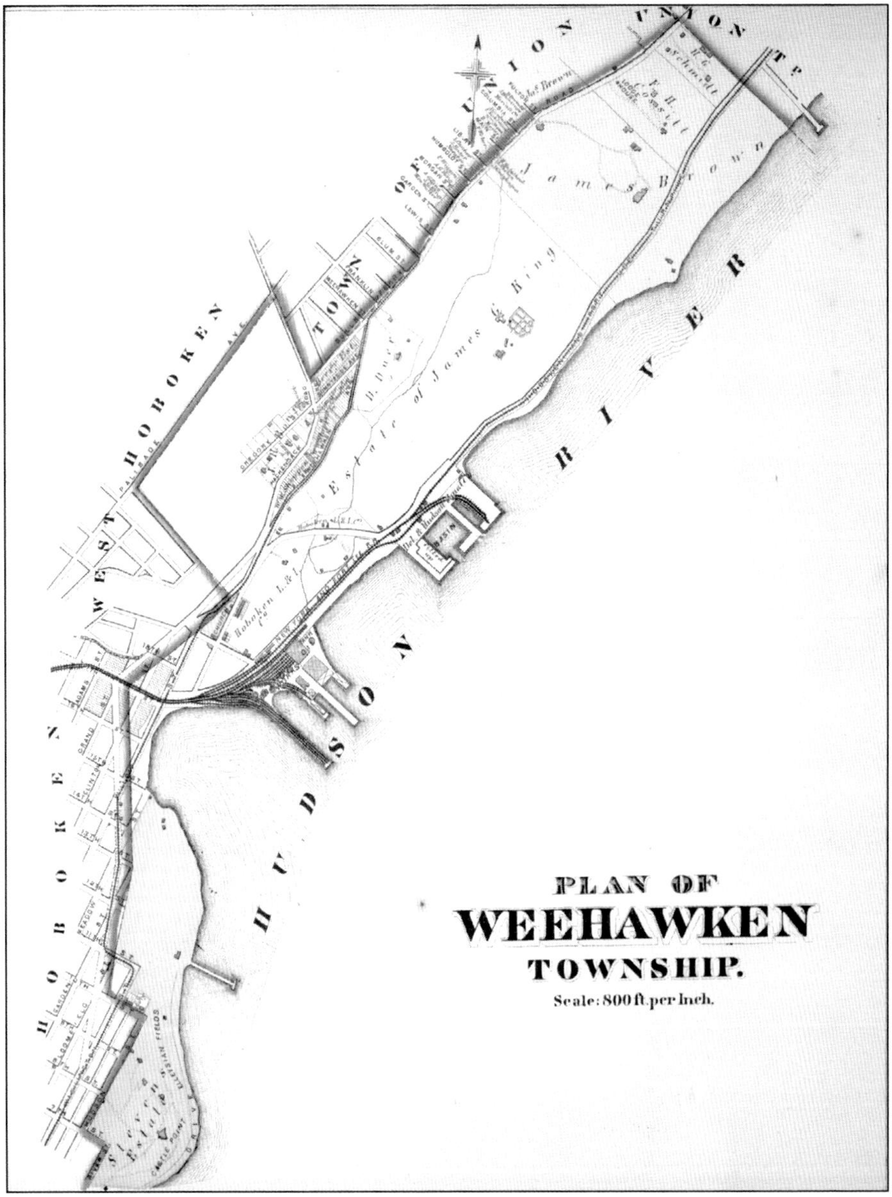

This map was part of an undertaking of surveys by G. M. Hopkins, civil engineer, in 1873. Though Hoboken, West Hoboken, and Union (Union City) were already bustling cities, most of Weehawken remained a series of large estates owned by wealthy New York businessmen who either lived in Manhattan and chose Weehawken as their summer home or had relocated here. Among the largest estates were those of James Gore King (1791–1853), whose property was the most extensive; James Brown (1790–1877); and Denning Duer (1812–1891). Frederick H. Cossitt (1811–1887) and Henry G. Schmidt (1827–1881) owned smaller estates, and the Hoboken Land and Improvement Company owned smaller but valuable parcels adjacent to the Hudson River. The Heights section encompassed the large properties of John H. Bonn (1829–1891) and William W. Shippen (1827–1885). The waterfront area was already quite developed with the construction of various railroad lines, oil tanks, and the Delaware and Hudson Canal Company's coal basin. (Library of Congress.)

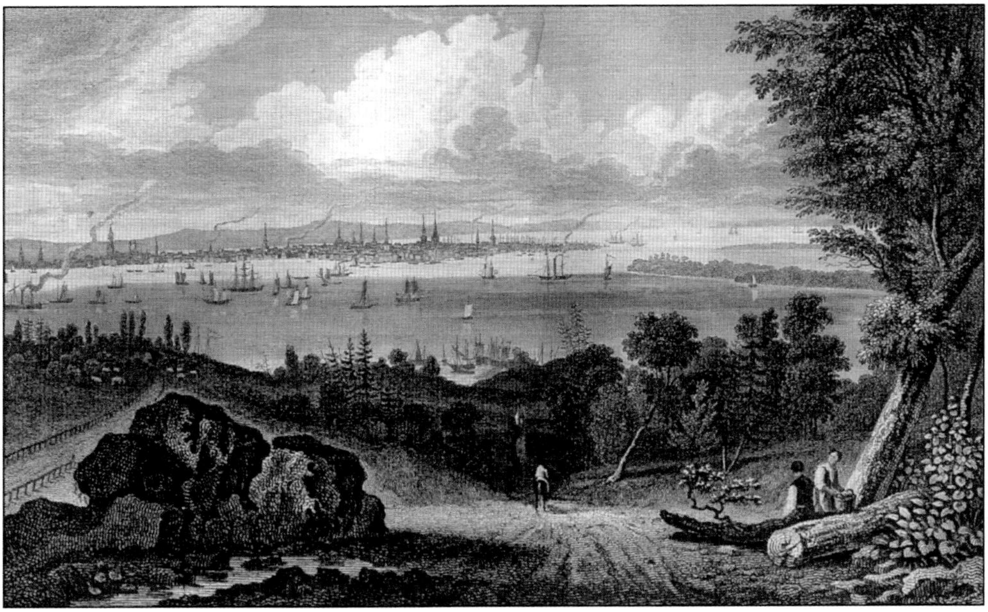

This German engraving, with its long view of the Hudson River across to lower Manhattan, illustrates the bucolic splendors of the area in the mid-19th century. An active Hudson River (then the North River), rustic country roads, and a picnicking couple in the foreground are romantically depicted. The right mid-ground includes a view of Castle Point, annexed to Weehawken from 1859 until 1876 when it was reassigned to Hoboken. (Lauren Sherman.)

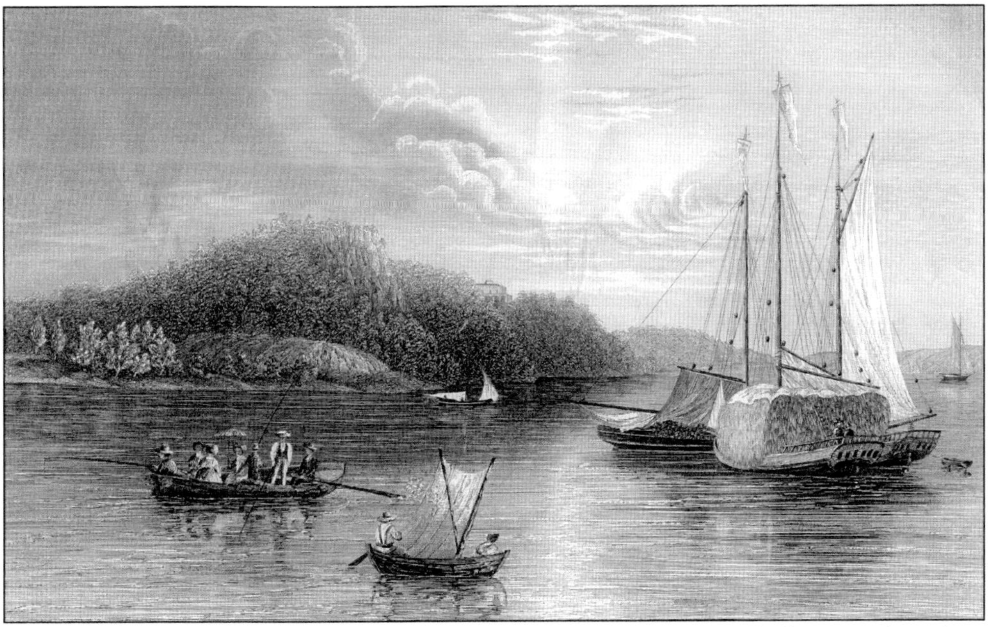

On the west riverbank of the Hudson River, the hills gently rise to the bluff or "Devil's Pulpit" as it was sometimes called, with Highwood in the distance. At right, two boats are engaged in transporting a large load of salt hay, a valuable crop used for insulation, construction, and as packing material. Harvested in salt marshes, it was then cut, dried, and loaded onto a shallow scow and towed by pole boats to be shipped to market. (Charlesworth family.)

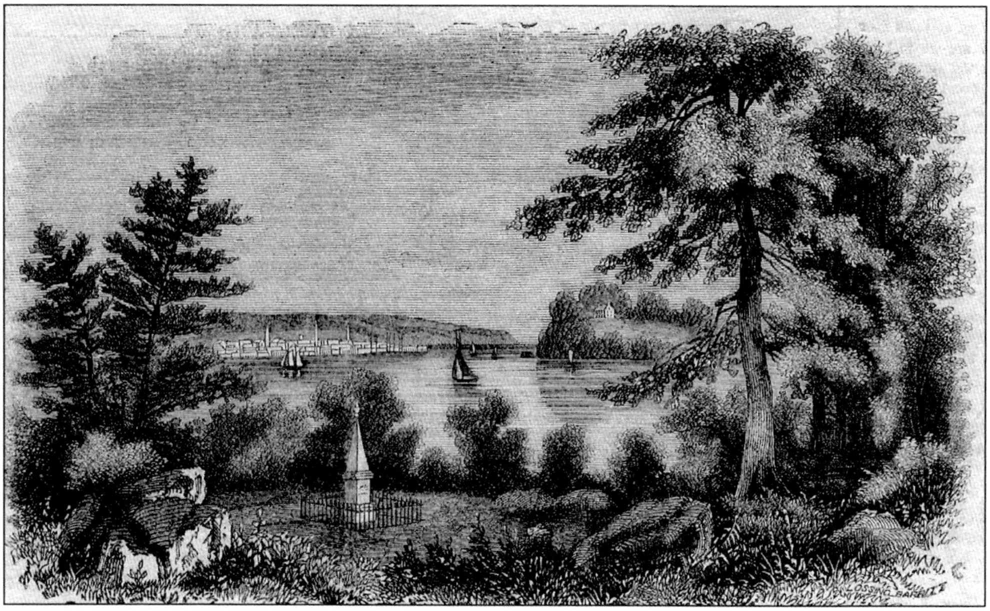

When Alexander Hamilton died in 1804 after the infamous duel with Aaron Burr, there was a great hue and cry among New Yorkers and an invigorated discussion of the evils of dueling. In 1806, the St. Andrew's Society of the state of New York, of which Hamilton had been a member, erected this first memorial, a marble cenotaph with an obelisk on top. This memorial remained in place on the dueling grounds for the next 15 years.

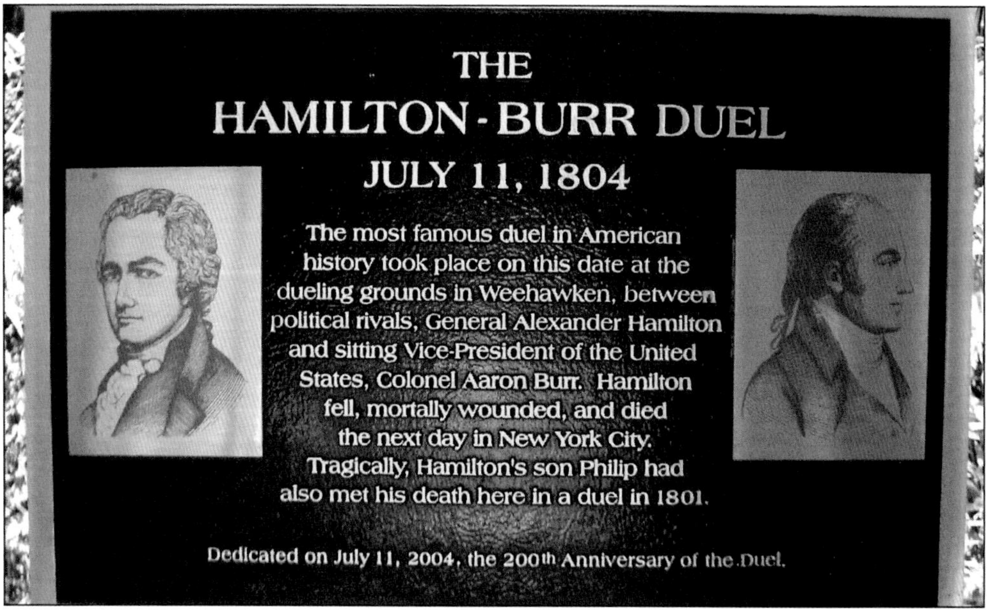

Aside from the two duels above, there were 16 other documented "affairs of honor" that took place on an isolated, wooded ledge located on the Palisades, about 20 feet above the Hudson River. This plaque marks the 200th anniversary commemoration of this notorious duel. Participating in the dedication were Hamilton and Burr family members, the Aaron Burr Association, the St. Andrew's Society of the State of New York, Mayor Richard F. Turner, and the Weehawken Township Council. (Ellen Robb Gaulkin.)

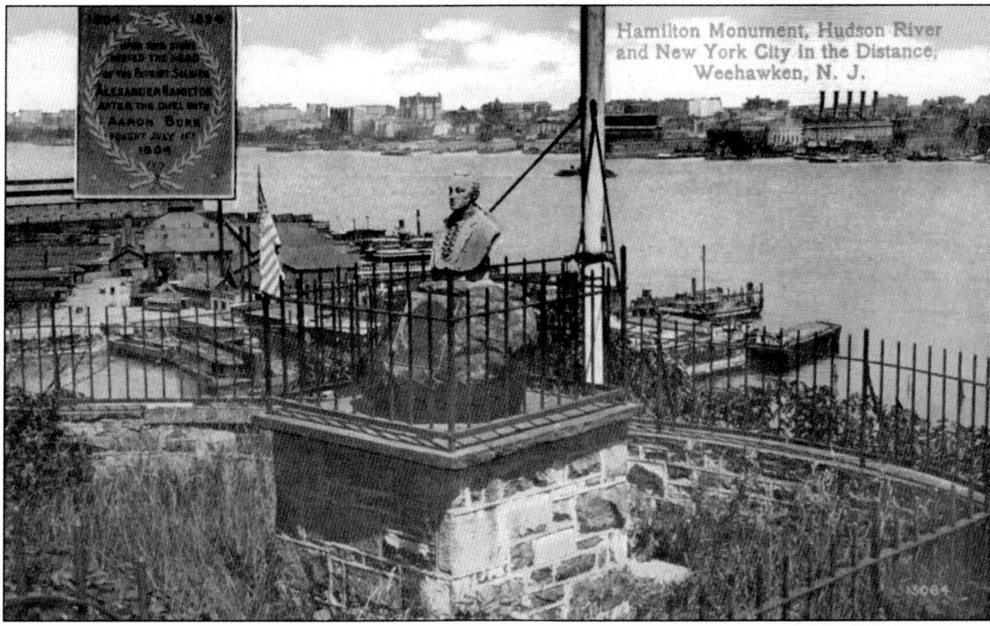

The St. Andrew's monument was destroyed by anti-dueling protesters in 1821, and the dueling grounds were cut away from the Palisades to accommodate the railroads in the late 1850s. In 1894, a new memorial to Alexander Hamilton was erected on Hamilton Avenue to replace the original. The monument included a stone bust and the rock that Hamilton was said to have laid his head on after having been mortally wounded. In 1934, the weathered bust was vandalized and soon replaced with a bronze bust by local sculptor, John Repetti, who designed the soldiers and sailors monument nearby. The memorial, shown at right in a 1950s postcard, was refurbished with the Hamilton Park and Boulevard East promenade renovations in the 1990s. (Al Berg.)

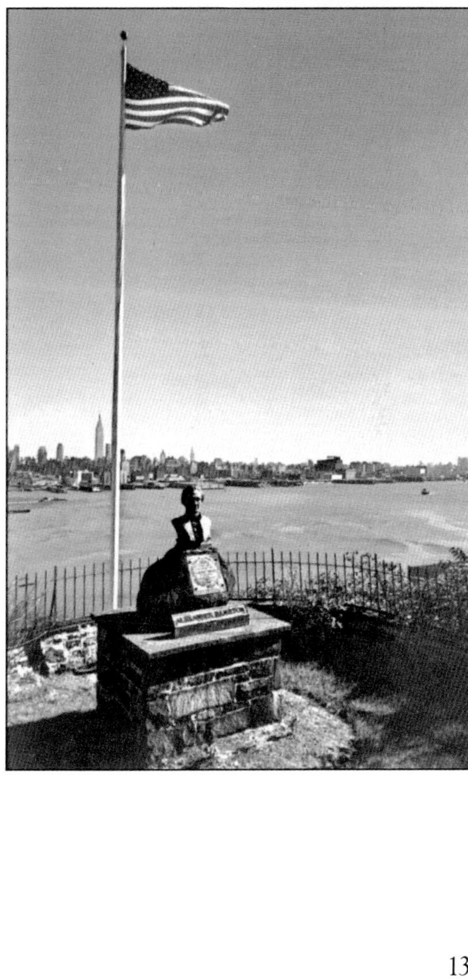

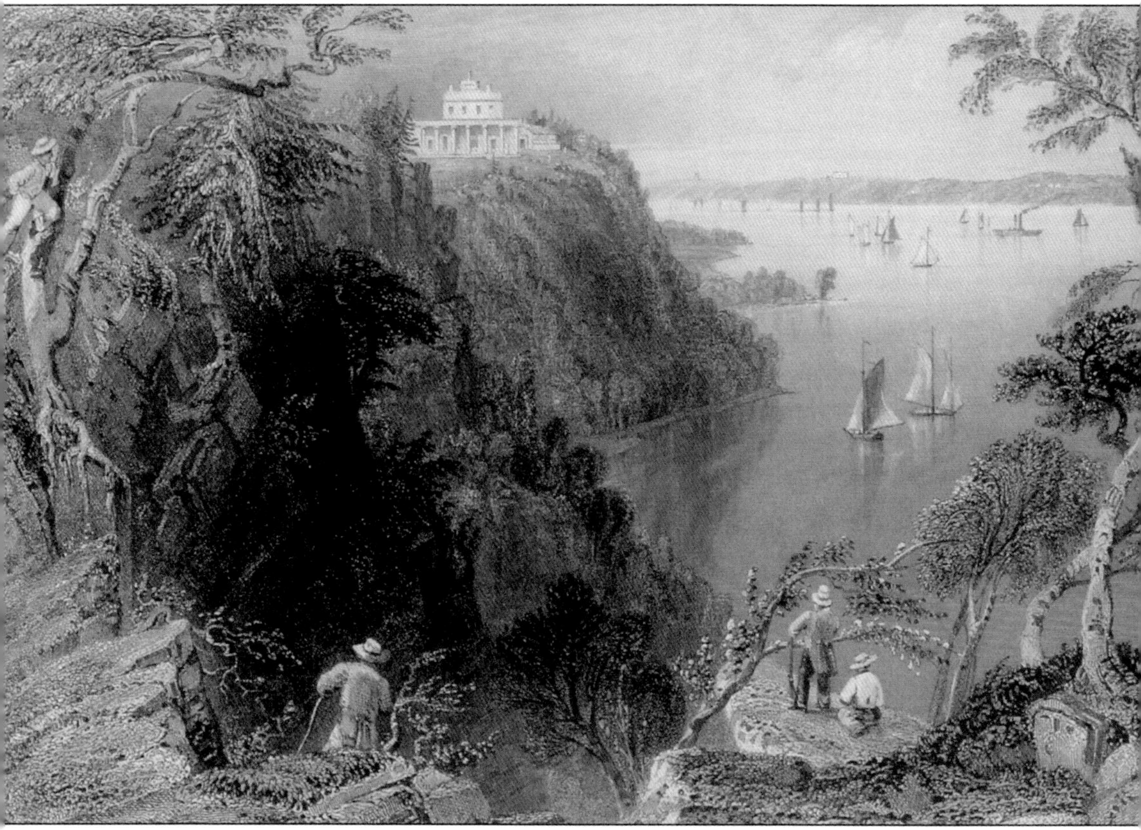

This engraving by W. B. Bartlett, titled *Villa on the Hudson*, with its view of the Hudson River and the Palisades, illustrates the unspoiled nature of the environs in 1836 pocketed with adventurous sightseers climbing their way to picturesque spots. Highwood, built near the edge of the bluff, was the home of James Gore King. Born in 1791 the son of Rufus King, a United States senator and statesman, James was a New York banker of influential Wall Street firm James G. King and Sons. He was also president of the Erie Railroad for a time and served in Congress. Built in 1832, Highwood became a gathering place for the wealthy in New York society. Frequent guests included Charles Dickens, Washington Irving, Daniel Webster, and the poet Fitz-Greene Halleck. Though the home was rather plain, the grounds were spectacular, with extensive gardens, fruit orchards, rustic bridges, and streams and paths winding through King's Woods. James died in 1853 while at Highwood after a brief illness. (Ellen Robb Gaulkin.)

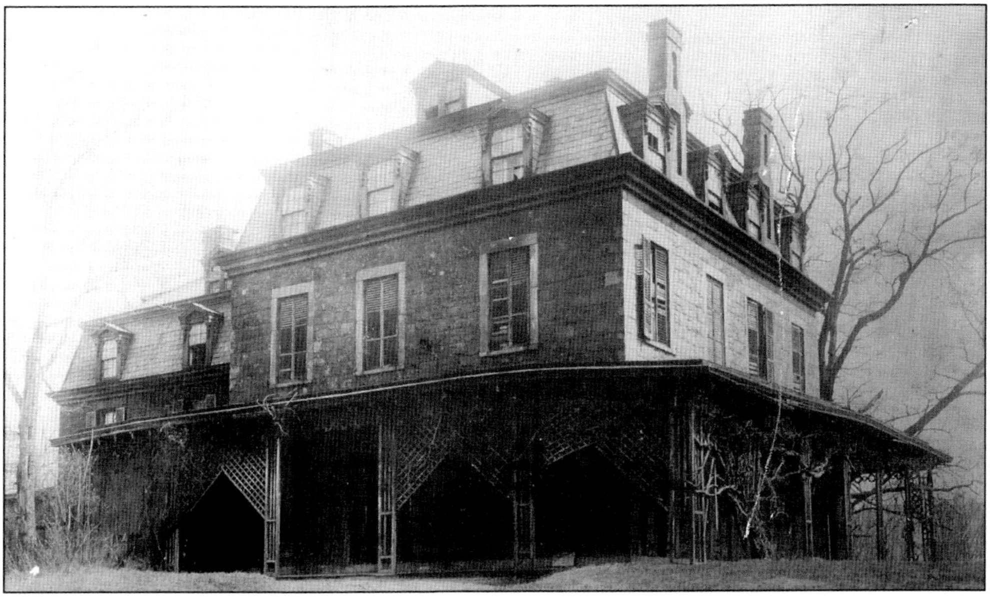

Hauxhurst was the country residence of Denning Duer, a New York banker and the son of William A. Duer, a president of Columbia College. Denning's father-in-law, James Gore King, built the mansion in 1848 for his daughter, Caroline and her husband; soon thereafter, Denning joined King's firm. The house was situated near the intersection of Sterling Avenue and Denning Place where Woodrow Wilson School now stands. This photograph from about 1900 shows the house in a state of disrepair, about nine years after Denning's death.

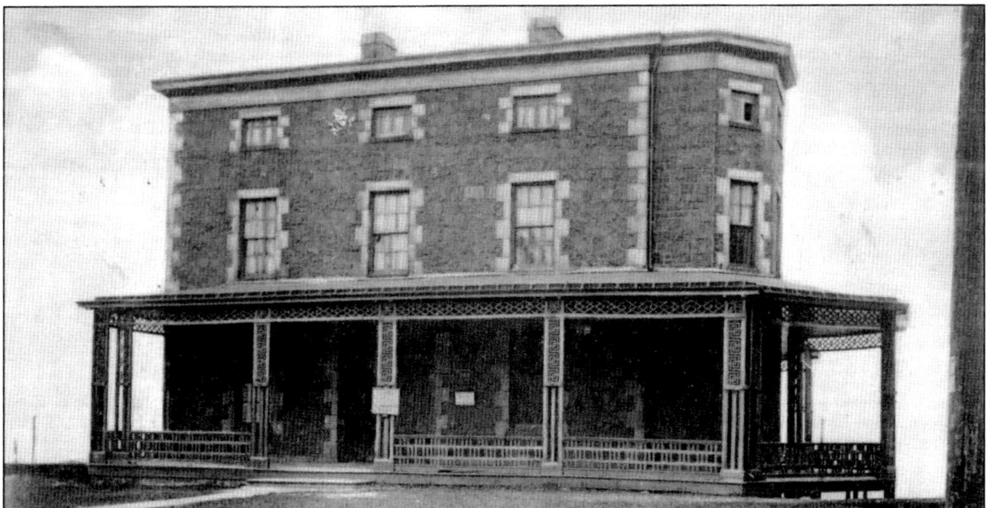

The Brown mansion is probably the oldest extant building in Weehawken. The original part of the house still stands behind Louisa Park and belongs to the Shri Swaminarayan Mandir, a Hindu temple. Once the country home of James Brown, owner of the New York banking firm Brown Brothers and Company, it was called Clifton, and the area became known as Clifton Park. His daughter Mary Louisa married Howard Potter, and both lent their names to surrounding streets. After Brown's death, the building was enlarged as the Clifton Chapel of the Grove Reformed Church in 1913. For a time, it was also a Christian Science Church until changing hands in 1986. (Al Berg.)

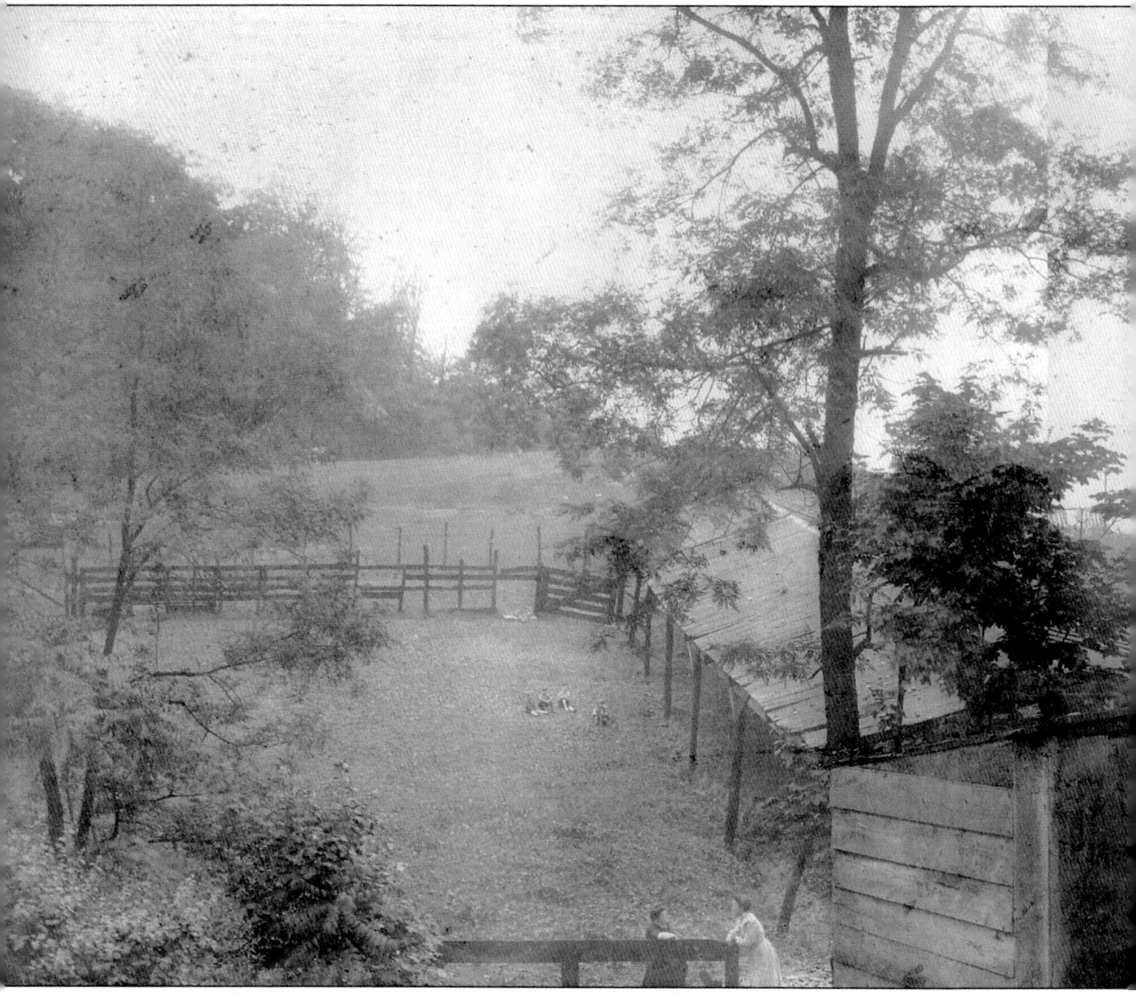

This pastoral scene photographed in about 1895 was called Cunningham's Hill, an area located near the foot of the river between the helix to the west and the beginning of the rise of the Palisades at the bluff. Visible are cattle sheds and farm animals, a pair of women talking over a rustic fence, and children at play. Within a few years, the area was transformed; the Erie

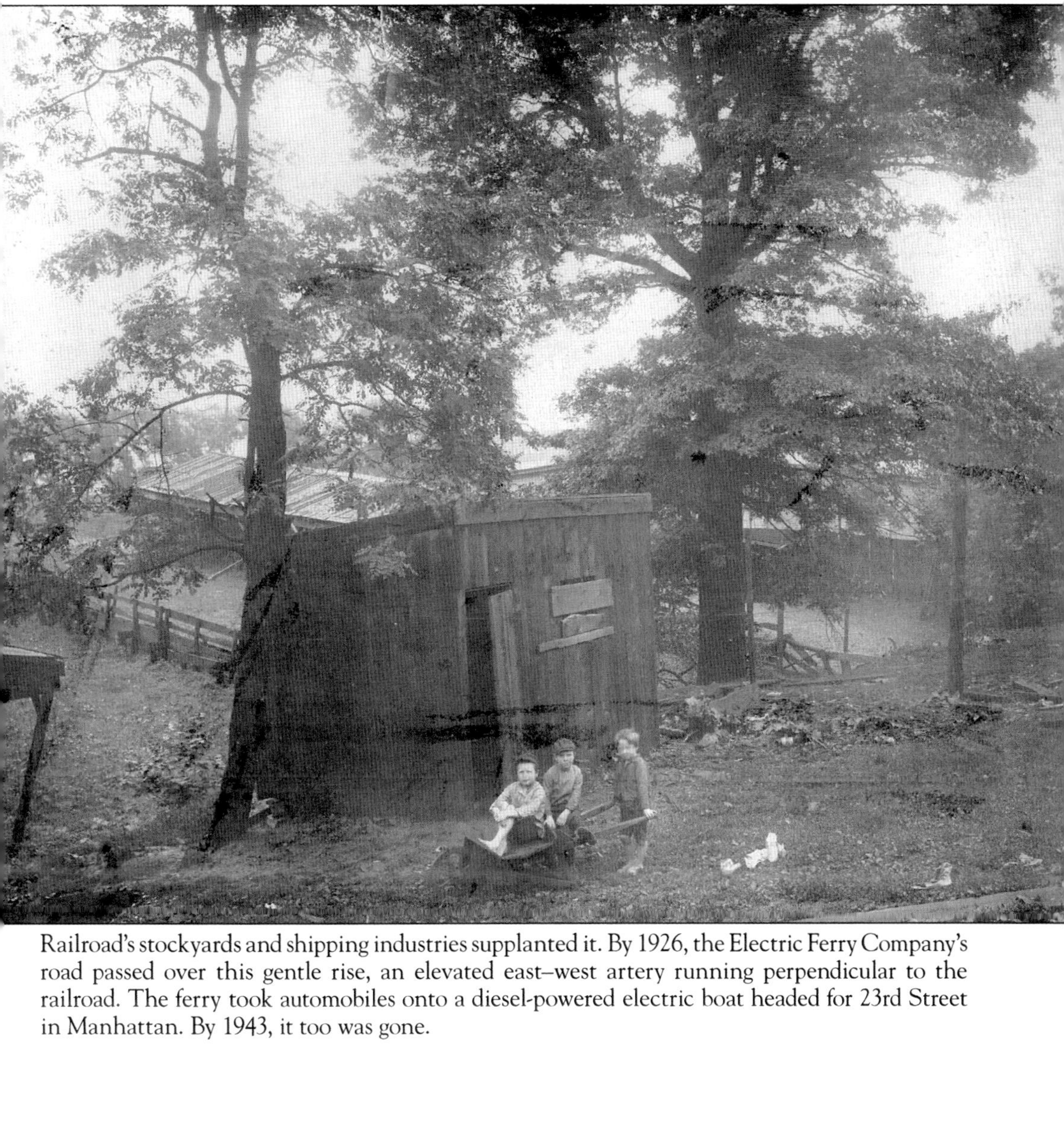

Railroad's stockyards and shipping industries supplanted it. By 1926, the Electric Ferry Company's road passed over this gentle rise, an elevated east–west artery running perpendicular to the railroad. The ferry took automobiles onto a diesel-powered electric boat headed for 23rd Street in Manhattan. By 1943, it too was gone.

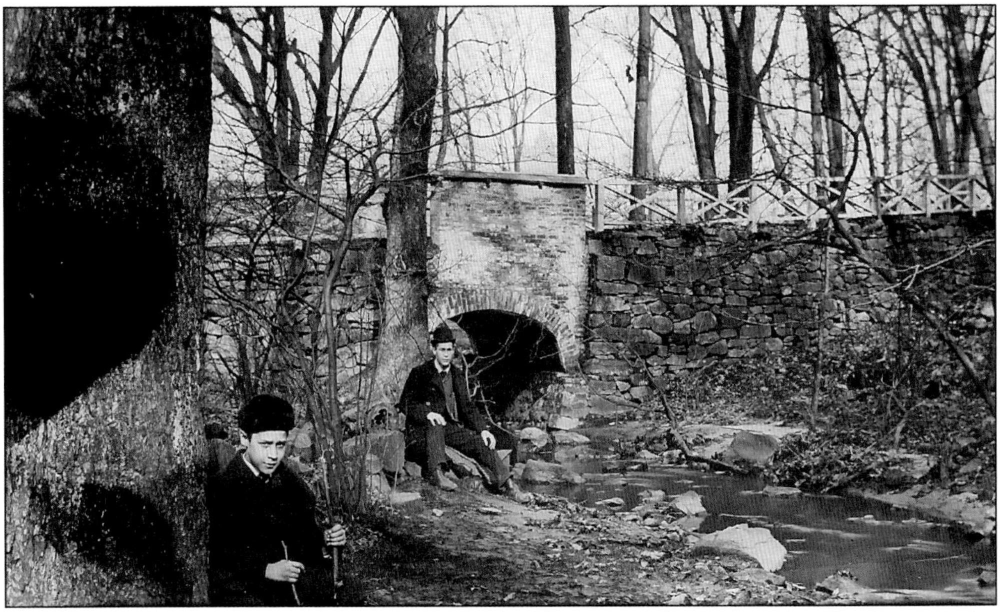

Pictured above are two young nature lovers backed by a rustic bridge and wooden fence in the Kingswood area of Weehawken. From the 1830s through the early 1890s, upper Weehawken was wooded and unspoiled. This brook once ran from the Highwood estate of James Gore King down towards the current site of the Lincoln tunnel helix. Below, further along the brook that leads down into the valley, three well-dressed gentlemen in bowler hats are perched on the rocks above. It was said that the brook was so plentiful with trout that one could cast a line and just pull them in. These views were photographed in the early 1890s by C. J. Ahrnke, who lived at 17 Bonn Place.

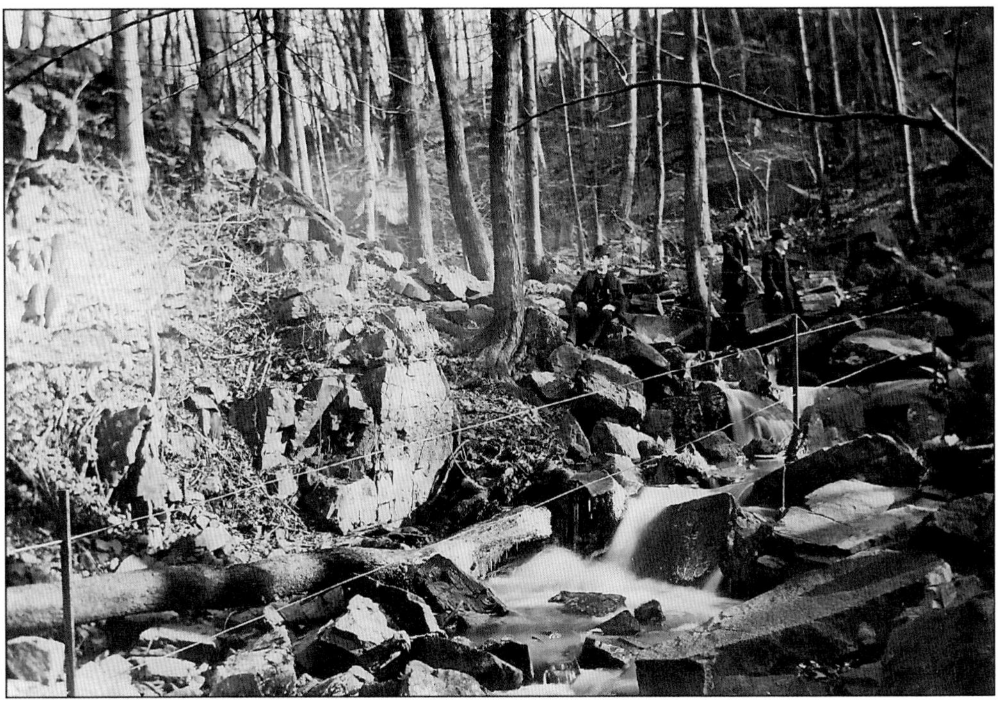

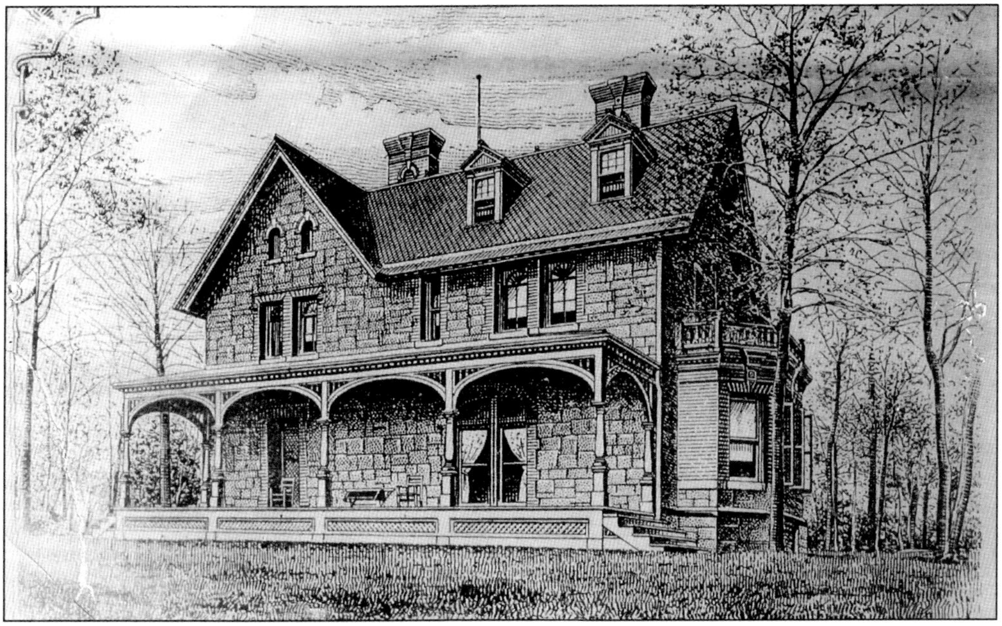

The Bluff, or Highwood Bluff, was the home of Archibald Gracie King, son of James Gore and Sarah Gracie King. He married Elizabeth Denning Duer, once again uniting these two powerful families and estates. The late Victorian stone house was located on Kingswood Road midway to the end of the bluff. Archibald died in 1897 of bronchitis, and after a long illness, his wife died in 1900. Both the Bluff and Highwood were destroyed by fire.

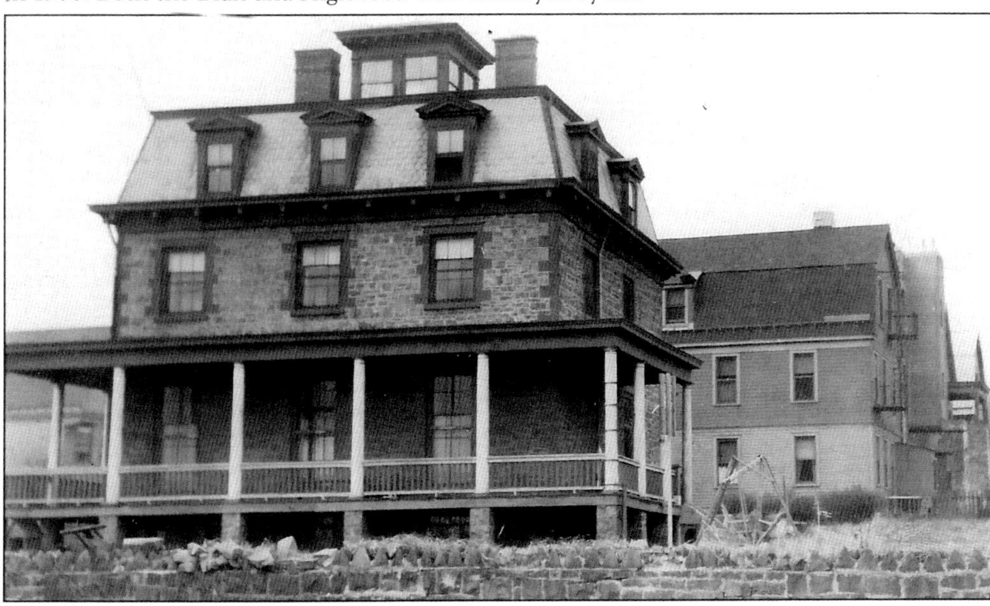

Now headquarters for Weehawken Elks Lodge No. 1456 at 50th Street and Boulevard East, this was once the home of Henry G. Schmidt, or "Champagne Schmidt," as he was called, a wealthy wine merchant and importer who died in 1881. H. G. Schmidt and Company's New York offices were located at 38 Beaver Street; this was his country home at the northern border of Weehawken. This view from the boulevard shows the stone house as it appeared before renovations in 1935.

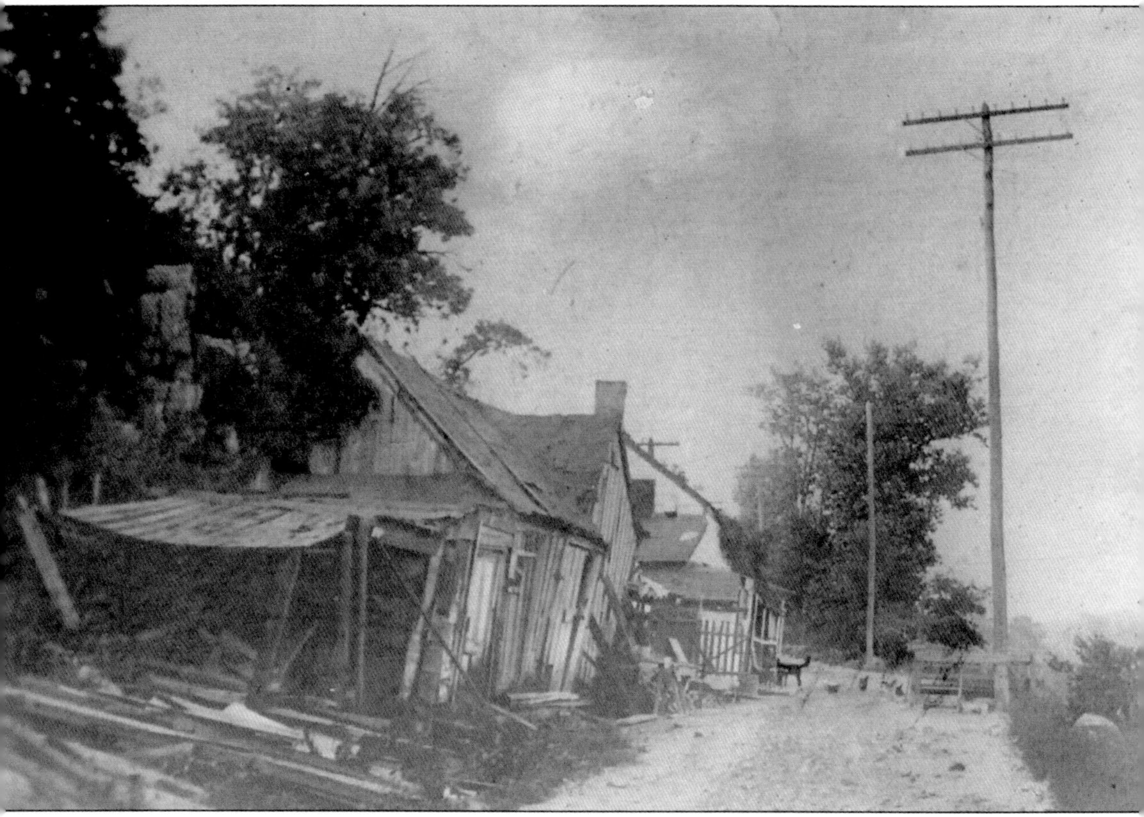

Hackensack Plank Road, one of the earliest roads from Colonial times, was laid out in 1718. The old plank road, also known as the Hackensack or Bergen Turnpike and built with a surface of plank decking, took travelers from Hoboken up through Weehawken, North Bergen, and on to Hackensack. It became a toll road in 1802, with tolls costing three-quarters of a cent for single vehicles and one-and-one-half cents for horses. It had a travel speed of three miles per hour. The tollhouse and gate were located where the road begins its climb upward from Nineteenth Street. From 1840 until 1875, Sam Ryer was the toll keeper. He was succeeded by William Miller, who was toll keeper from 1876 until he died in 1925. This photograph, showing a dog, chickens, and a dilapidated building, was probably taken between 1916 and 1924. The building was razed in 1927.

Two

THE WATER TOWER

In the early 1880s, Weehawken counted 1,100 citizens, whereas Hoboken, just to the south, was already a booming waterfront city of 30,000 and needed a sanitary water system. The Hackensack Water Company, a fledgling private water company in Bergen County, was contracted to provide the means for pumping Hackensack River water to a new reservoir to be built near Hoboken. Weehawken offered ideal conditions for the reservoir, as ample open space was available, and more importantly, its height on the Palisades allowed water to flow by gravity from there down to low-lying Hoboken.

In addition, a 175-foot water tower would be constructed next to the reservoir for greater height to provide sufficient water pressure to serve the upland communities in north Hudson. The expanding Hackensack Water Company commissioned prominent New York architect Frederick Clarke Withers (1828–1901) to create an architectural solution to handsomely promote the company's corporate image as well as store a 165,000-gallon iron tank at the top of a tower, which could also accommodate pumping equipment, administrative offices, and employee apartments below the tank.

Withers was well known for his Gothic Revival–style ecclesiastical and residential buildings, but his 1875 design for the Jefferson Market Courthouse in New York's Greenwich Village was highly acclaimed as a public and commercial complex and presaged the possibilities for the Weehawken project. The tower design, an elegant reminiscence of a European medieval guard tower, held true to Withers's Gothic Revival aesthetic, while employing innovative utilitarian structural principles to hold a 650-ton water tank aloft. Upon its opening on September 29, 1883, the water tower was extolled as a significant engineering milestone in industrial architecture.

In the 1970s, the entire complex was sold for a shopping mall development and condemned for demolition. Weehawken citizens and the Weehawken Environment Committee, recognizing its architectural significance as well as its iconic stature, succeeded in saving the tower and having it placed on the National Register of Historic Places in 1980. In 2000, ownership was transferred to the township. The exterior has been faithfully restored, and the tower remains a beloved landmark of Weehawken.

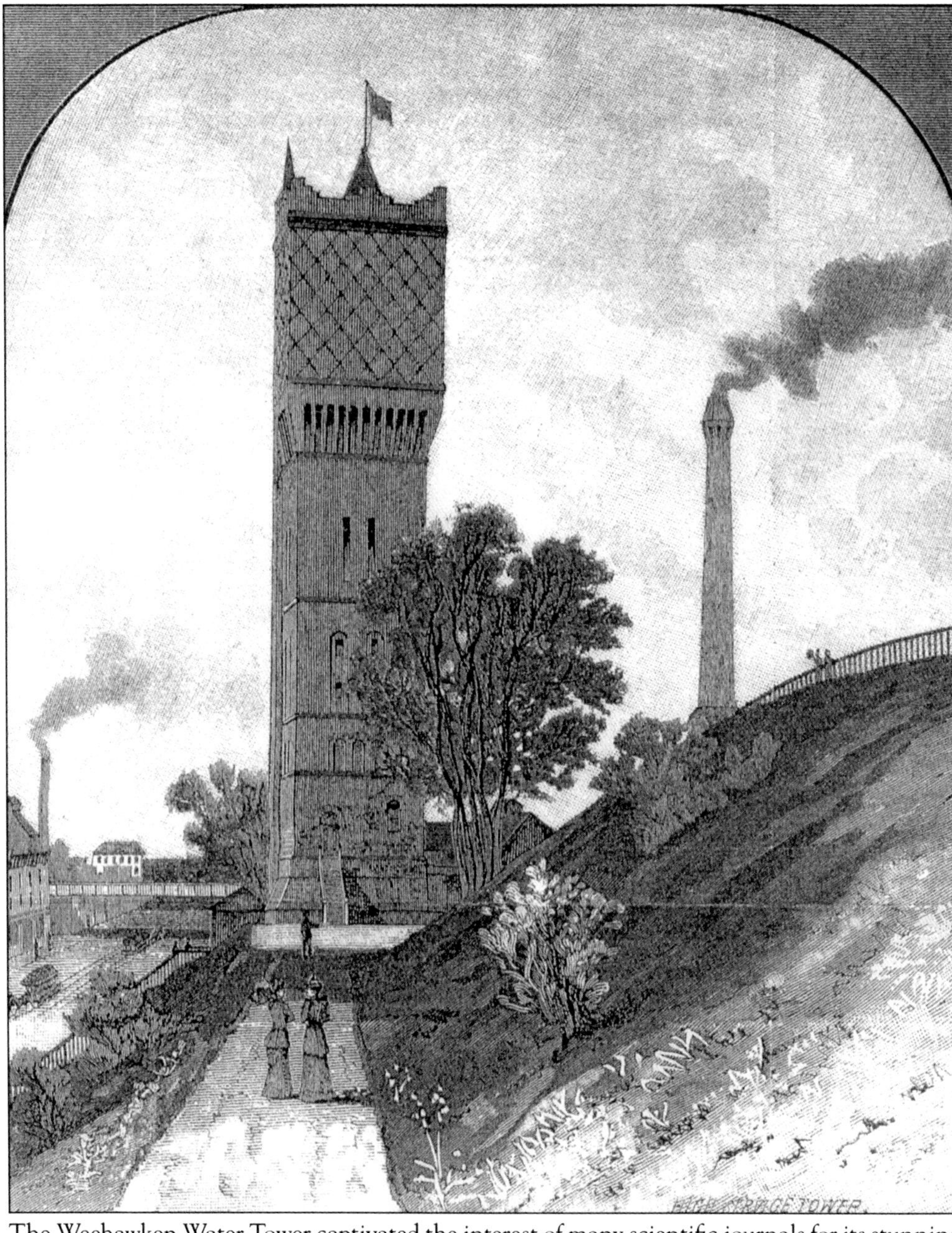

The Weehawken Water Tower captivated the interest of many scientific journals for its stunning beauty combined with its extraordinary innovation in industrial design. In this 1892 rendering from *Scientific American* looking north along Bulls Ferry Road (Park Avenue), the setting is still bucolic though other mechanical buildings have been added to the complex, including the furnace room smokestack at right. Note the trolleys of the Weehawken and Hoboken Horse Railway Company in operation on Bulls Ferry Road since 1861. The railroad trestle crossing the roadway, at left in the distance, is the extension of the great passenger elevator line coming from the waterfront to a station at Liberty Place and Bulls Ferry Road where excursionists heading for the Eldorado amusement grounds disembarked. The rail line then crossed Bulls Ferry Road and veered north to the Guttenberg Racetrack.

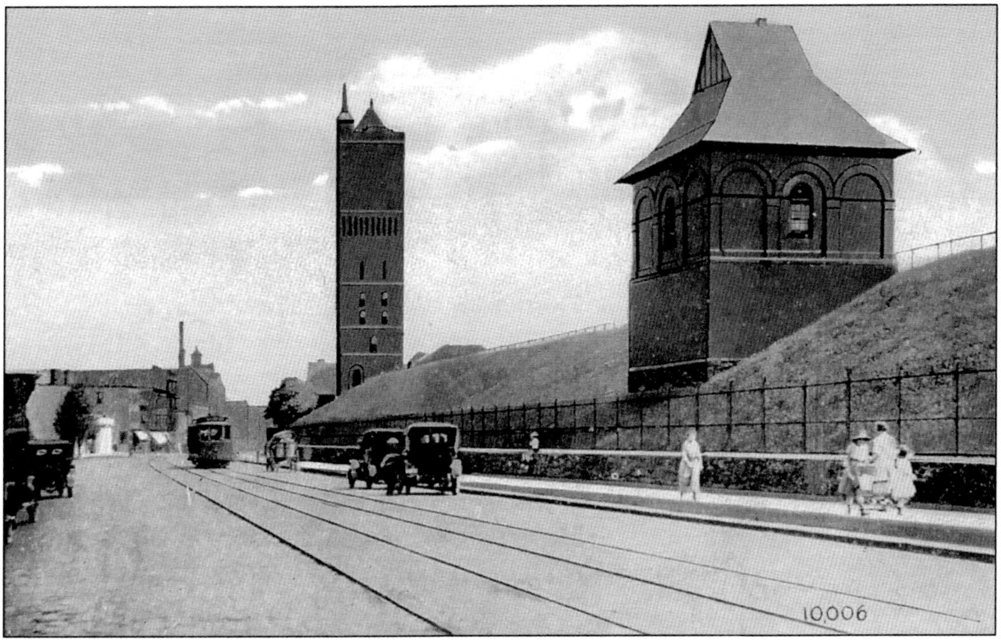

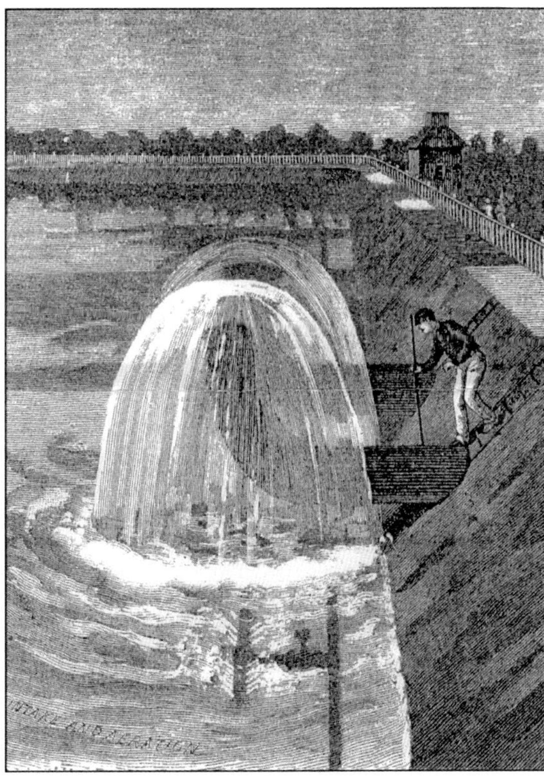

The charming gatehouse, also designed by the water tower's architect, Frederick Clarke Withers, was situated at the southern end of the Hackensack Water Company complex on Bulls Ferry Road, straddling the reservoir. The water made its way through 20-inch pipes from the Hackensack River, 14 miles to the west, to the Weehawken plant, filling the reservoir to its 15 million gallon capacity. From this height in Weehawken, the water could flow by gravity into Hoboken. The gatehouse held components that monitored the flow of water in and out of the reservoir. At right, the reservoir, constructed above the street level, was fabricated of an earthen embankment lined with brick. Fountain pipes within the berm circulated the water, introducing oxygen to retard the growth of algae and other contaminating matter in the open-air holding basin. (Above, Steve Dorio.)

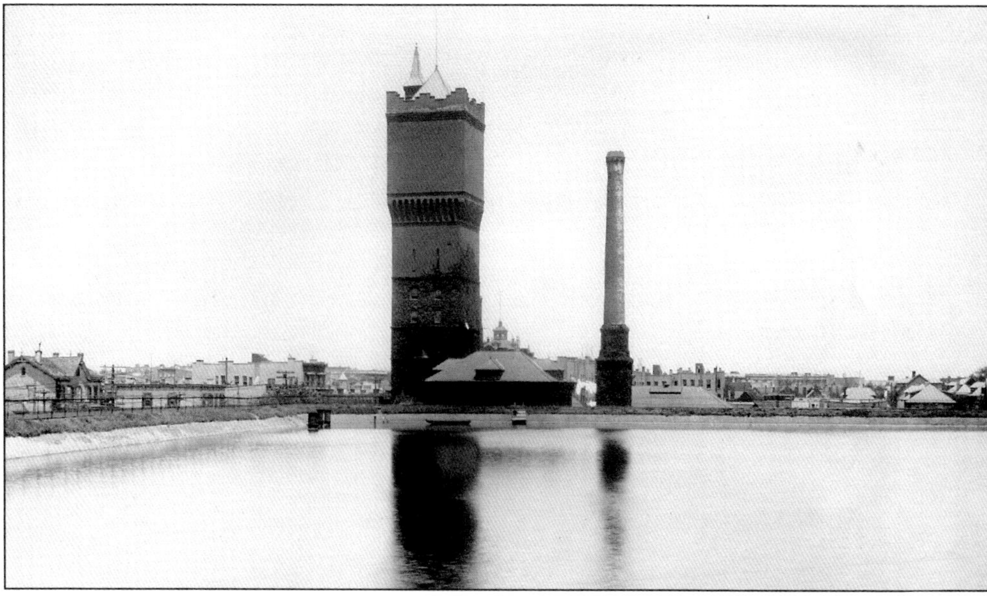

Whereas the reservoir served Hoboken, the 175-foot water tower was built to provide enough pressure for gravitational flow to Weehawken and the surrounding communities atop the Palisades. The tank section can be identified on the tower exterior by its larger volume above a more slender shaft beginning at the band of projecting masonry arches about a quarter of the way down from the top. The 30-foot-in-diameter tank sits at that level, its weight supported by the thickness of the walls and eight large masonry Gothic arches within the seventh-floor level just below the encircling decorative arches. Below, the water tower rises above the sweep of Park Avenue and the trolley line around 1920. The street entering Park Avenue from Union City on the left is Fortieth Street, which is opposite the present entrance into the Tower Mall parking lot. (United Water.)

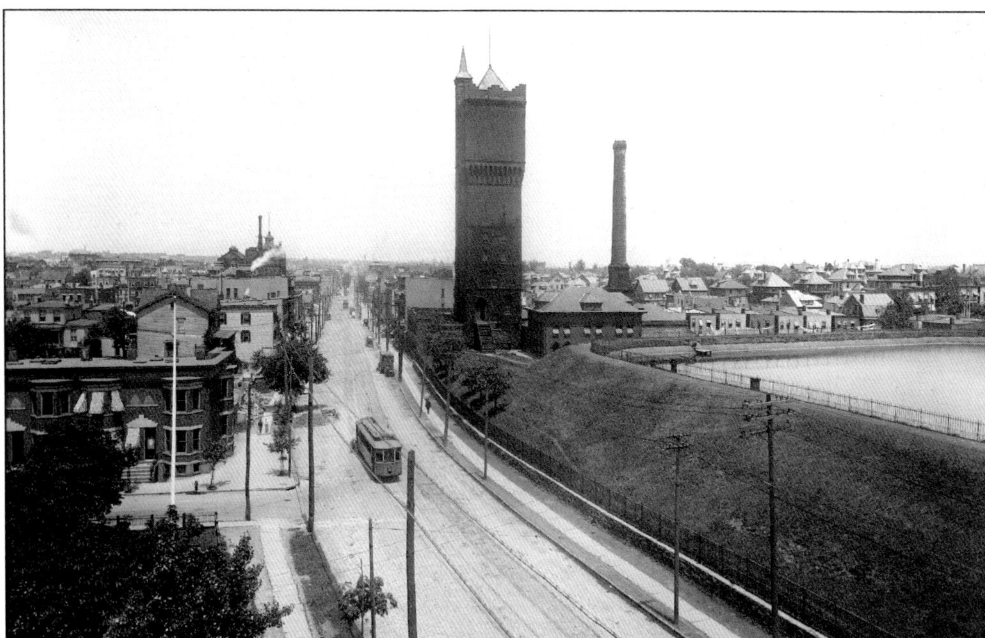

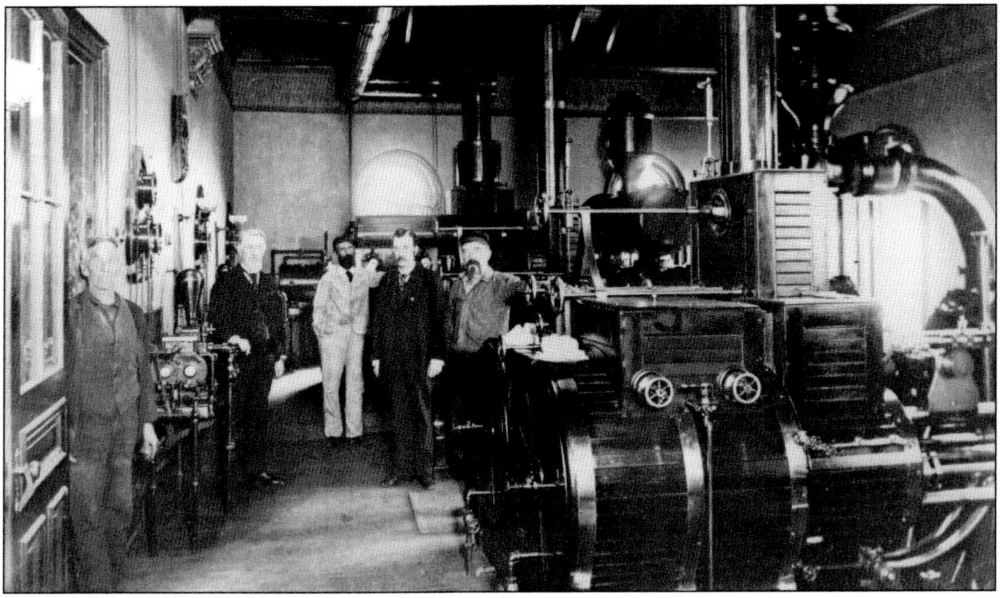

In addition to storing 165,000 gallons of water in an iron tank, the tower housed two Worthington pumping engines on the third level, shown here in 1885. The water came from supply mains below the street, entered the tower on the Bulls Ferry Road side, and was pumped through 10-inch pipes to the storage tank at the top. Each engine could pump 2 million gallons a day. Below the engine room on the second level were the boilers, which supplied steam to the engines, and below that at grade level were the furnaces that heated the boilers. (United Water.)

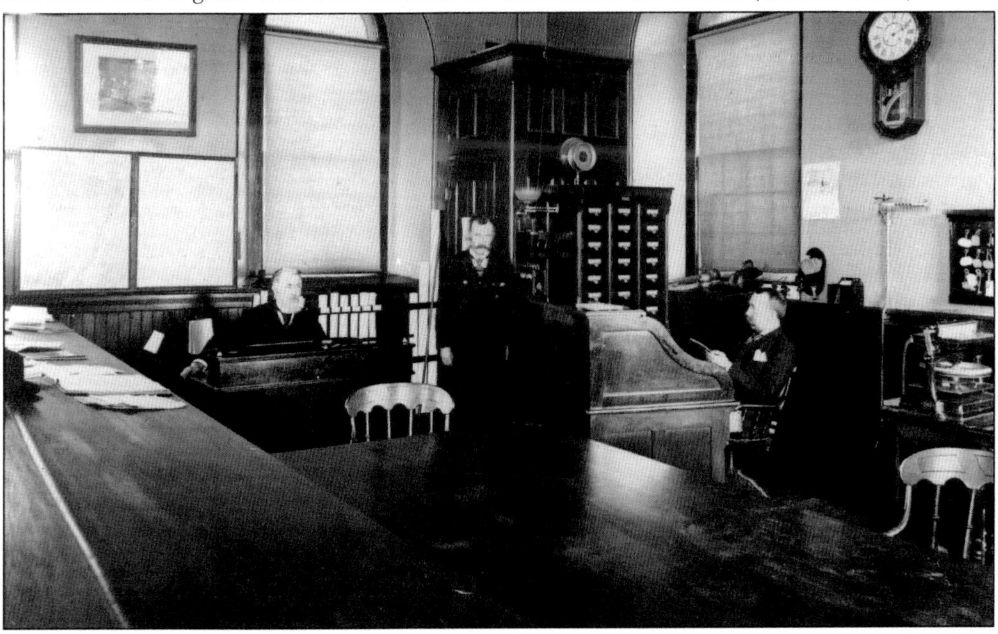

Upon completion of the tower in 1883, the Hackensack Water Company centralized its headquarters in Weehawken. In 1885, the first chief engineer, Charles E. Brush, is seated at right in the fourth floor office over the engine room. There were two apartments for employees on the two floors above. All of the mechanical equipment, office, and living spaces were quartered beneath an iron water tank that weighed 640 tons when filled. (United Water.)

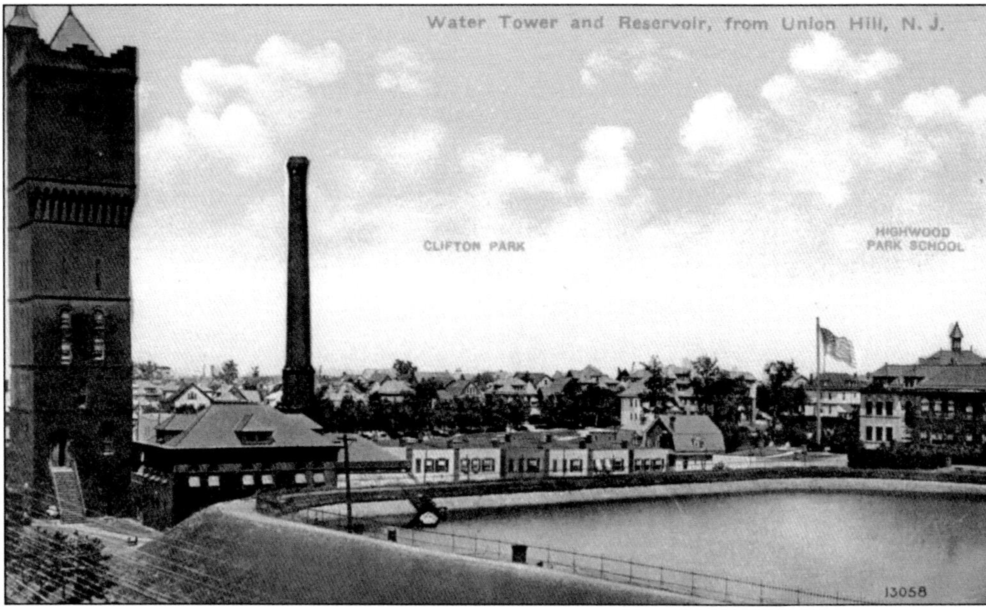

In 1892, the operation expanded with the addition of a new engine room, coalhouse, and boiler room, and a smokestack clustered around the tower at left with the Clifton Park section of Weehawken in the background. In 1895, a larger office building was constructed on Park Avenue just north of the tower. For all its stunning engineering innovation, the water tower was decommissioned in 1904, with newer technologies having evolved to serve a burgeoning population. The reservoir stayed in use, but the tower and outbuildings were appropriated for other purposes or closed; the smokestack was demolished in 1936. The Hackensack Water Company continued to thrive and remained headquartered in the administration building until the 1970s. The company ultimately merged with other local water systems, becoming United Water. Pictured below is the Hackensack Water Company's men's basketball team in the company's halcyon years of 1928 to 1929. (Above, Al Berg; below, United Water.)

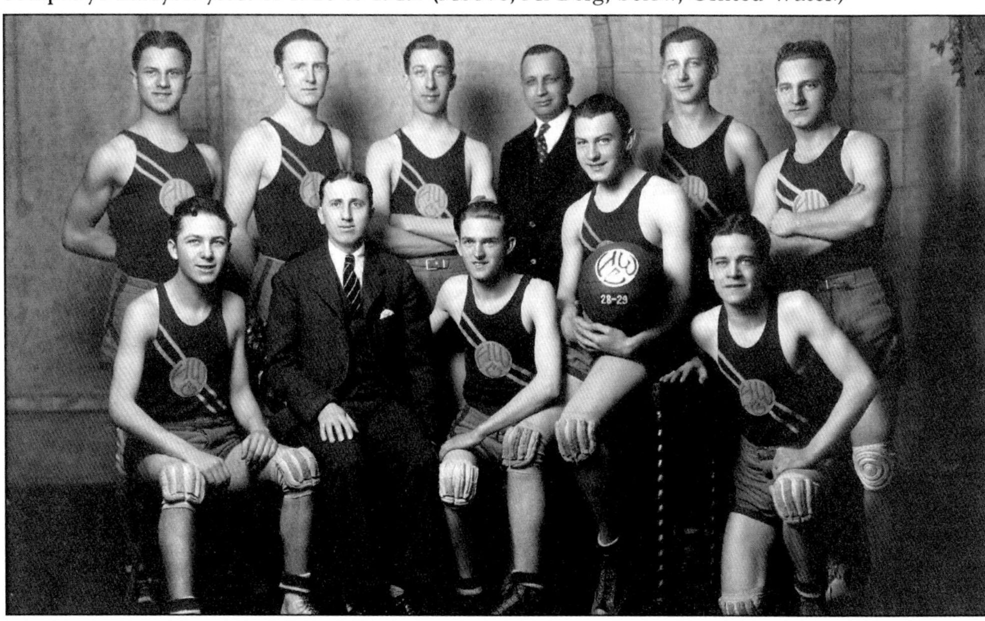

Three

Eldorado

Eldorado is the elusive, mythical city filled with gold and precious jewels beyond compare. Hungarian-born impresario Bolossy Kiralfy envisioned a shining entertainment venue as he looked west across the Hudson River from New York towards Weehawken's Palisades.

In 1890, a group of prominent businessmen formed the Palisades Amusement and Exhibition Company, whose officers included Herman Walker of Guttenberg and two sons of John H. Bonn, president of the North Hudson County Railway Company. Kiralfy was on the board of directors and held the title of amusement director.

Fifteen acres were purchased, encompassing the area from the edge of the cliffs overlooking the Hudson River west to Highwood Avenue and from Duer Place to Liberty Place. The entertainment complex included a Moorish inspired casino, a Rhenish castle, a 30-foot-high fountain replete with mythological figures, a music pavilion, bandstands, and an 8,000-seat amphitheater. The first season opened on June 27, 1891.

The grounds were magnificently appointed to soothe weary urban eyes, with shaded outlooks and pathways strung with colorful pennants fluttering in the breezes. The long arcades were lined with little electric lamps and hung with sparkling glass prisms. And the view was spectacular.

During the afternoon hours, a circus performed in the amphitheater. Acrobats, jugglers, hot-air balloonists, aerialists, and other unique entertainments delighted patrons as did band and opera concerts conducted by Nahan Franko or a young Victor Herbert, of operetta fame. The evening featured outdoor spectaculars. The inaugural production, written and directed by Maestro Kiralfy, was *King Solomon and the Destruction of Jerusalem*, employing dance, pantomime, and choral singing to portray the story. A cast of nearly 1,000 performers amazed audiences as did the lavish costumes and elaborate scenic effects. After the show, a fireworks display over the Palisades was accompanied by live music.

In the second year, access to Eldorado was simplified with the addition of a giant passenger elevator. Despite the throngs attending the first season (over 1 million, it was said) and the success of the next several seasons, Eldorado was unable to turn a profit. Its extravagant production costs were not covered by the modest fees charged to visitors. In 1894, the park closed and faded away into history.

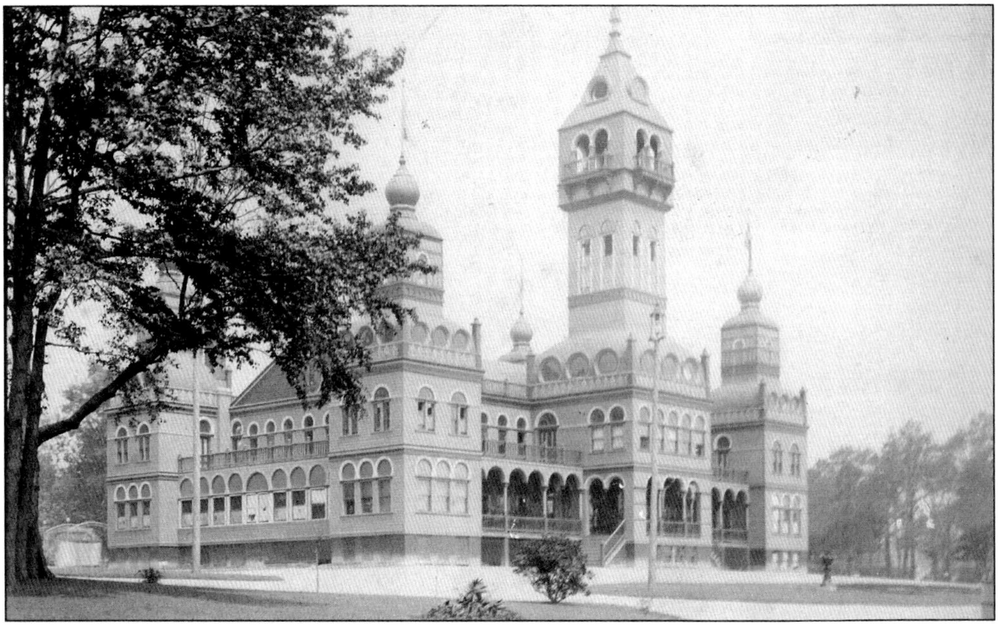

The casino, built in 1891, was the most spectacular building of the Eldorado complex. Of Moorish design, the expansive building was 125 feet long by 85 feet high, with the central tower reaching 110 feet and the corner towers topping off at 70 feet each. Aside from the several eating and drinking venues, there were bowling alleys, shooting galleries, conversation and smoking rooms, a café, and the observatory, a place from which to view the river and New York beyond.

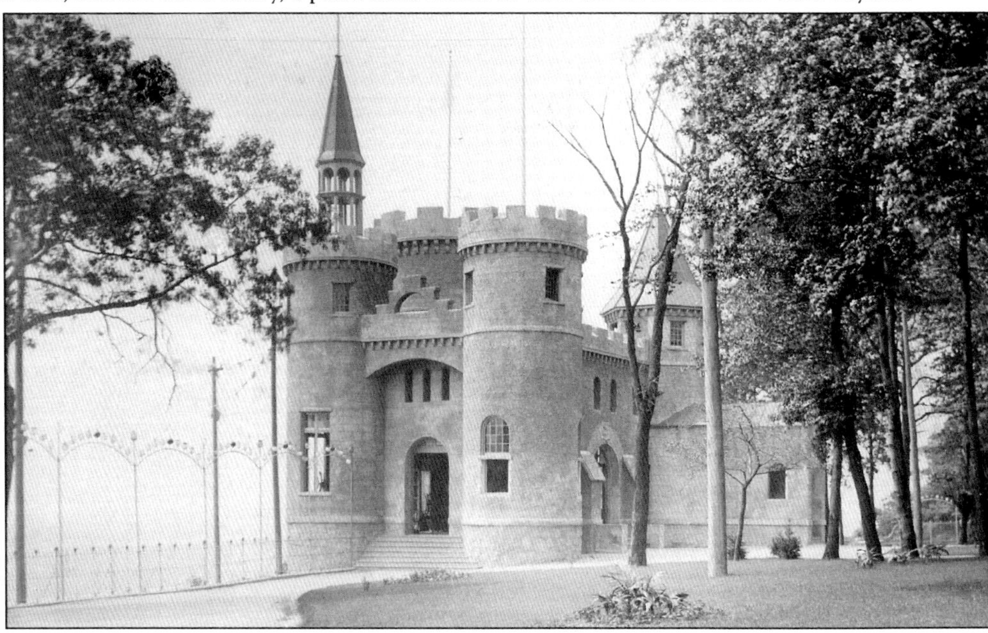

The Rhenish castle at Eldorado, with its dramatic turrets and bastions, was perched at the southeastern edge of the grounds overlooking the Palisades and the Hudson River. It contained a Viennese-style café along with a small stage for more intimate entertainments. In 1896, after the demise of the Eldorado, famed sculptor Karl Bitter purchased the building and some adjoining land and turned the castle into his atelier.

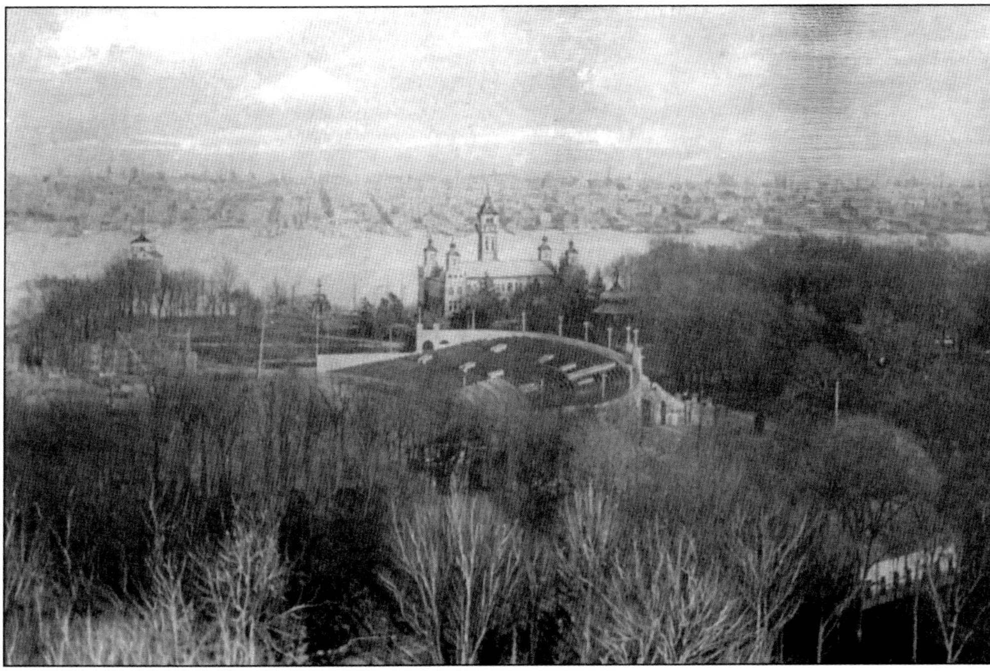

This Eldorado souvenir booklet aerial view of the grounds, Hudson River, and New York City beyond was taken from the Weehawken water tower, which stood just west of the property. The Roman-style 8,000 seat amphitheater hosted events day and night during Eldorado's four seasons; as financial returns diminished, specialty acts were scheduled and added to the spectaculars to entice visitors to spend the day and evening. (Al Berg.)

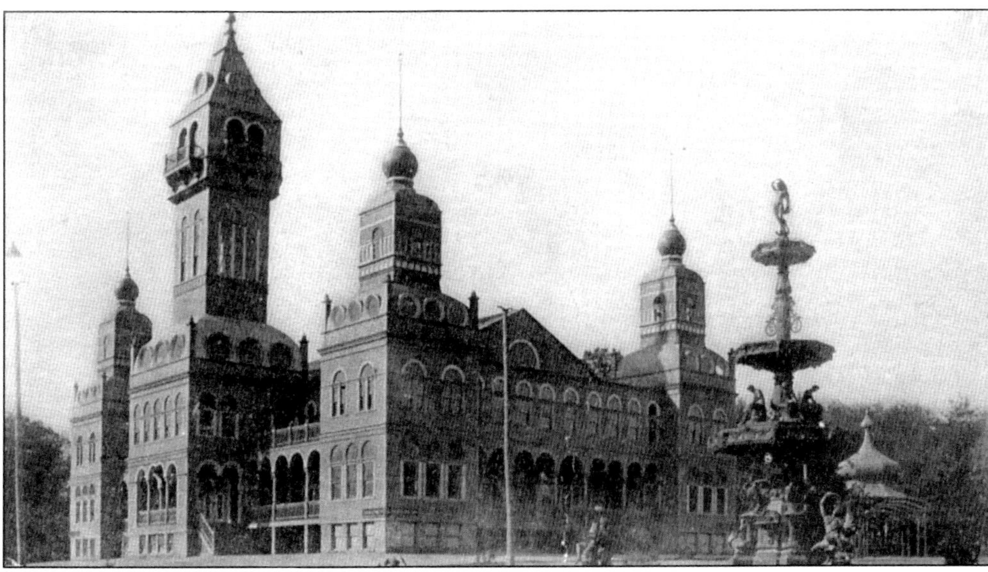

Located on the north side of the casino was the 30-foot-high fountain, designed with mythological creatures and men and women who appeared to be shampooing their heads in the fountain's spray. In the large circular basin below the three tiers were gold and silver fish. The fountain, said to be the largest in the world in 1891, was manufactured by J. L. Mott Iron Works of New York.

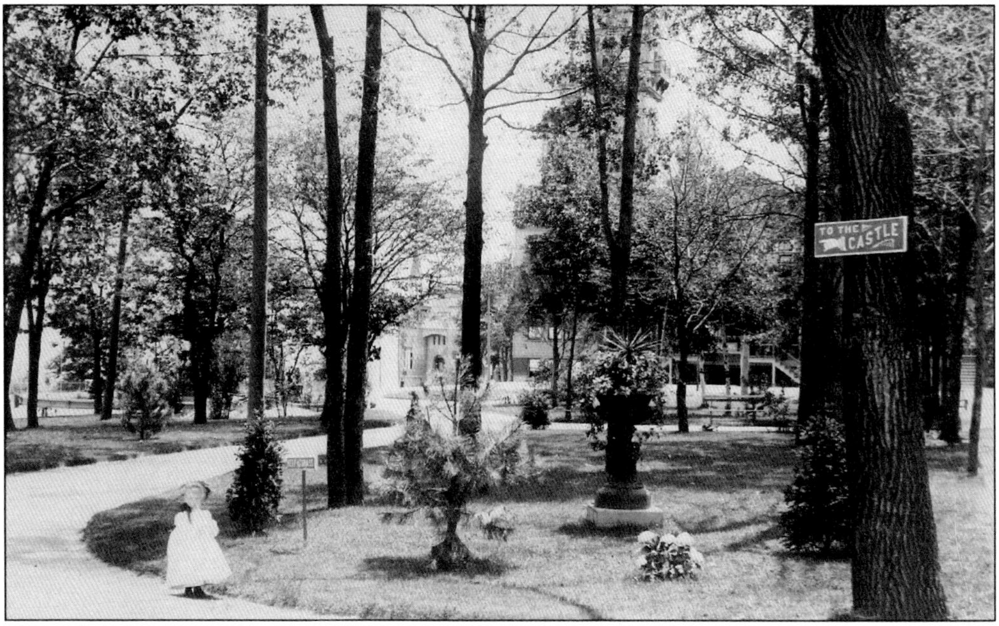

Eldorado's attractions were noted by the *New York Times* just after its opening in June 1891. The site's natural beauty was improved with the addition of meandering walks, shady spots for lingering, and an array of shrubs and flowers bordering the smooth paths. Then, suddenly, a visitor might be thrust upon a height to view the expanse of the river and city beyond. This little girl must have run ahead of her parents on the way to the castle.

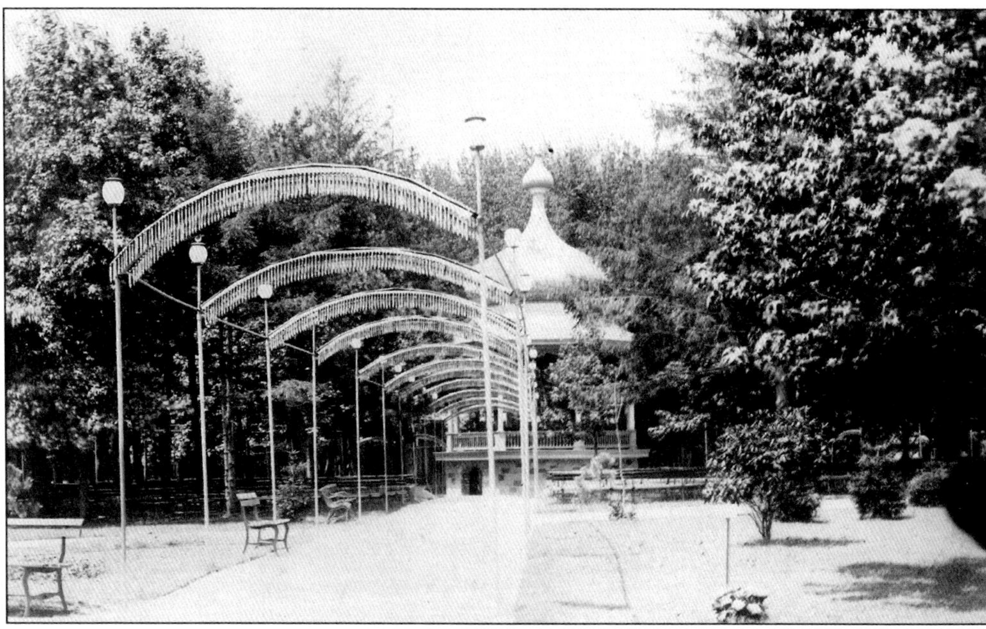

There were several bandstands at the Eldorado as well as a music pavilion for the larger concerts. During the 1891 and 1892 seasons, the Eldorado Band of Fifty, led by Nahan Franko, played, with the likes of virtuoso Jules Levy soloing on the cornet. In the 1894 season, a young Victor Herbert took over conducting duties with the famous P. S. Gilmore's 22nd Regiment Band and introduced his popular *Eldorado March*.

Looking back from a turret atop the Rhenish castle are the towers of the casino. In front is the manicured lawn with "Eldorado" spelled out in Victorian-style flowers and flanked by two large urns. At right in the mid-ground is a view of the elaborate fountain.

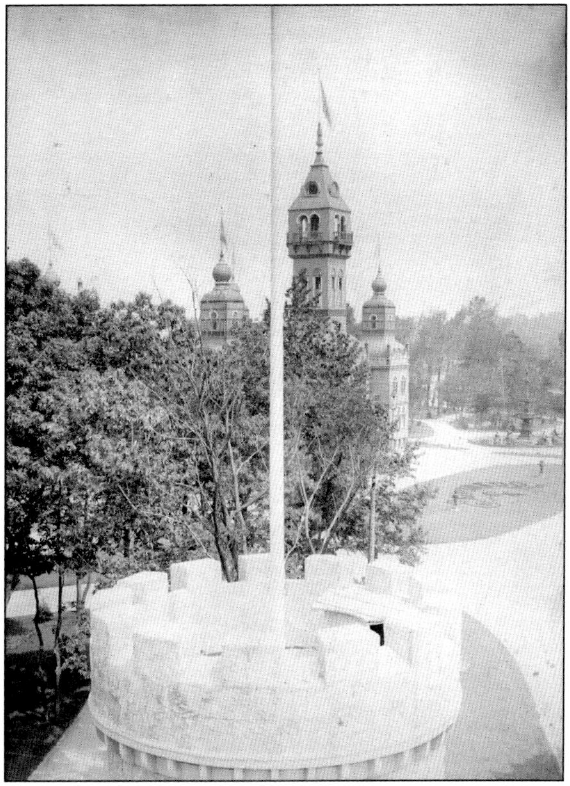

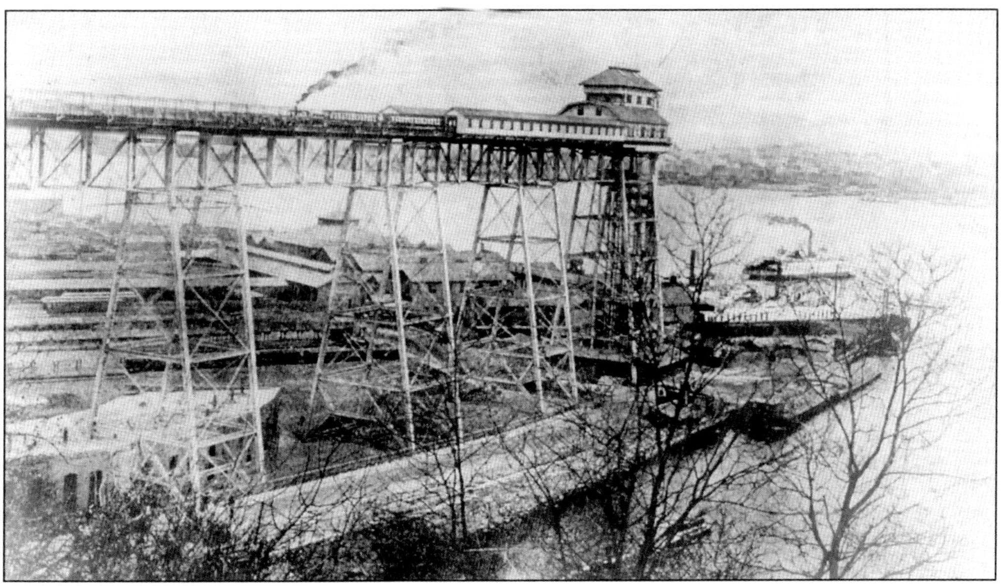

The elevator stood 197 feet tall at the end of a 900-foot trestle connected to the Palisades. From here, trains took Eldorado visitors across to Eldorado station and northbound patrons to the Guttenberg Racetrack. In this photograph from about 1892, ferries are arriving and departing from the terminal just north of the elevator, and a train chugs across the trestle's span. What is left of the entrance to the railroad cut at the top of the cliff near Liberty Place is still visible today.

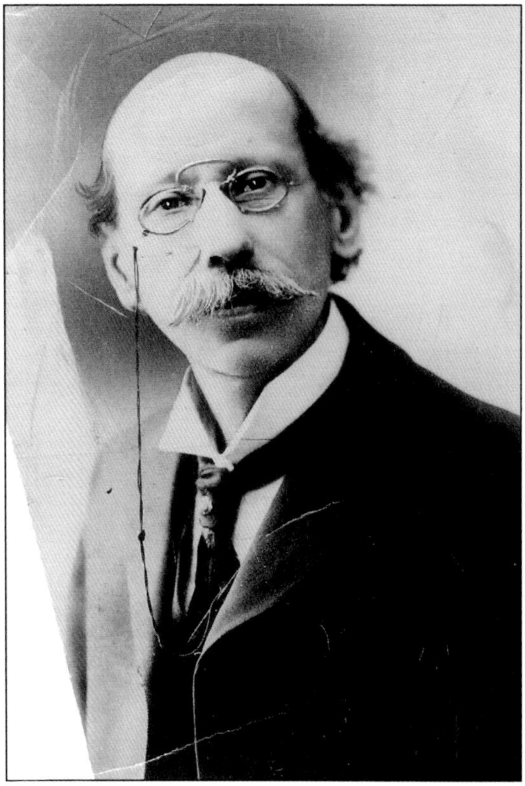

It was Bolossy Kiralfy's artistic vision that made the Eldorado amusement park possible. Born in Budapest in 1847, he and his older brother Imre toured the capital cities of Europe from the tender ages of four and six. Dazzling audiences with their versions of traditional Hungarian dances, the family soon became a traveling troupe. In 1869, the Kiralfys immigrated to the United States where the two brothers collaborated as entrepreneurs of the late-19th-century spectacular genre of epic stories, elaborate scenery, and 1,000-member casts. In 1887, the brothers' business partnership dissolved, and they never spoke again, though each one continued to produce theatrical extravaganzas. In 1891, in partnership with the Palisade Amusement and Exhibition Company, Bolossy launched his Eldorado. (Jean Kiralfy Kent.)

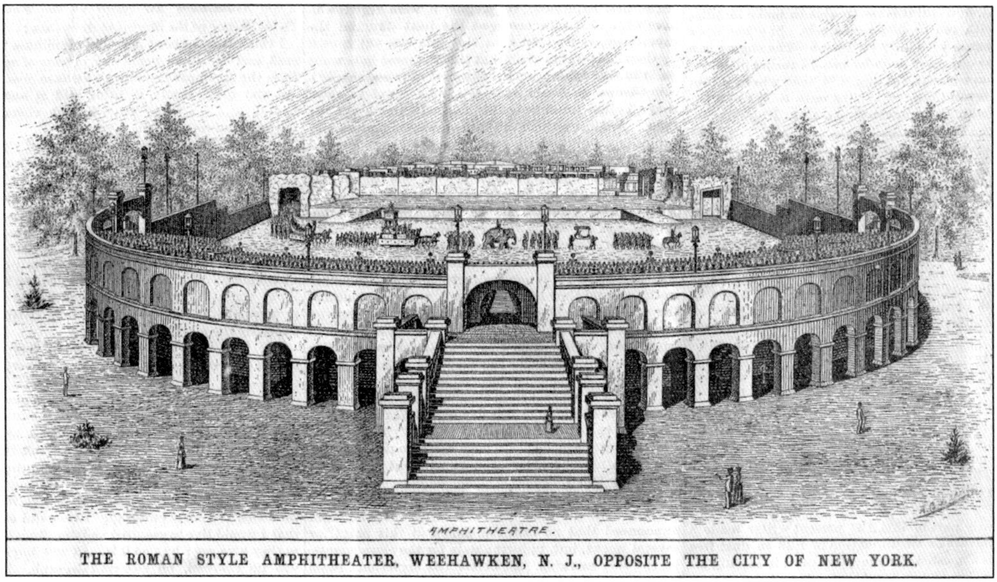

Scientific American published this image of the Eldorado amphitheater on October 31, 1891. Modeled after the Roman Coliseum and designed by the renowned theatrical architectural firm J. B. McElfatrick and Sons at the cost of $75,000, it was said to be the largest stage ever built. Constructed of wood, it was covered with cement and crushed stone, giving it the appearance of masonry. Electric lights encircling the top wall of the 8,000-seat theater furnished illumination for evening performances. (Al Berg.)

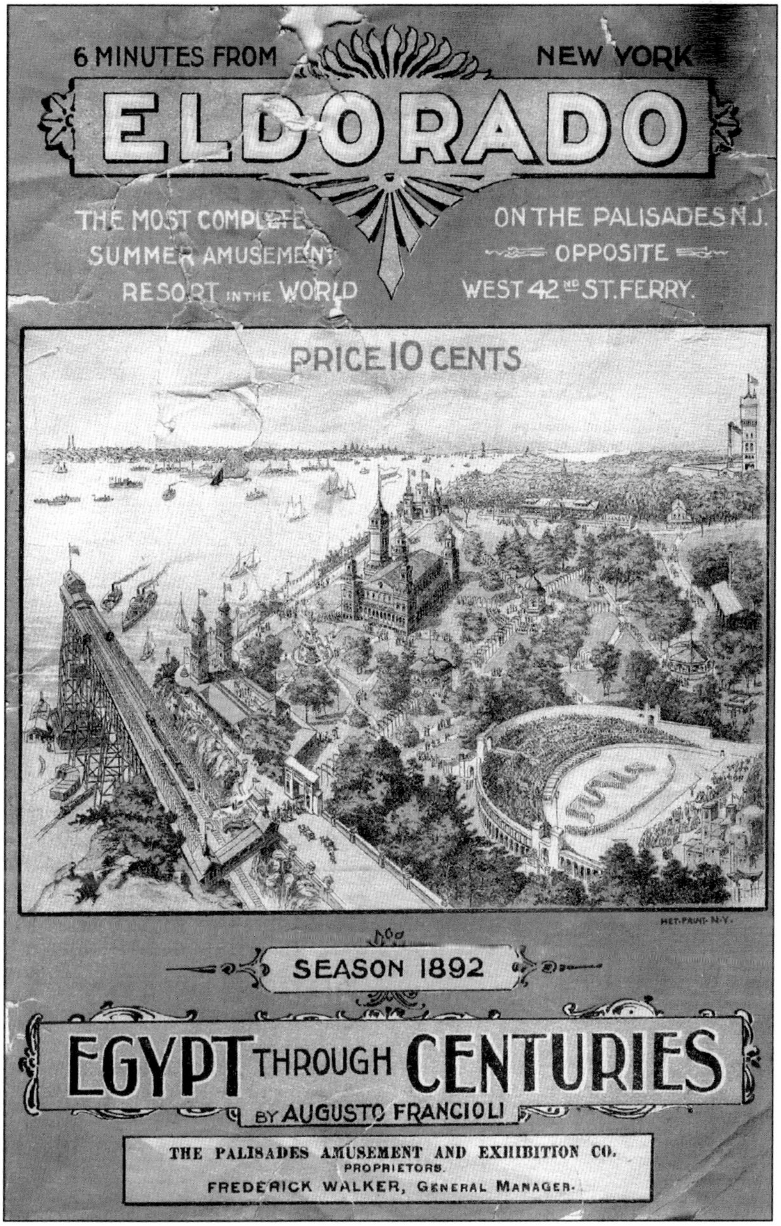

Due to a dispute between Kiralfy and the amusement company's producers, he and his *King Solomon* did not return for the 1892 Eldorado season. Instead, the amphitheater's spectacle was *Egypt Through Centuries*, penned and directed by Augusto Francioli, an Italian ballet master and assistant director at La Scala Opera House in Milan and the Metropolitan Opera in New York. The five-act extravaganza covered 110 centuries of Egyptian history including highlights of the sacrifice of 100 virgins to Osiris, the great pyramids and the first pilgrimage to Mecca, the birth of Moses, Cleopatra and her court, the Suez Canal, and the fall of Alexandria. Featured were fire eaters, jugglers, camels, donkeys, an army on horseback, cannons, and fireworks. This cover from the libretto provides a visual overview of the Eldorado complex. Interestingly, it inaccurately sites the Hackensack Water Company tower south, rather than west of the amphitheater, in order to fit the landmark in the picture. (Willie Demontreux.)

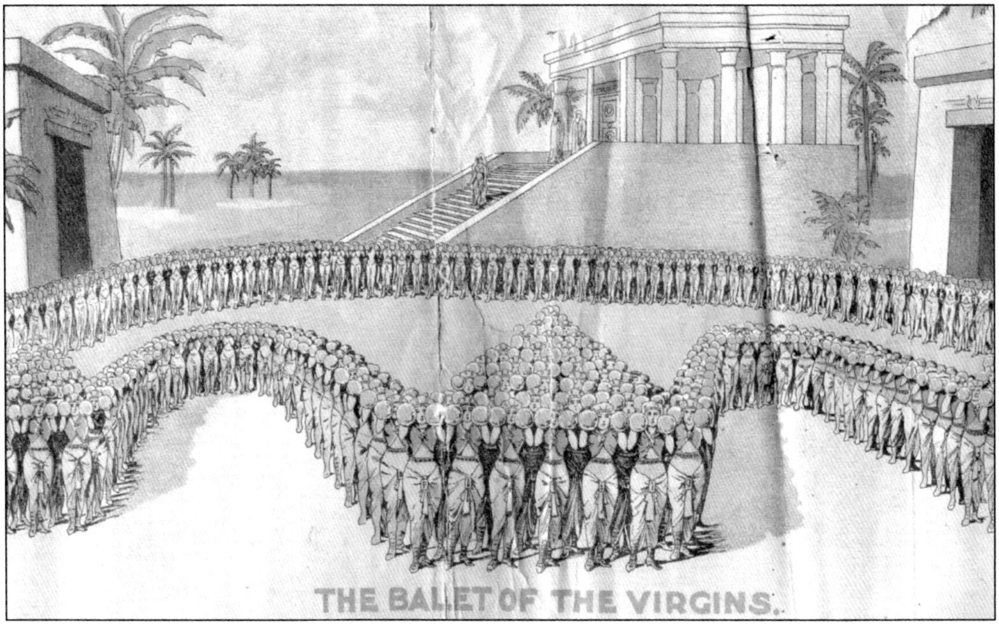

The ballet of the virgins was one of the typical numbers in Augusto Francioli's five-act spectacular *Egypt Through Centuries*. The ballet involved the sacrifice to Osiris of hundreds of virgins who, by dancing their way into the Nile River to their deaths, caused the riverbanks to overflow and sustain the crops. (Willie Demontreux.)

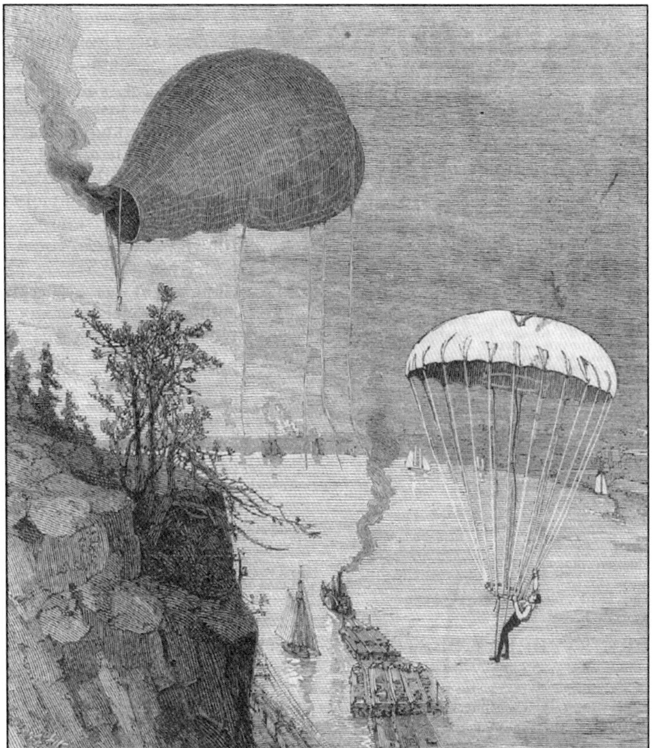

Ballooning was especially dramatic at Eldorado, as seen in this *Scientific American* illustration from 1891. A Montgolfier balloon was inflated with gas, to which was attached a 28-foot-diameter parachute, with the aeronaut holding on to the bottom ring. As the balloon was released, the aeronaut ran towards it and ascended. When sufficient height was reached, he cut himself loose with a knife and began to descend quickly until air caught in the parachute and slowed his fall. One Eldorado aeronaut was M. L. MacDonald, known as "Daring Donald" for reasons that should be obvious. Ballooning was a popular, if unpredictable entertainment. (Al Berg.)

Four

STREETSCAPES

Weehawken's land area is less than one square mile. Within that small space several distinctive neighborhoods have evolved out of topographical constraints, historical circumstances, and political and entrepreneurial developments.

The soaring Palisades stand between the upland residential districts and the Hudson River waterfront. High on the bluff, Kingswood, Hauxhurst, Highwood, and Clifton Park were named after a handful of early 19th-century estates. The Eldorado subdivision grew out of the failed 1890s amusement park and necessitated the construction of Boulevard East.

In the 1930s, the decision to locate the Lincoln Tunnel entrance plaza in Weehawken with an express approach road through town cut the north end of the municipality from the south end of the Palisades. That project solidified the Heights's singular identity south of the tunnel cut. On the site of the earliest settlement, the Shades's few blocks are tucked under the cliff in the southern lowlands on the Hoboken border. The 100 steps, erected up the Palisades from the Hackensack Plank Road, connected this insular enclave to the Heights above.

The gritty, industrial waterfront below the Palisades was a land apart, a jumble of railroads and ship yards. Pershing Road steps leading down to the 42nd Street ferry were the sole access to the riverfront for many years. The long-abandoned rail yards are now being replaced with what will someday be an urban village with its own contemporary style.

Maintaining the oneness of this tiny township has presented challenges over the years. The challenges will persist; solidarity has always prevailed.

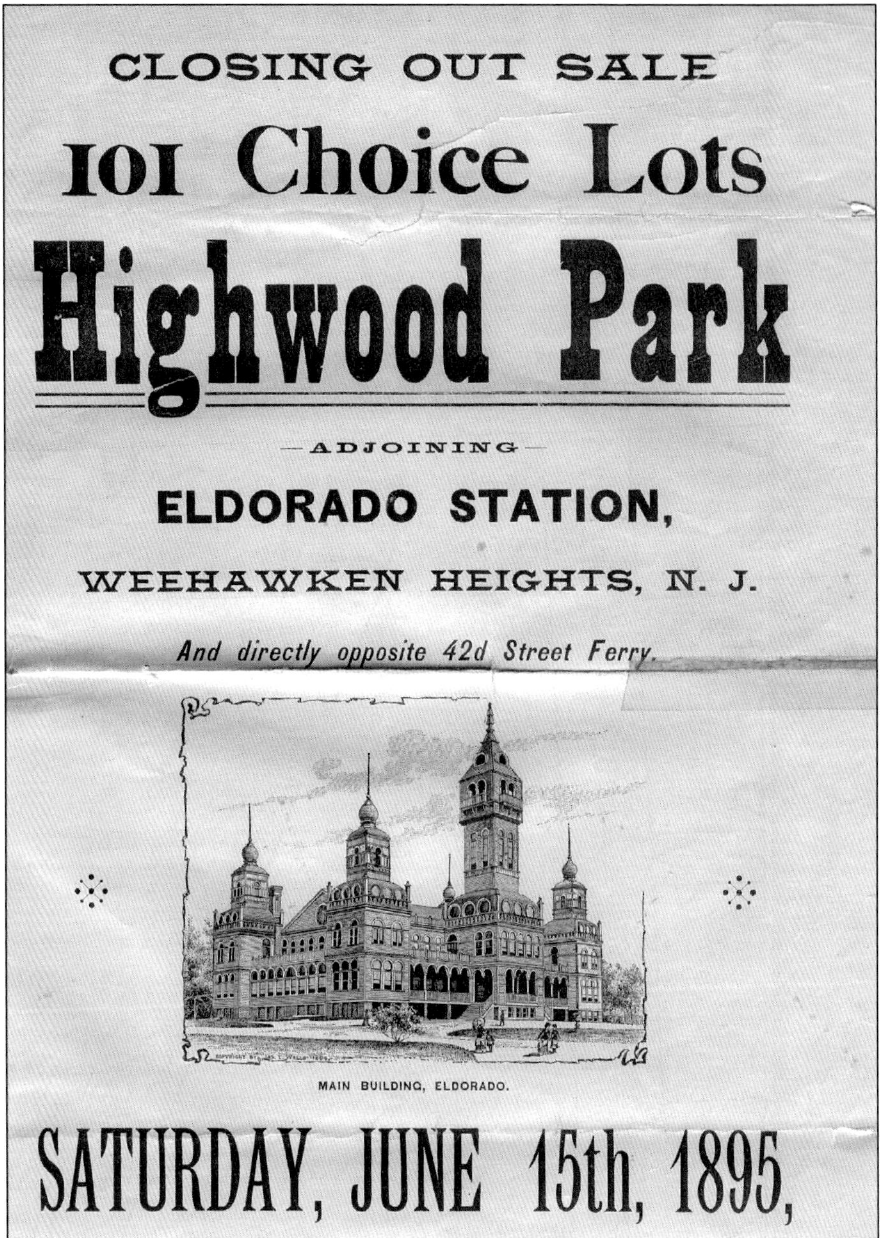

This sales announcement for a new development called Highwood Park, which was part of the old James Gore King estate, followed an auction offering of 293 lots in May 1894. The balance of 101 lots was still available to be snapped up by savvy investors with easy terms of payment, including a free title and a discount for cash. The auctions were conducted by James L. Wells of 59 Liberty Street in New York, whose company provided lunch in a large tent before the sale. The prospectus extols the natural advantages of Highwood Park, the romance of the Hamilton Burr duel site, the new monument just erected in 1894, and the new county road to be constructed along the top of the Palisades with its commanding views of the Hudson River and the easy commute to New York City. It took only 10 minutes to get to West 42nd Street via the West Shore Ferry.

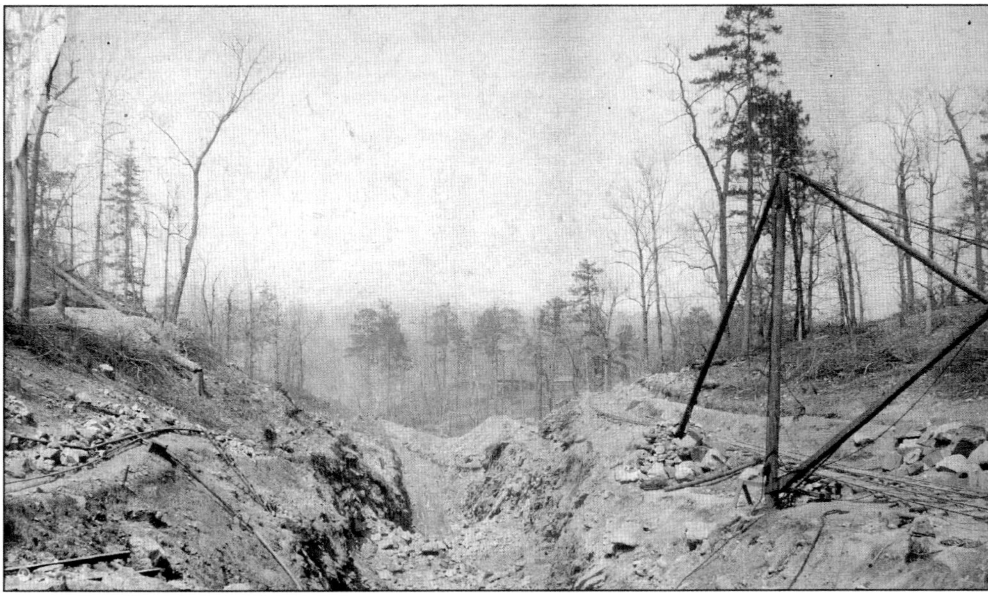

This 1896 image shows the construction of the county road (Boulevard East) from just below Highwood Terrace looking down towards the valley. By this time, the Eldorado was closed, though the buildings remained. The King estate had been broken up into seven parcels, which were then subdivided into building lots and auctioned off in 1894 and 1895 to home builders and real estate investors, of whom Hugh N. Camp was the largest. The beautiful new roadway was one of the improvements advertised to lure prospective buyers.

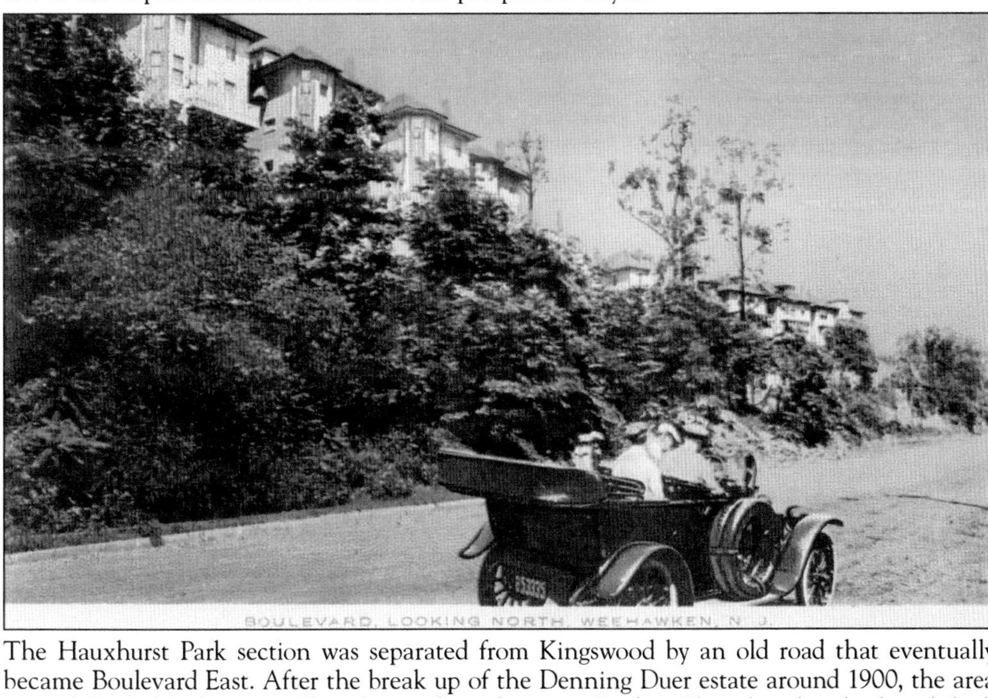

The Hauxhurst Park section was separated from Kingswood by an old road that eventually became Boulevard East. After the break up of the Denning Duer estate around 1900, the area was subdivided for housing. These houses have fronts on Sterling Place, but their backyards look across to Kingswood. This open car carries a group out for a spin north along Hudson Boulevard. (Steve Dorio.)

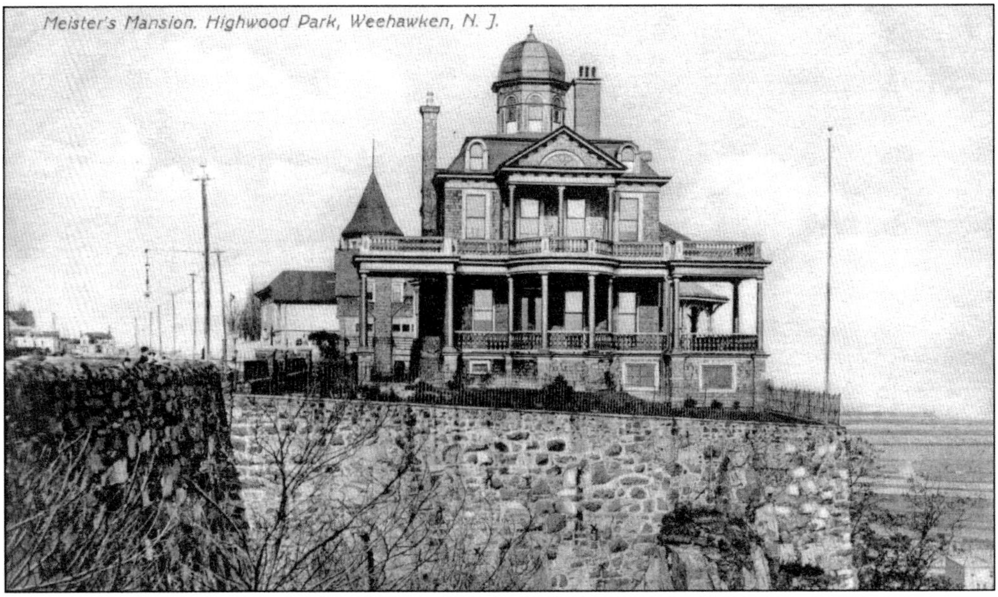

The Meister home was located at the south end of what is now Hamilton Park. The impressive house with wrap-around porches and an elaborate cantilevered gazebo on the north side was one of the first eight built in the area. The Meisters, who owned extensive real estate, moved from New York to Weehawken in 1895 with little John G. Meister, who grew up to serve as mayor of Weehawken for 18 years. The house was demolished around 1927 along with the Bitter buildings to make way for Hamilton Park. (Al Berg.)

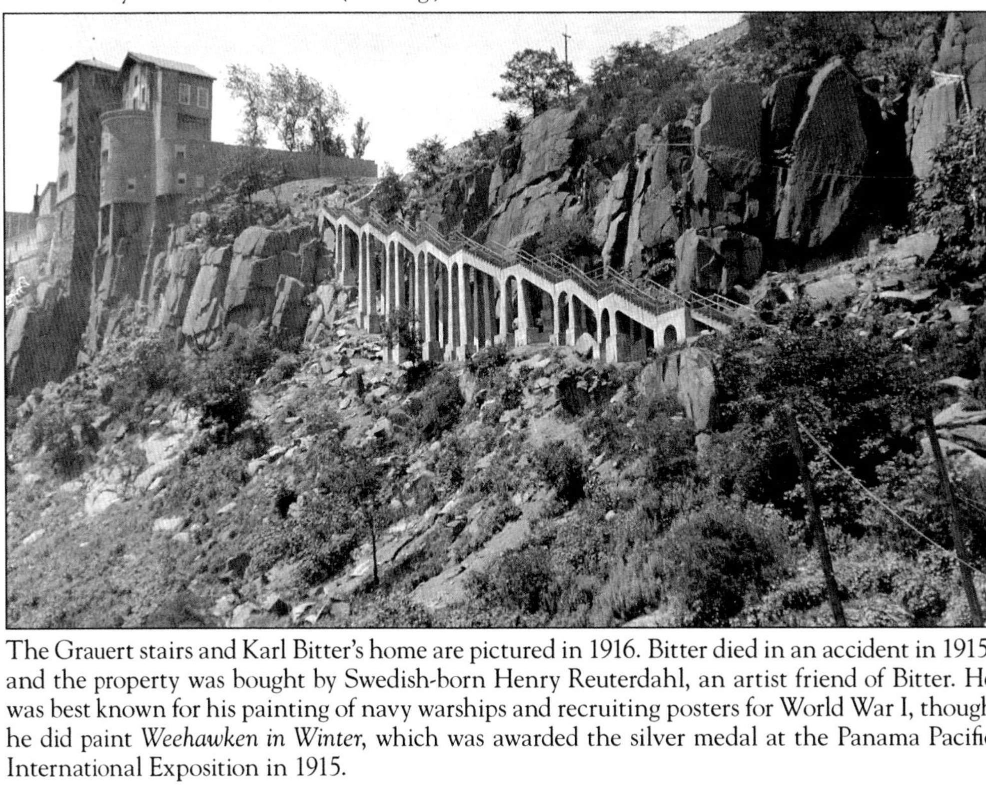

The Grauert stairs and Karl Bitter's home are pictured in 1916. Bitter died in an accident in 1915, and the property was bought by Swedish-born Henry Reuterdahl, an artist friend of Bitter. He was best known for his painting of navy warships and recruiting posters for World War I, though he did paint *Weehawken in Winter*, which was awarded the silver medal at the Panama Pacific International Exposition in 1915.

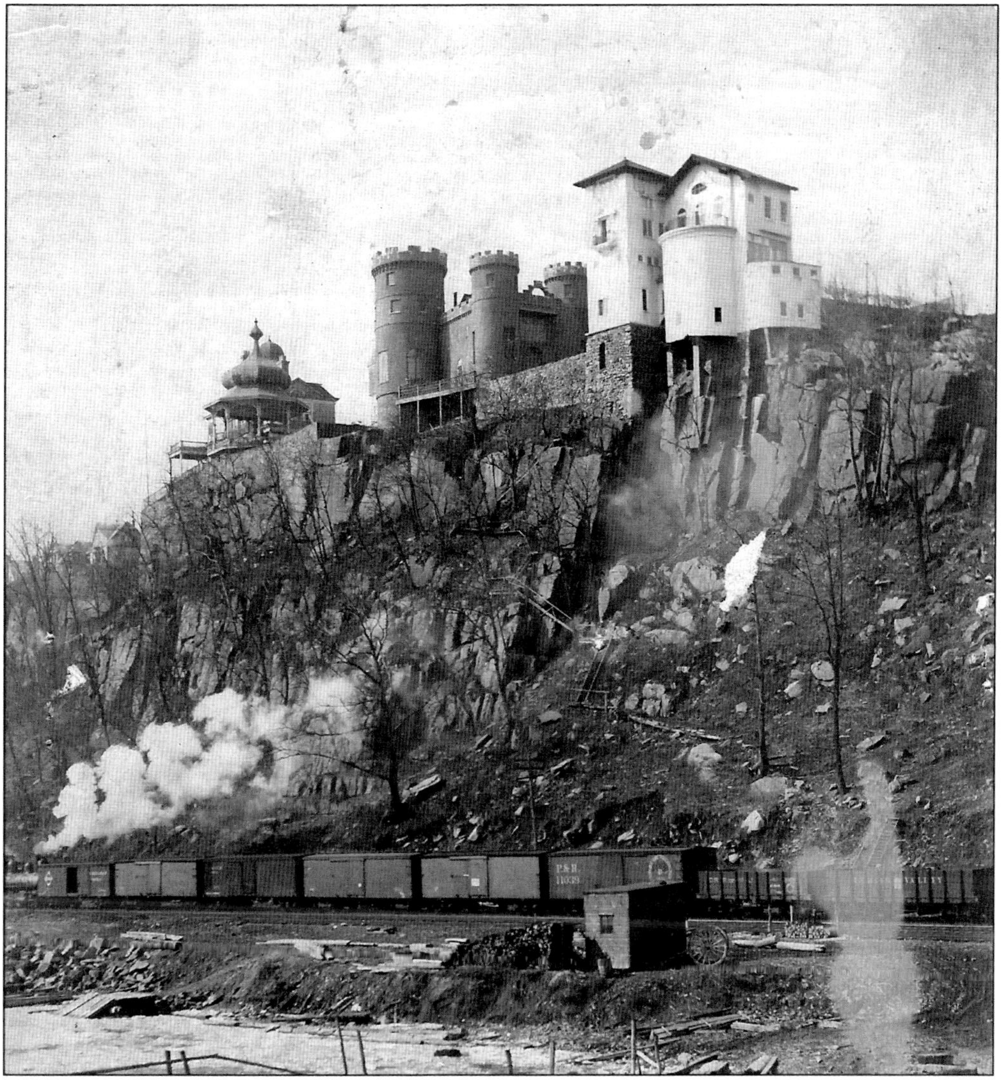

In 1896, the renowned Viennese sculptor Karl Bitter purchased the Rhenish-style castle (center), which was a feature of the short-lived Eldorado amusement park, for a studio. He retrofitted the building with joists and pulleys to lift his bronze sculptures; proximity to the railroad allowed direct access to freight cars below for shipment of his largest works. He built his home (right) adjacent to his atelier, where he lived until 1909 when he moved back to New York. However, he continued to work at the Weehawken atelier until his untimely death. The building at the far left was the residence of the parents of John G. Meister, mayor of Weehawken from 1932 to 1948. This view from about 1900 shows the extensive bluestone retaining walls and piers needed to hold the buildings straddling the edge of the Palisades. The stone walls still exist as part of the foundation of Hamilton Park. Looking closely, a rickety set of wooden stairs from the stone walls traversing the cliff down to the bottom can be seen.

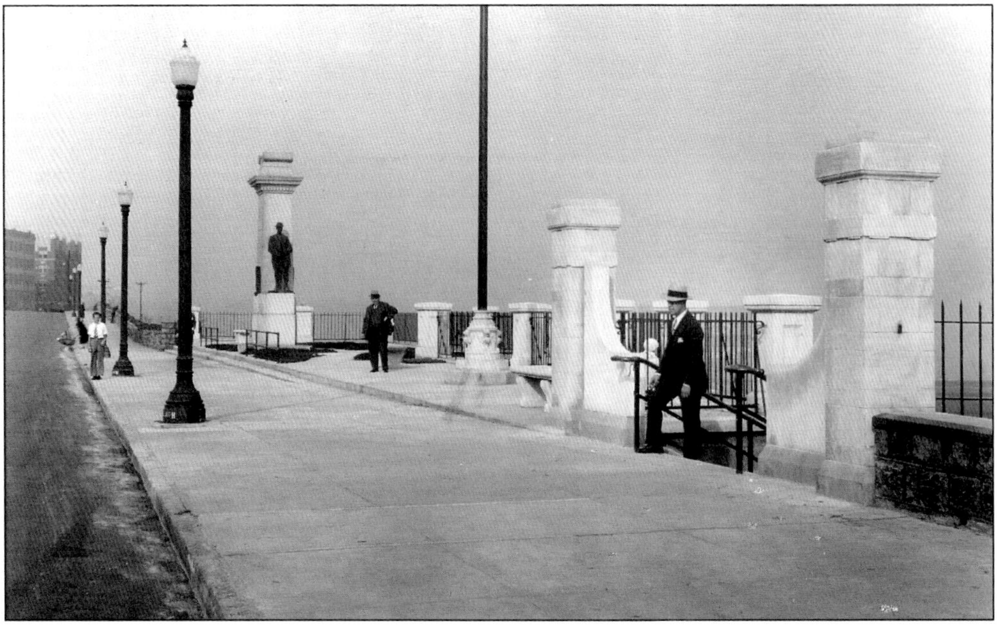

This is the newly created Hamilton Plaza and soldiers and sailors monument as it appeared in 1930. The man at the top of the stairs has just made his way up from Pershing Road via what was known as the Grauert Causeway, erected under Mayor Emile W. Grauert's administration. Today the Rapetti-designed soldiers and sailors monument is flanked by World War II, Korean, and Vietnam War memorials.

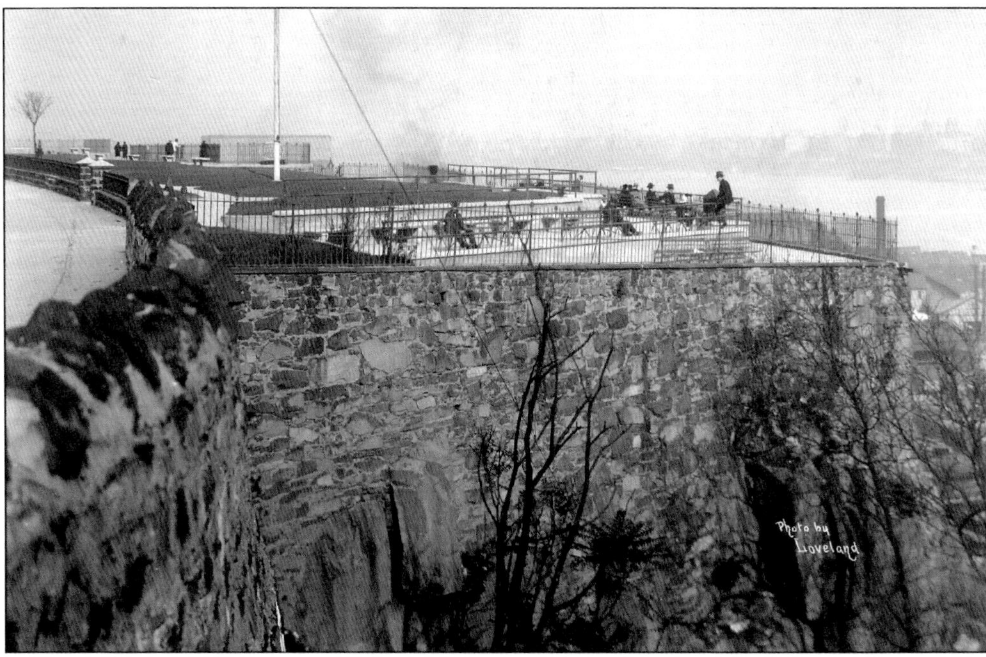

This 1930 photograph shows the newly completed Hamilton Park looking north from Hamilton Avenue. The extensive stone foundation was part of the Meister house, which was demolished three years earlier. There was not much in the way of landscaping other than several lawn and seating areas, but people, then as now, were drawn to the magnificent view.

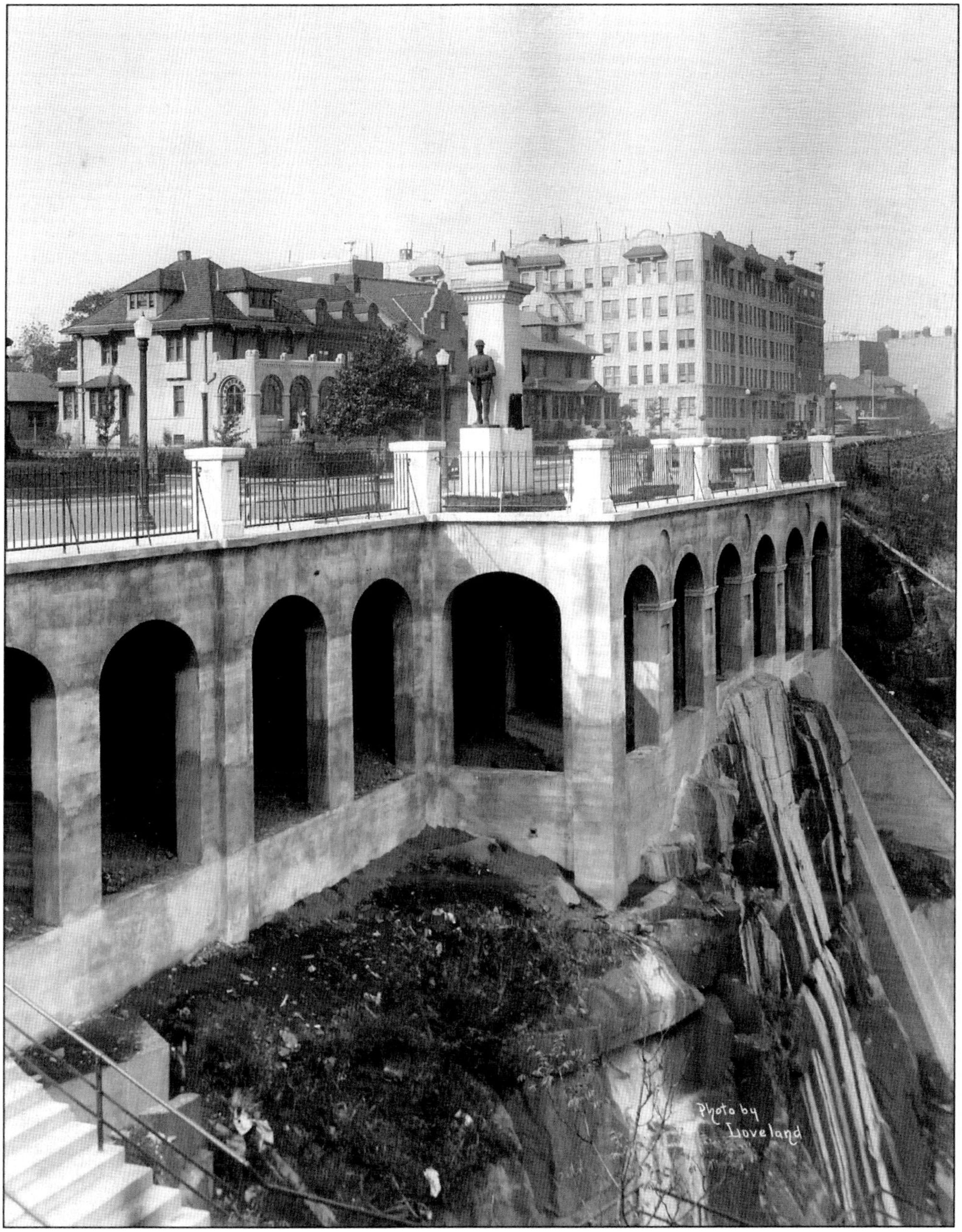

The township bought the old Bitter property from marine painter Henry Reuterdahl's family in 1926 and then acquired the Meister property in 1927 for the purpose of creating a town park. The buildings were razed, the foundations shored up, and a series of giant concrete arches were built to support Hamilton Plaza and the World War I soldiers and sailors monument. Just visible at the lower left is the beginning of the Grauert stairs. By 1930 when this photograph was taken, the west side Boulevard East included new homes and apartment buildings, all taking advantage of the extraordinary view and looking very much as they do today.

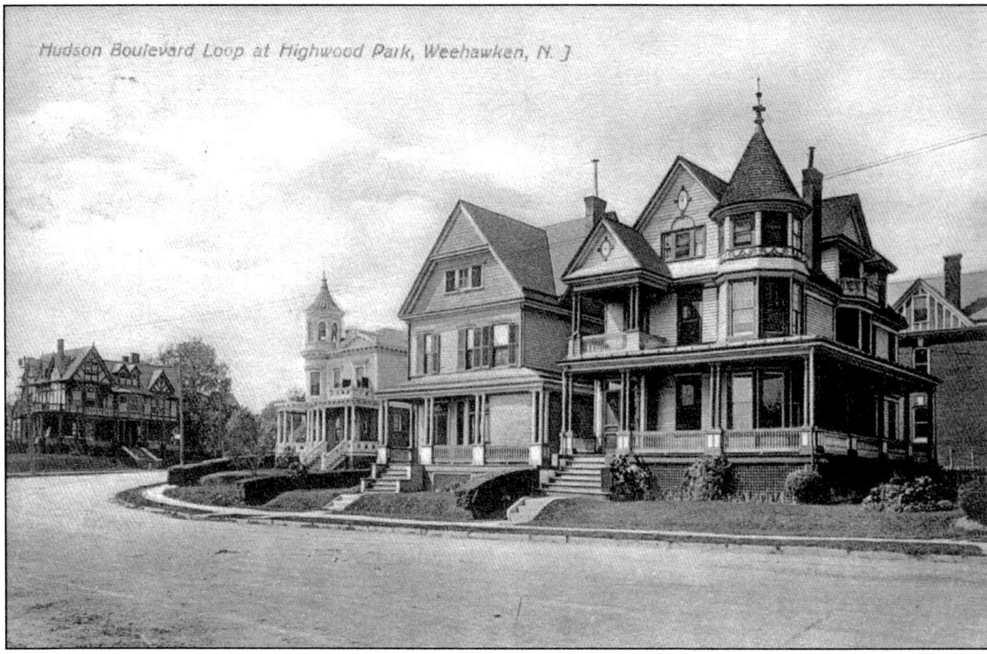

These large, late Victorian-style homes were built as part of the Highwood Park development, which began its initial offering in June 1894 during the last season of the Eldorado amusement park. Given the unobstructed views of New York City, the properties along the boulevard would have been snapped up first. (Al Berg.)

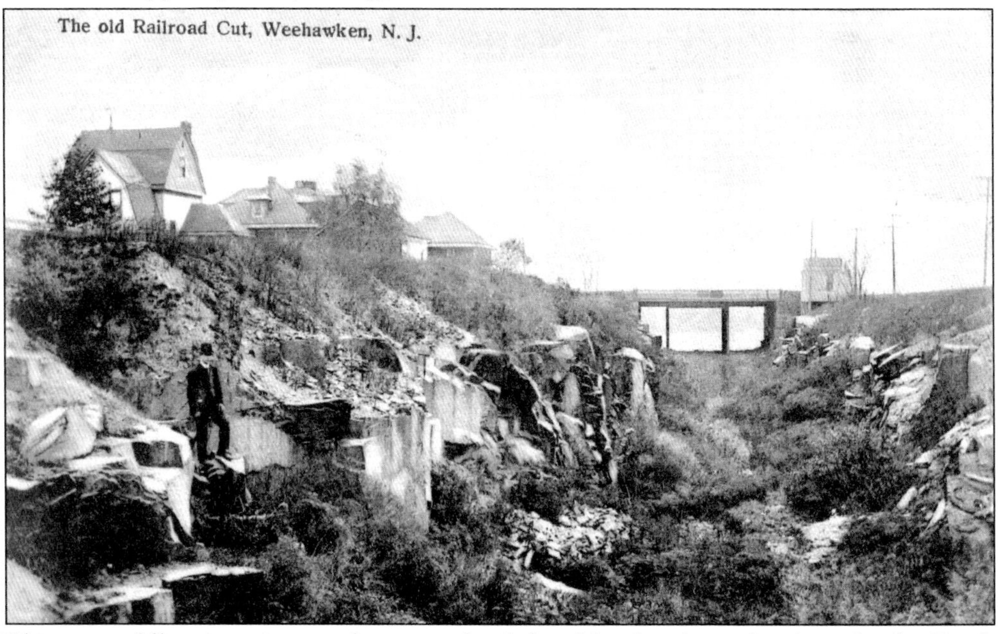

This young fellow is posing on the west side of the old railroad cut that brought the North Hudson Railway Company trains through the Palisades from the trestle attached to the giant elevator. Looking east, the homes seen at left are on the south side of Clifton Terrace. The railroad lasted only a few years, partially due to inexpensive and convenient trolley service from the West Shore Ferry terminal up Clifton Road, introduced in 1895. (Al Berg.)

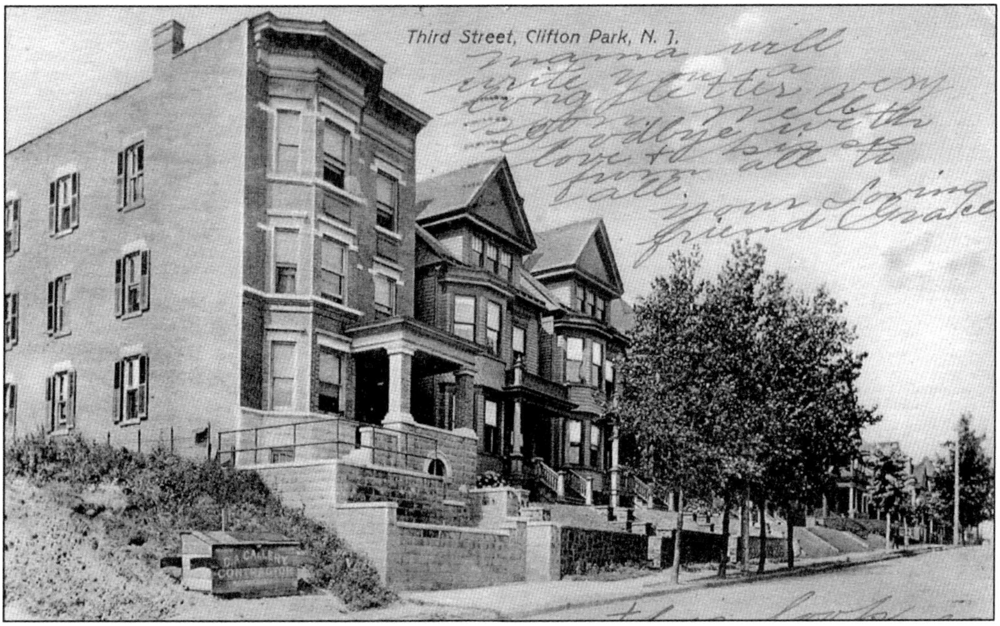

This is an early view taken from Boulevard East of tree-lined Third Street (today's Forty-seventh Street) in what was then called Clifton Park before the apartment building on the southwest corner was built. The construction container belonged to a C. A. Callery and a Mr. Murphy who were general contracting partners in the 1905 North Hudson business directory. (Barbara Hansen.)

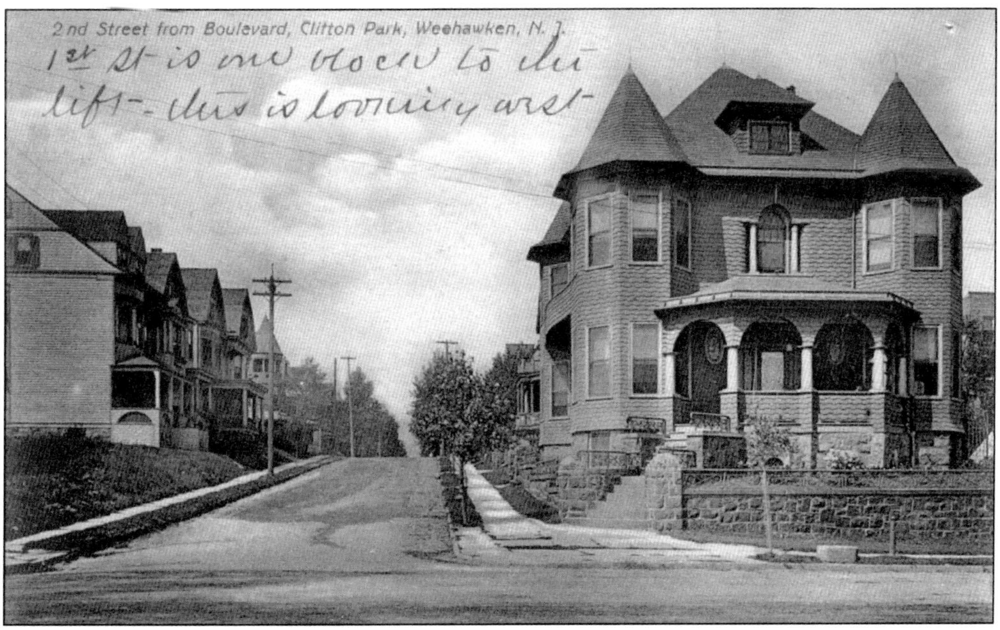

A Mr. Von Biela was the first owner of this house on the corner of Second Street (today's Forty-sixth Street) and Boulevard East. The house was one of the first built in what was called Eldorado Heights by the Eldorado Realty Company, a developer that purchased the site of the defunct amusement park. Its prospectus touted the newly completed Hudson County Boulevard, suggesting it rivaled Riverside Drive in New York. (Al Berg.)

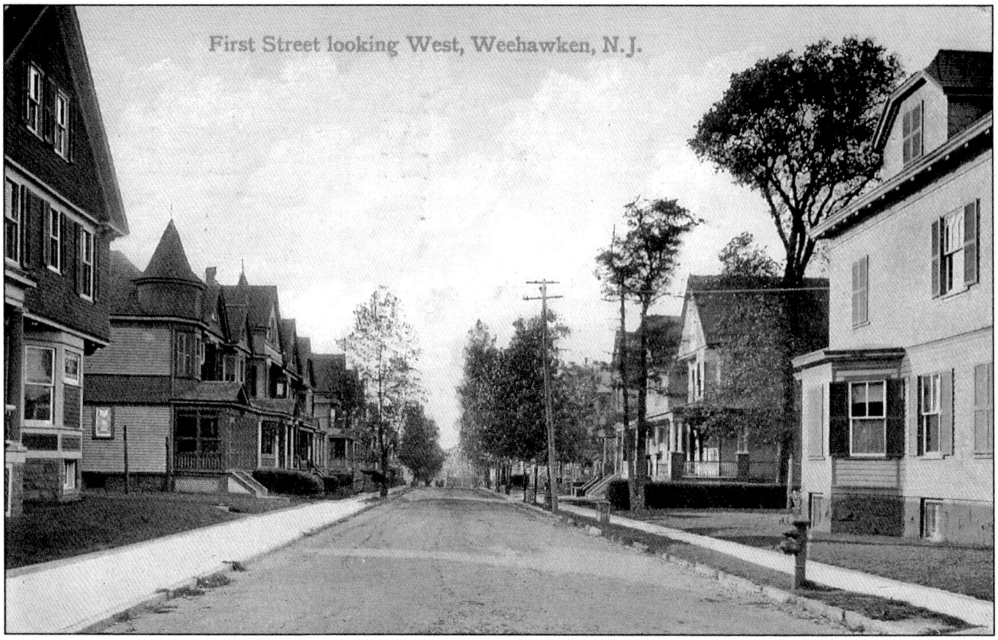

This postcard view, taken from Louisa Place, shows First Street (later Cooper Place) around 1900. Though the road appears unpaved, there are well-appointed houses on both sides of the street. Several of the houses on the north (right) side were demolished to make way for the Roosevelt School in 1927. First Street was renamed in 1940 after Alvah Cooper who was, at 85, the oldest resident on the block, having lived there for 41 years. (Lauren Sherman.)

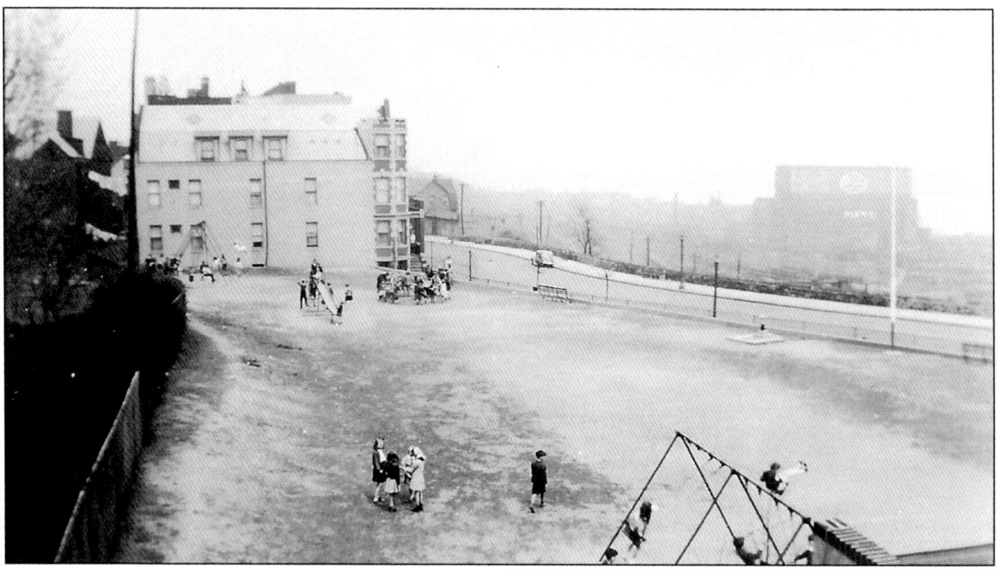

Louisa Park was built on land that had belonged to the Brown estate; the old house is just west of the playground property. Shown in 1943, there is not much equipment other than a couple of sets of swings and a small sliding board, but its location near Roosevelt School made it a convenient place for children to gather and play. On the waterfront looms the giant grain elevator. (Cheryl Burns Mansfield.)

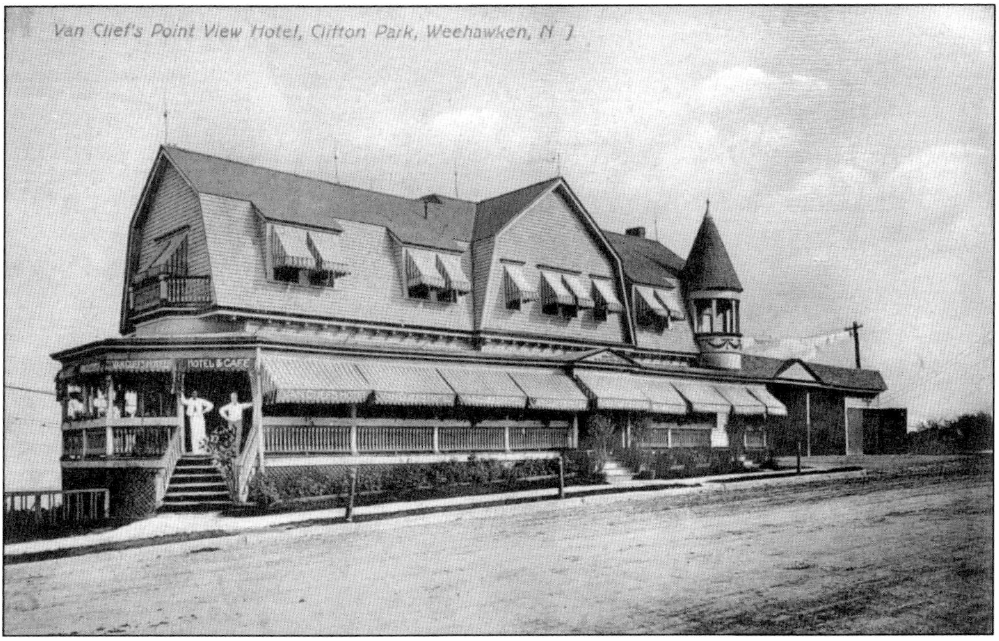

This old roadhouse, located on Boulevard East at the corner of Clifton Road (now Pershing Road), was first owned by master politician Simon Kelly. After his death in 1900, the business was taken over by a Mr. Van Clief and remained Van Clief's Hotel and Café for the next several decades. The building was remodeled over the years, losing its porch, awnings, and Queen Anne tower but retaining the Dutch-inspired gambrel roof and general profile. The building has been a restaurant for over 100 years since it first opened. (Al Berg.)

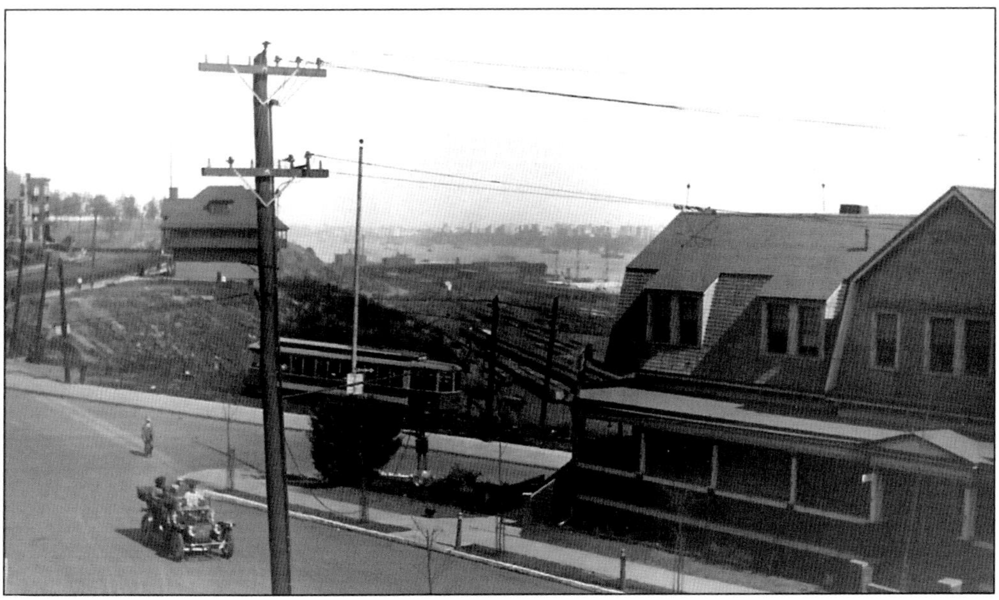

The intersection of Boulevard East and Clifton Road was a busy one in the early part of the second decade of the 20th century. Not only was the famous Van Clief's road house on the corner where one might stop for a drink or meal, but the trolley stopped there and took passengers to and from the West Shore Ferry Terminal. In the distance is Clifton Hose Company No. 3.

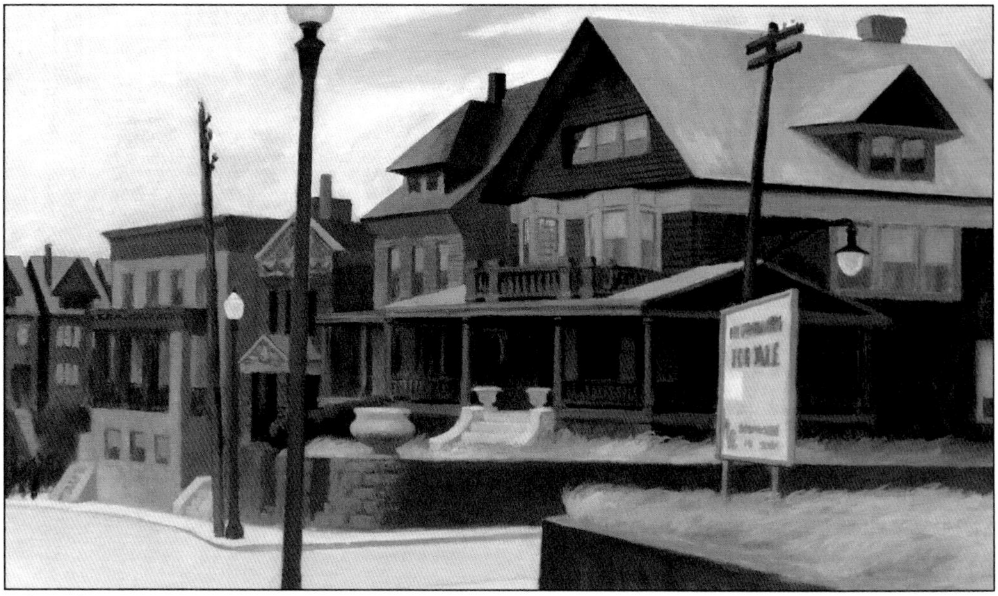

Edward Hopper's painting *East Wind Over Weehawken*, depicting the corner of Forty-ninth Street and Boulevard East, was painted in 1934 after a series of eight sketches he did of the site. Hopper found inspiration in the urban scenes of the city and occasionally ventured across the river to Hoboken and Weehawken. The corner does not look much different today; the concrete urn still sits at the corner retaining wall directly across from the American Legion lot. (Pennsylvania Academy of the Fine Arts, Philadelphia, Collections Fund.)

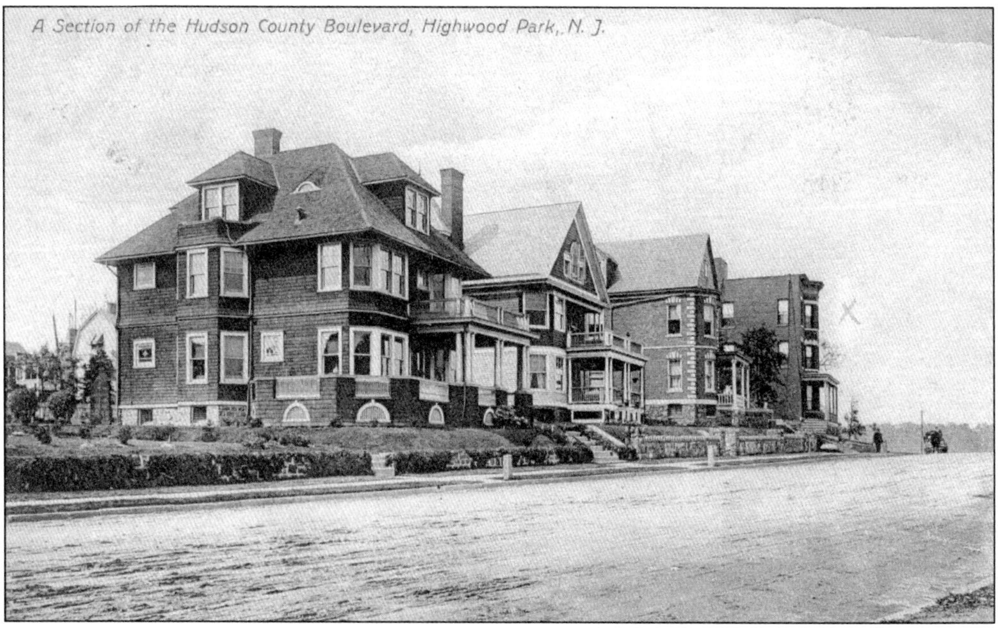

The Eldorado Realty Company's intention was to sell lots developed with homes in order to retain control of architectural style and construction quality, but they also built to purchasers' plans. So sure that the amenities of Weehawken would be apparent to new buyers, they built some homes on a speculative basis. Pictured above are Boulevard East houses between Forty-ninth and Fiftieth Streets. (Al Berg.)

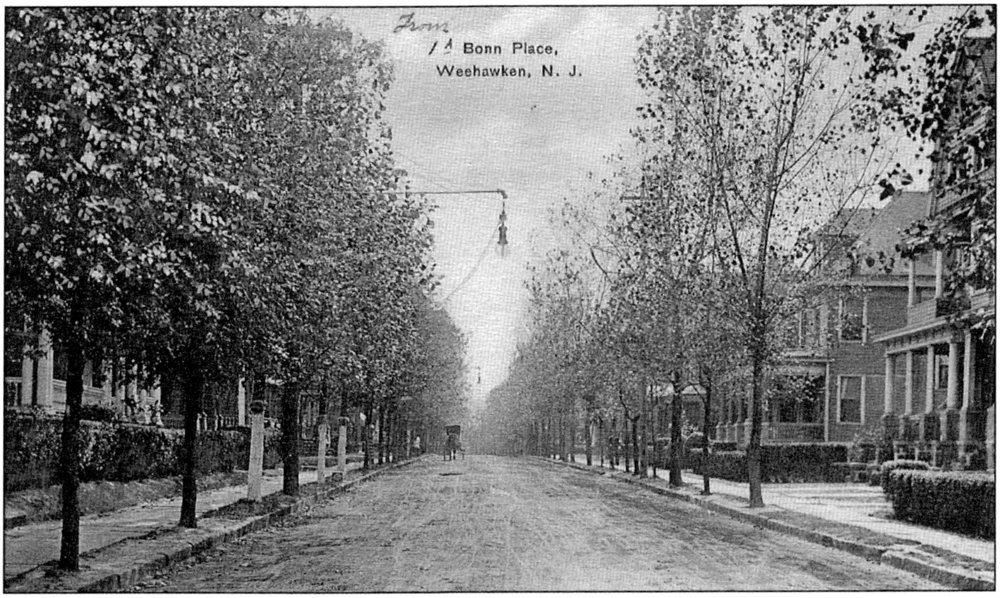

Highwood Park was the earliest residential development to appear after the sell off of the King estate. First offered for sale and then auctioned in 1894 by Hugh N. Camp, a New York real estate developer, lots were quickly sold, and large, gracious homes on tree-lined streets were erected. Bonn Place, pictured here, was named for Weehawken resident John H. Bonn, a German immigrant who conceived the transit system of surface and elevated railroads in north Hudson County. (Charlesworth family.)

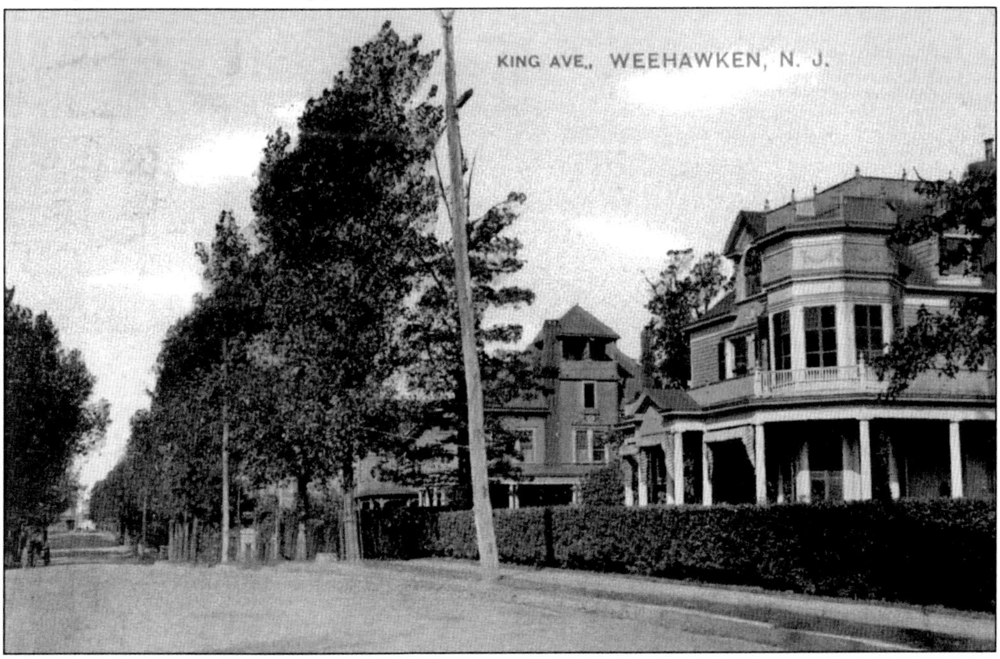

King Avenue, named for James Gore King, was the site of the original Highwood mansion, which had been located between Hamilton Avenue and Boulevard East in this first block. This view looks south toward Bellevue Street. The house in the foreground with two widow's walks was first owned by a Mrs. Brinkman. (Al Berg.)

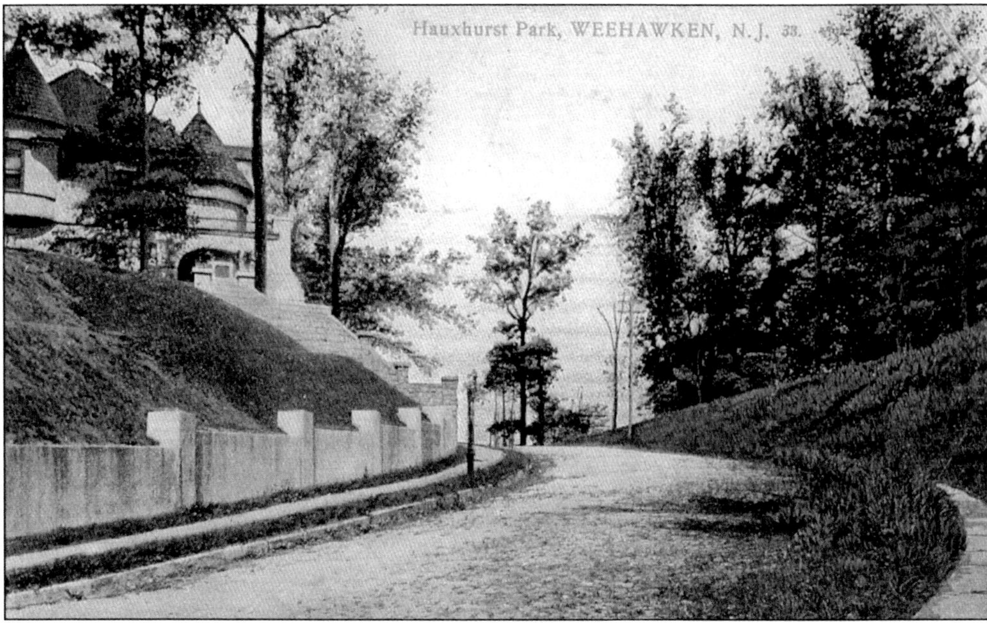

William Peter, a German immigrant who fled his homeland in 1850, is an iconic American success story. Apprenticed to brewers in New York and its environs, he quickly learned the trade and started his own small brewery in West New York in 1859, moving to Union Hill in 1862. His successful business grew over the course of 40 years until he was able to have a 17-room German-style castle built in Weehawken in 1904. At a cost of about $75,000, it was filled with marble, large stained-glass windows, custom tiles and woodwork, and several fireplaces. The building passed through several owners and was eventually sold to the Port of New York Authority during the Lincoln Tunnel construction. Since the port authority did not need the property, it was turned over to the township and transformed into the Weehawken library in 1942. The photograph below shows the home as it looked around 1920. (Above, Lauren Sherman.)

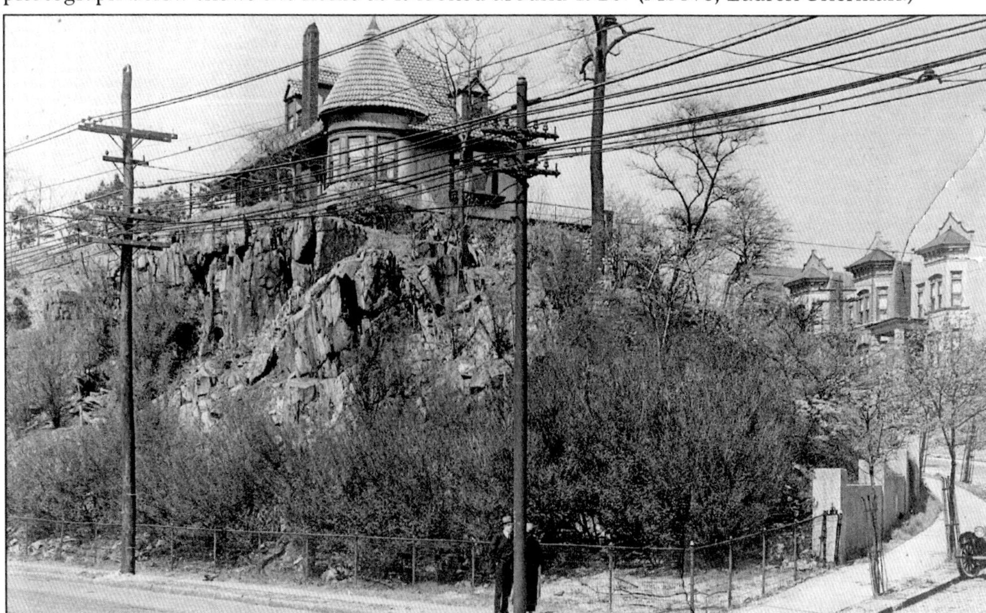

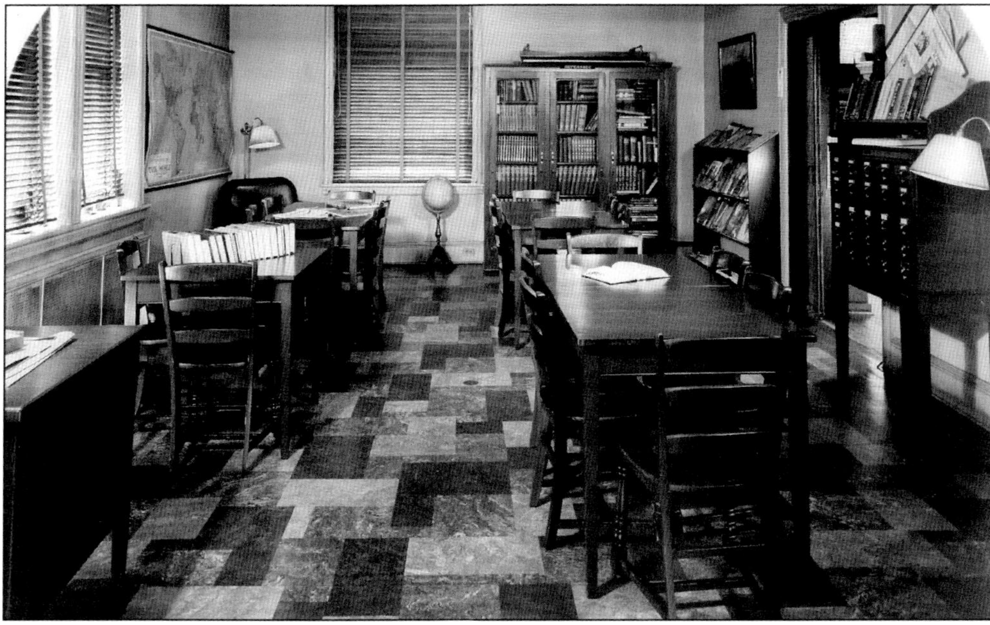

The Peter mansion was converted into the Weehawken library and is probably one of the more unique buildings used as a library. At its opening, the building was filled with books and artifacts donated by residents, leading to the development of a historical room that housed Weehawken memorabilia. Pictured is a room in the library around 1948. In 1997, the library closed for restoration and enlargement and reopened in 1999. (Weehawken Public Library.)

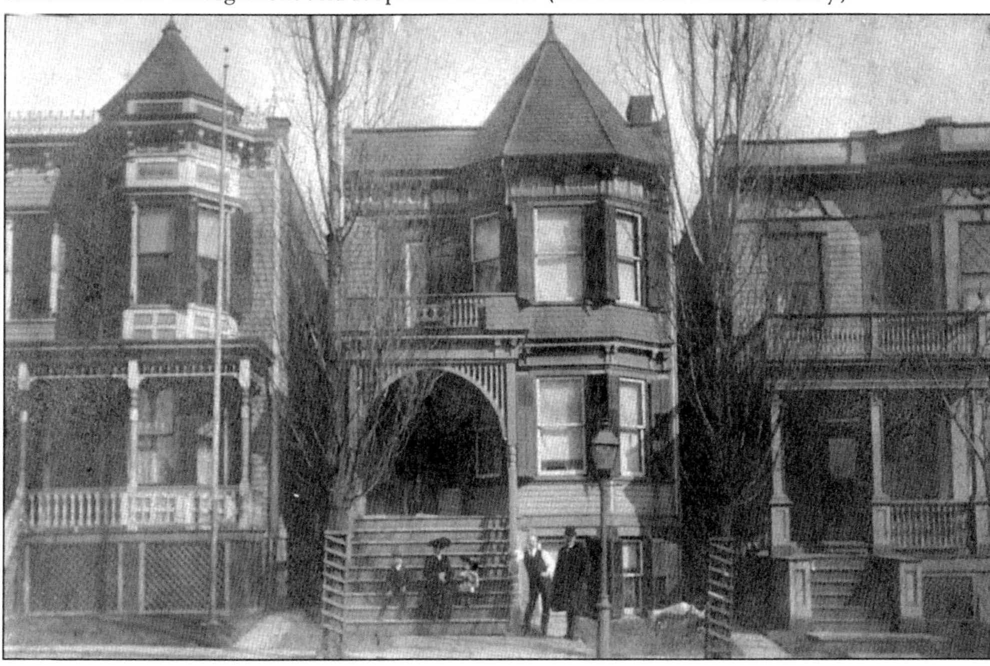

This view of 108 Hauxhurst Avenue (center) shows the Hauxhurst area as it was at the very beginning of the 20th century. All the houses wore their original wooden cladding and were ornamented with Victorian gingerbread decoration. Pictured are Mary and Richard Purcell with two unidentified children and Edward Hayden standing next to the gas lamp.

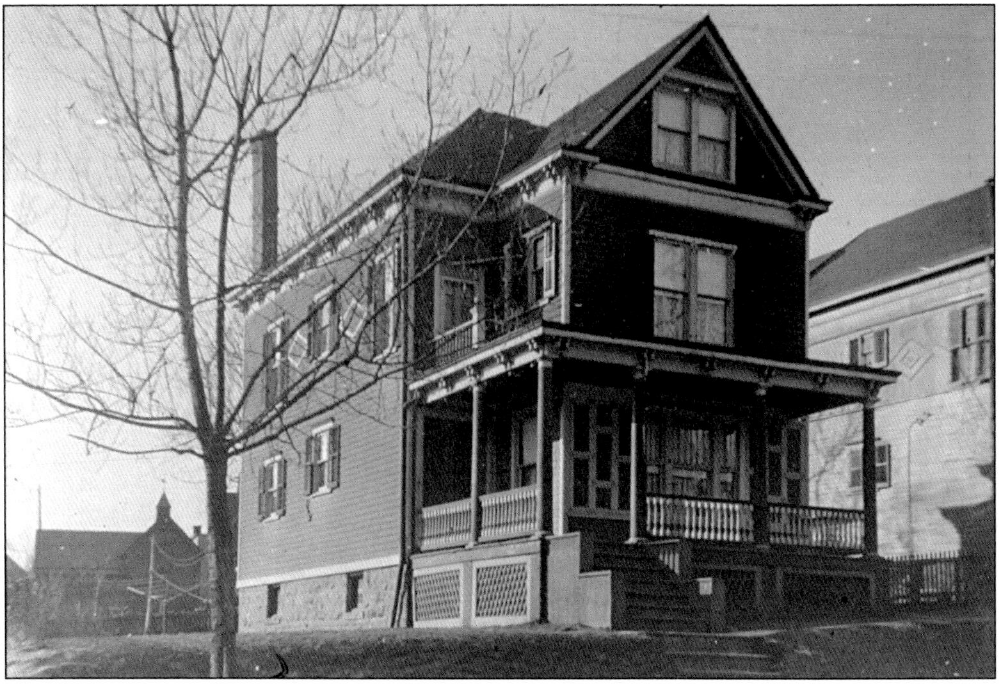

The house at 55 Highwood Terrace, east of Hauxhurst Avenue, was built by John M. Hannan who was born downtown on Nineteenth Street in 1875 and went on to serve as poormaster, tax assessor, and the only sheriff elected from Weehawken to serve in Hudson County. His brother Thomas was a Weehawken policeman, and another brother, James, was a detective. His son John J. was a councilman and member of the Weehawken Juvenile Conference Committee and also captured much of Weehawken's history with his camera.

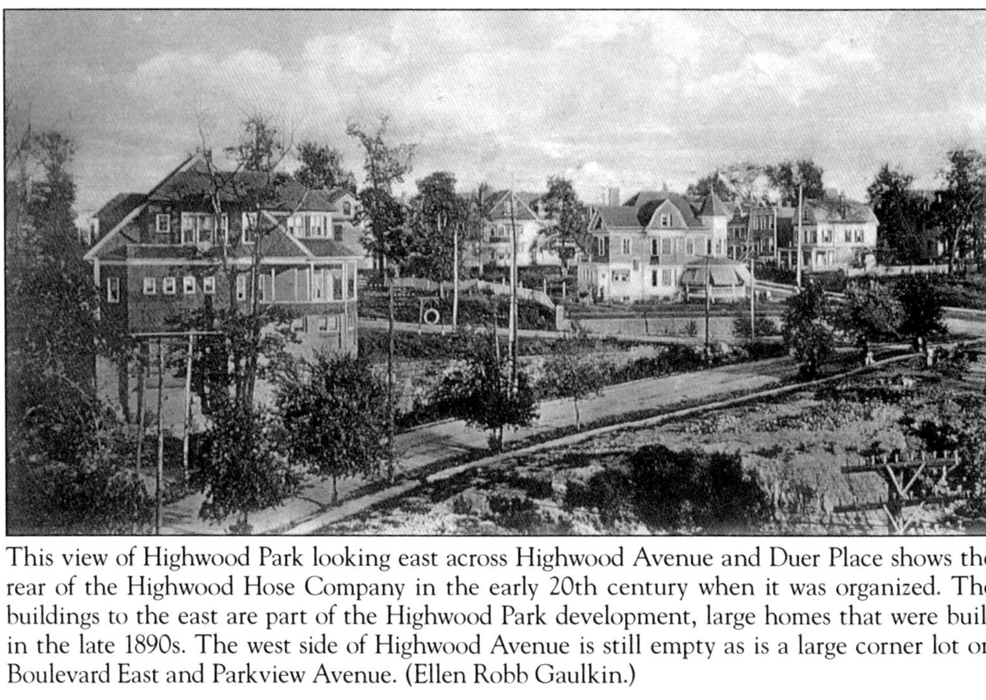

This view of Highwood Park looking east across Highwood Avenue and Duer Place shows the rear of the Highwood Hose Company in the early 20th century when it was organized. The buildings to the east are part of the Highwood Park development, large homes that were built in the late 1890s. The west side of Highwood Avenue is still empty as is a large corner lot on Boulevard East and Parkview Avenue. (Ellen Robb Gaulkin.)

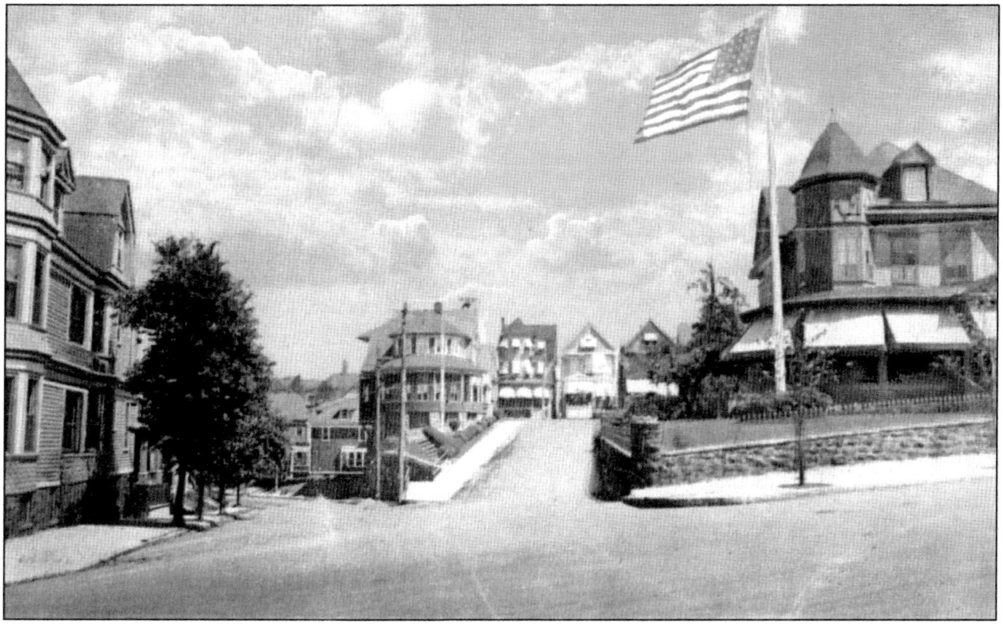

This somewhat later postcard looking north from the intersection of Boulevard East, Duer Place, and Highwood Avenue shows the changes in a few short years. By 1907, the fire tower of Highwood Hose Company was added (peeking out from the right side of the roofline) and Highwood Avenue was developed. The homes pictured still stands, though without awnings. (Al Berg.)

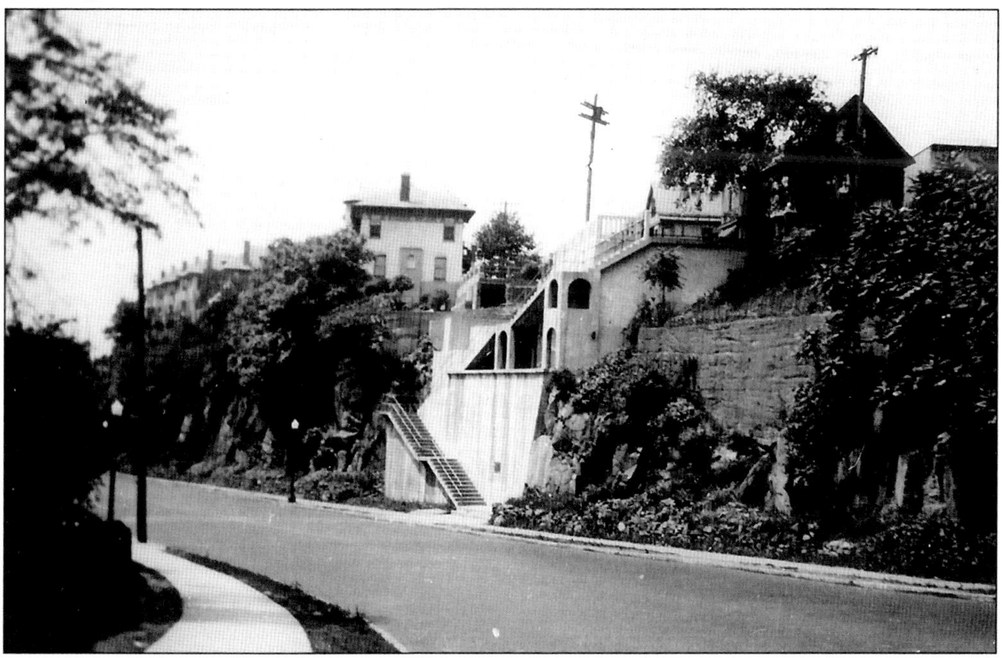

The Jefferson Street stairs were designed to make the Hauxhurst Park area easily accessible to the boulevard by foot without having to walk to Highwood Terrace and around. Linking Sterling and Jefferson Streets with Boulevard East, the concrete steps were completed under the administration of Mayor Emile W. Grauert in 1926 at a cost of about $15,000.

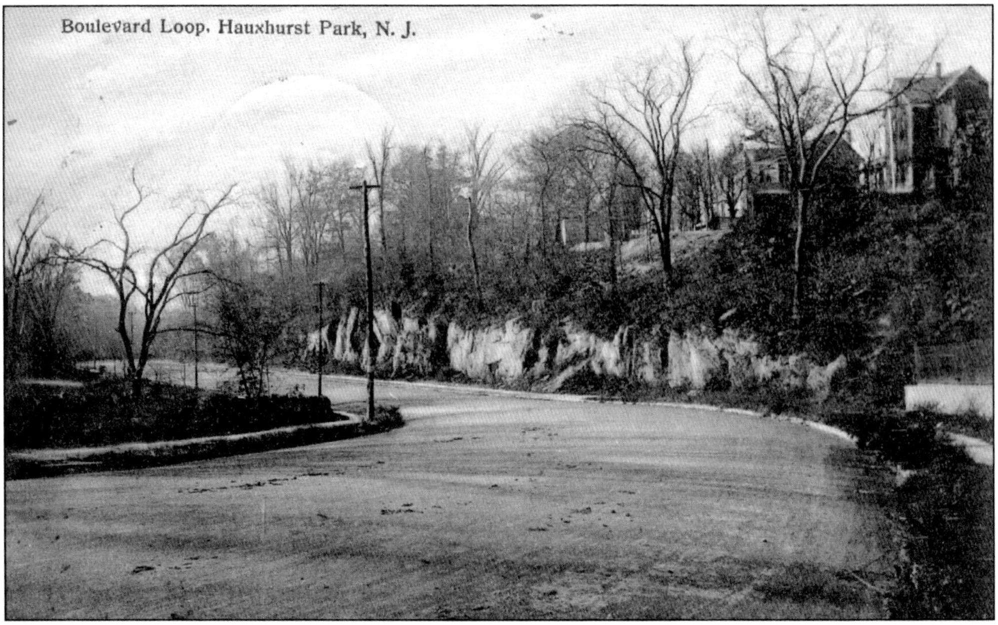

This view of Boulevard East looking south towards the valley, the low-lying land where the Lincoln Tunnel entrance plaza is today, shows several homes at the end of Jefferson Street prior to the bulk of homes built on Sterling Place between 1910 and 1915 and long before construction of the Jefferson Street stairs in 1926. The boulevard sidewalks are in, but the road is still unpaved. (Al Berg.)

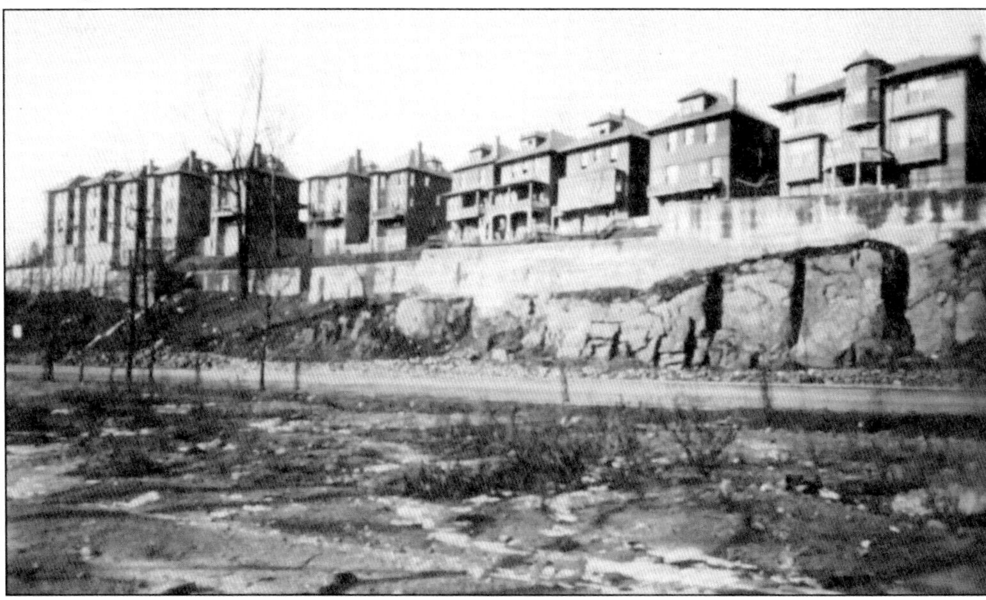

This photograph looks to have been taken just shortly after completion of the homes that front Sterling Avenue in Hauxhurst Park. Lots that had been accumulated by Samuel E. Renner and Thomas Henry were sold off to several real estate developers in 1911. The hillside was cleared of brush and trees, and the cliffs were stabilized with the construction of cement retaining walls. Across the boulevard is nothing but an empty tract of undeveloped land about where Hamilton House is today. (Al Berg.)

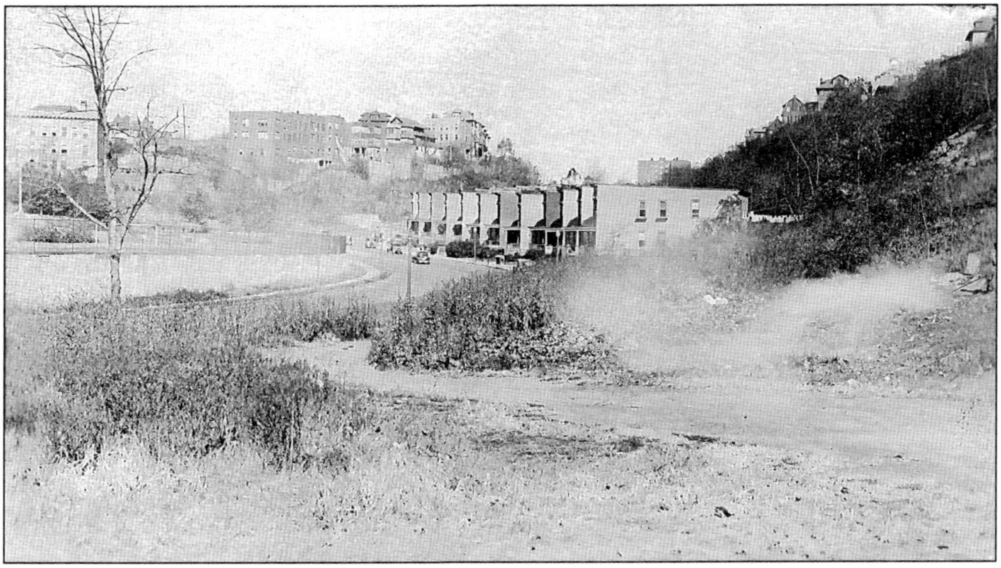

These homes along the right side of Boulevard East across from the valley playground were demolished as part of the Lincoln Tunnel construction. Seen near the top of this photograph from about 1930 are several homes and an apartment house on Sterling Avenue that also fell to the bulldozer. At far left is the two-year-old town hall.

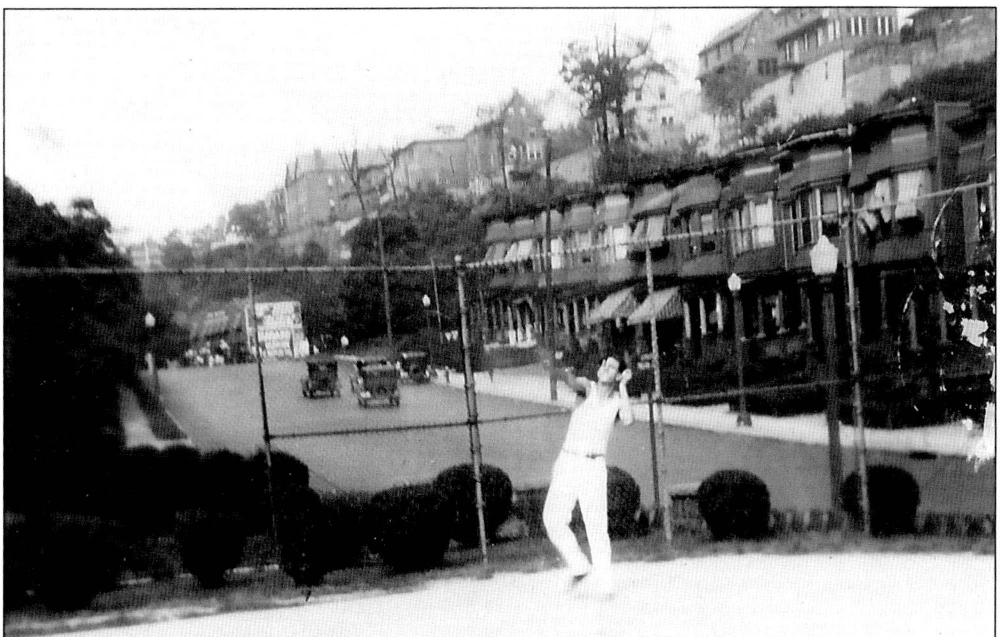

There were eight tennis courts along Boulevard East on the way down into the valley. All told, 26 homes along the east side of the street were demolished around 1934 to make way for the new access roads and helix of the Lincoln Tunnel. These homes were replaced by the Boulevard East exit ramp off of Interstate 495 West.

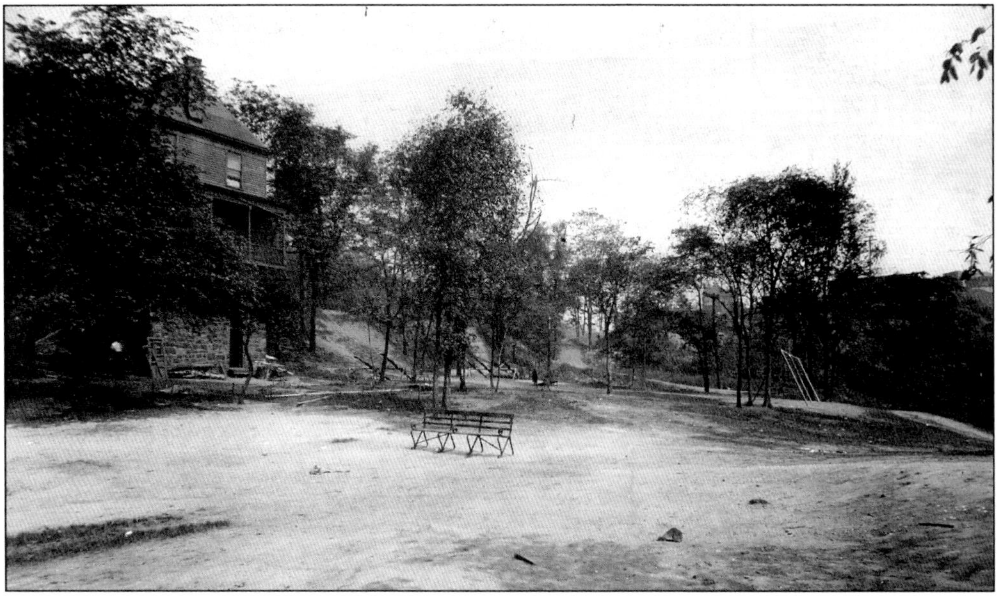

This is a 1920s view of the valley playground before the new town hall was built in 1928. The playground, a large, open multipurpose area with seesaws and a lone swing set was demolished as part of the Lincoln Tunnel construction; the 75th-anniversary celebration on September 28, 1934, was the last event held there. In 1938, the port authority built a new two-acre recreational center for the township, which included football and baseball fields, tennis and handball courts, a playground, and a concrete grandstand.

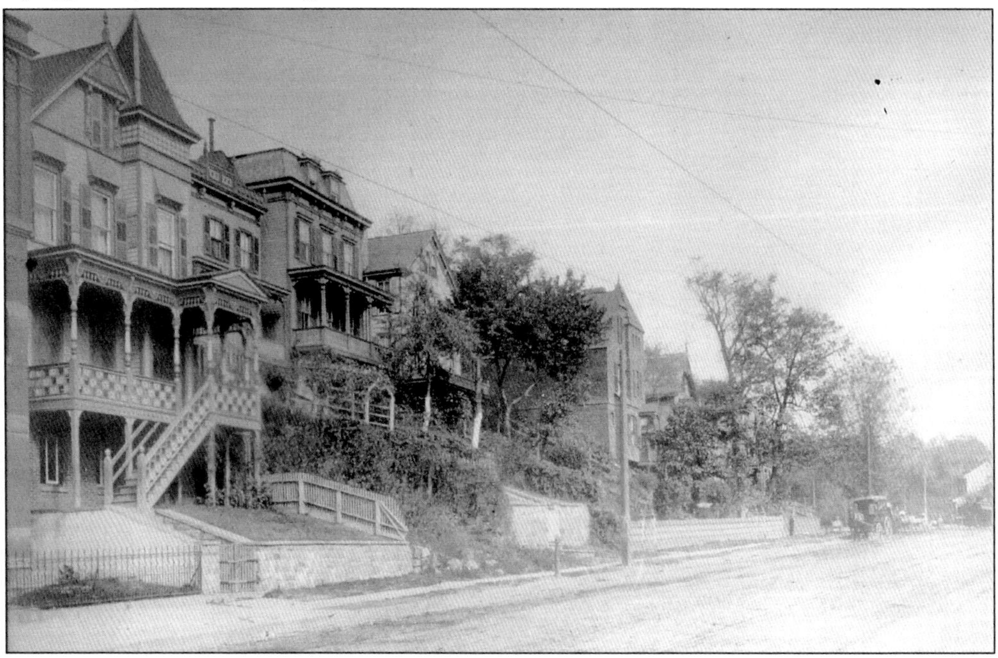

This view of lower Park Avenue, or Bulls Ferry Road as it was alternately known in the early 20th century, shows genteel houses with ornate Victorian decoration on the west side of the street. These houses are just north of the old town hall building. Up the road a bit, a delivery horse and carriage is making its way downtown to the Shades.

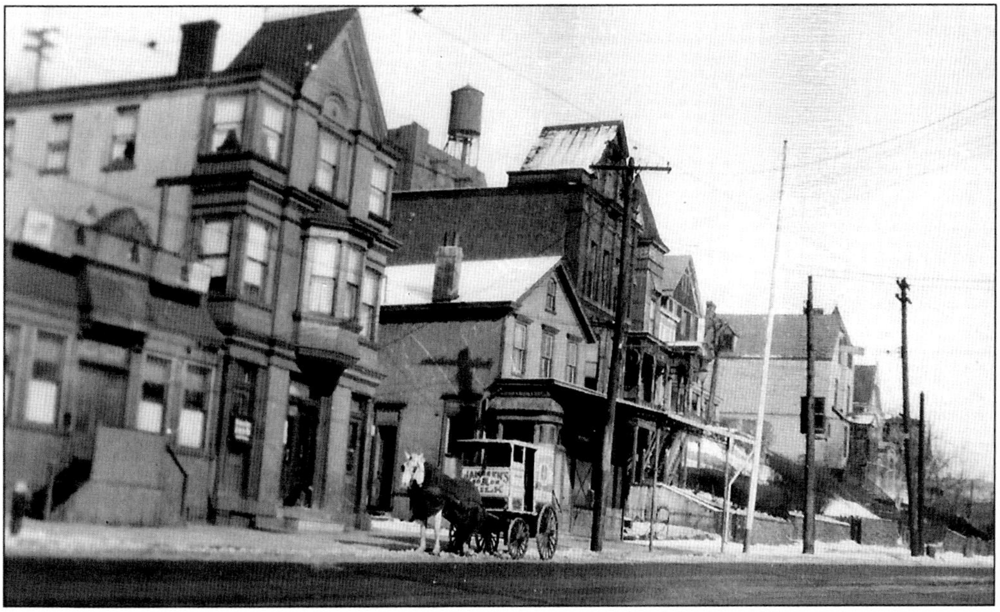

This 20th-century winter scene along lower Park Avenue with a blanketed horse shows Jamesen's A Milk truck making its deliveries. The milk wagon is just south of the old town hall, the three-story building with snow on its peeked roof.

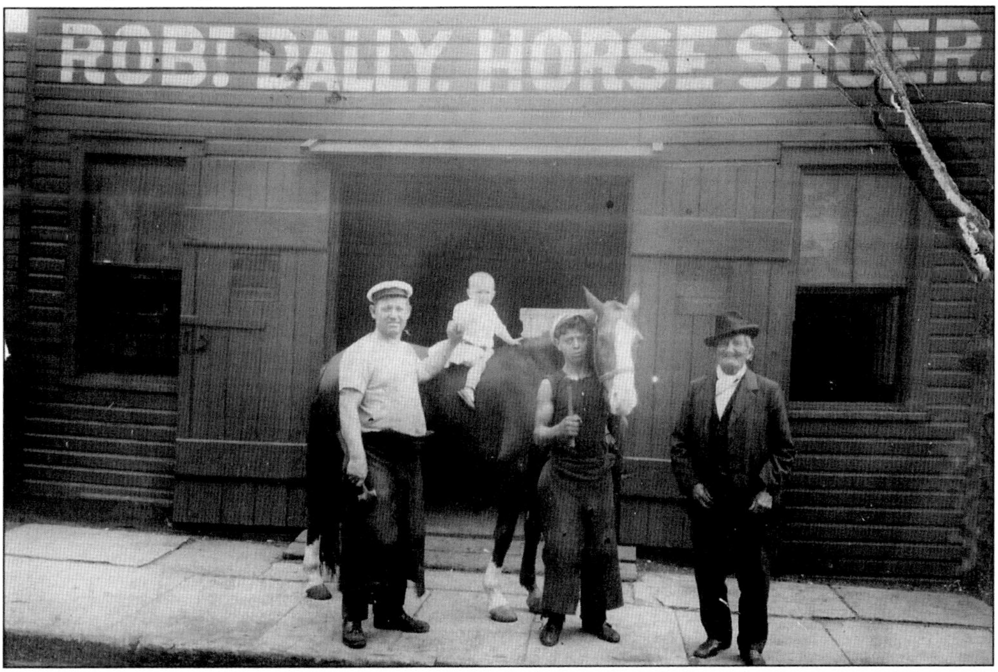

Robert Dally was a horseshoer in Weehawken and Union Hill from the late part of the 19th century until trolleys and cars made his business obsolete. The shop was located on the west side of Bulls Ferry Road across from the reservoir of Hackensack Water Company. Horses were dropped off, reshoed, and then delivered back to their owners, all in a day's work. Pictured from left to right are Robert Dally; Robert Dally Jr. on horseback, who grew up to be a Weehawken police sergeant; and two unidentified persons. (Cindy Dally Cimino.)

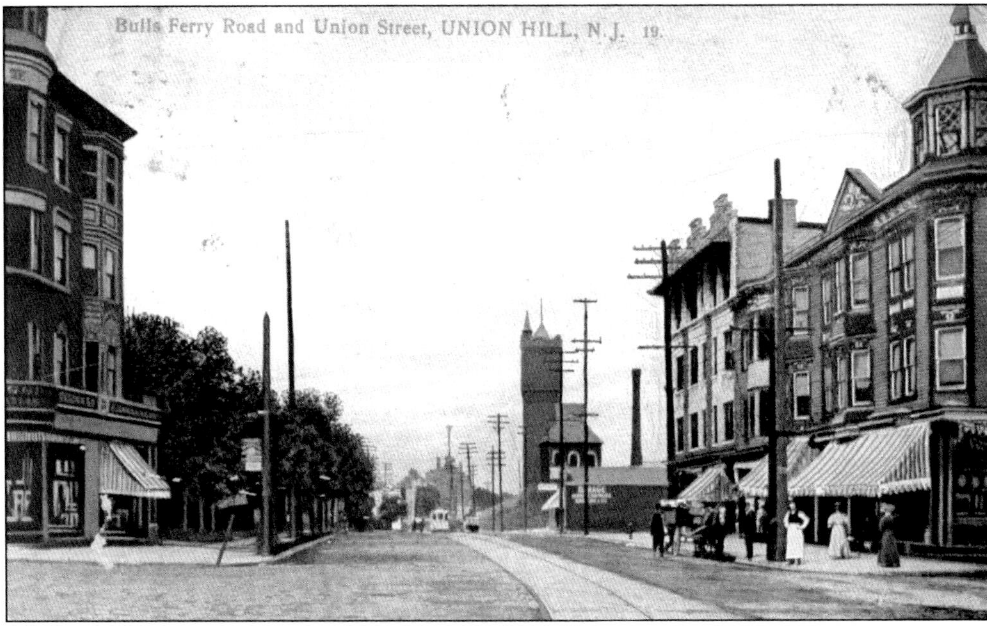

Looking north from the junction of Union Street (today's Thirty-seventh Street) and Highwood Terrace up Bulls Ferry Road is an active streetscape with a shopkeeper, shoppers, a peddler and his wagon, as well as a trolley disappearing towards the water tower. Directly south of the reservoir is a garage, which later became Jacobsen Power Motors and remained until the demolition of the reservoir in 1980. (Al Berg.)

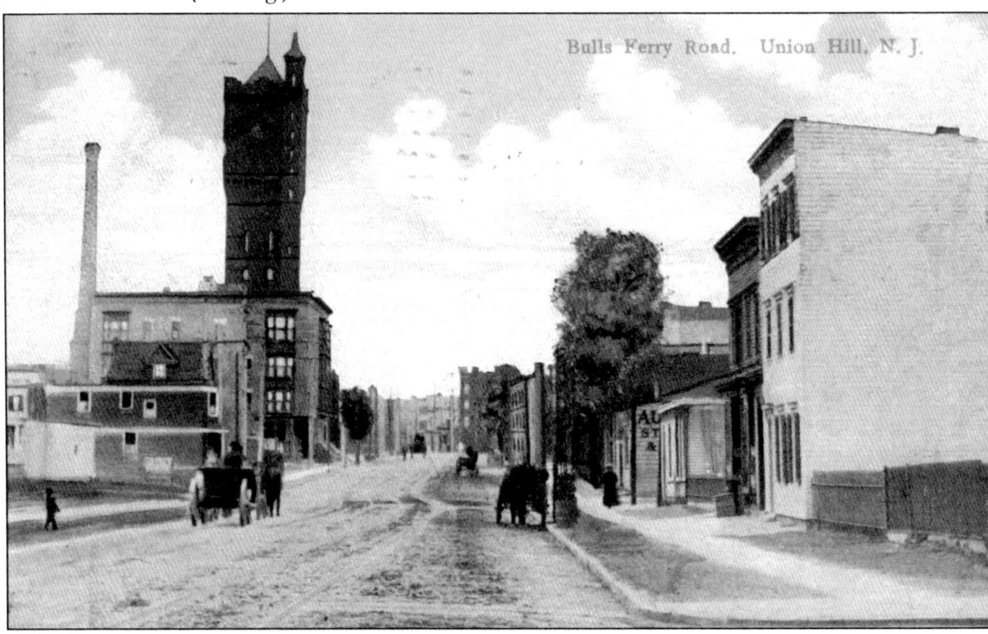

Looking south from Clifton Place down Bulls Ferry Road in the late 19th century shows a fairly rustic thoroughfare, especially considering it was the main commercial street for this part of Weehawken. The water tower and a few buildings near Liberty Place are here. Steel tracks are visible, but these are probably from the horse-drawn streetcars, the predecessor of the electric trolleys. (Al Berg.)

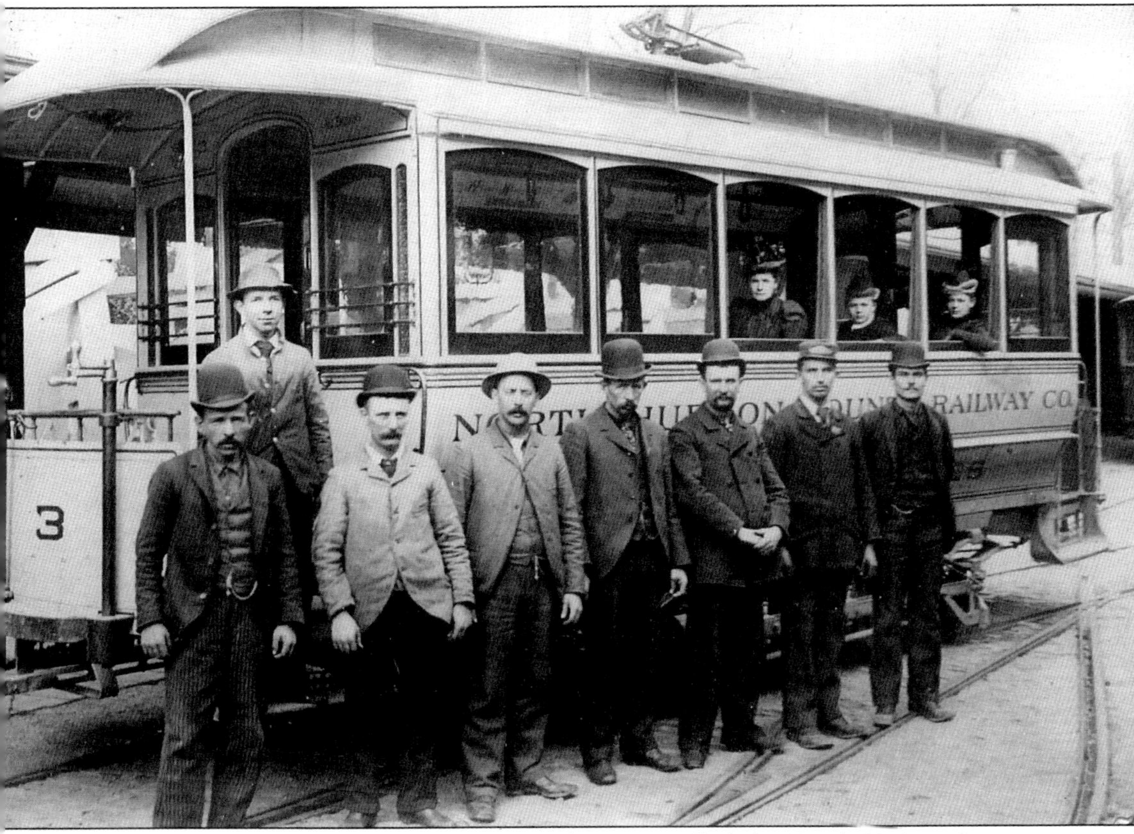

The first trolley car service to run in north Hudson was called the North Hudson County Railway Company. It operated along Bulls Ferry Road going to and from the Hoboken Ferry. Electric trolleys were preceded by the Union Hill-Weehawken horse cars, trolley cars that also ran on steel rails pulled by two horses. John H. Bonn was the impetus behind modernizing the transit system in north Hudson, starting with a series of street railroads in 1859 that were consolidated into the North Hudson County Railway Company in 1865. In the late 1880s, the invention of an electricity collection system from overhead wires made horse cars obsolete. This 1892 photograph shows Eldorado station, which was located at the foot of Liberty Place and Bulls Ferry Road (today's Park Avenue). Pictured in front of car No. 3 from left to right are John Bauer; unidentified; Louis Straube, conductor; William Wirtz, motorman; Charles Hess; Richard Fowler; Edward Johnson, Weehawken patrolman; unidentified; and three ladies on board.

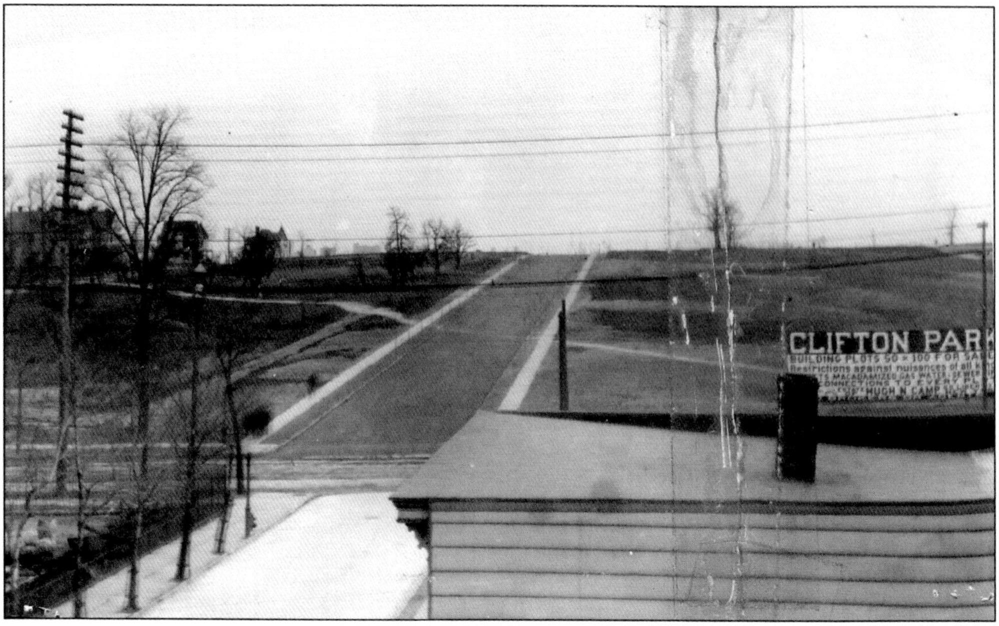

Hugh N. Camp's estate offered for sale 50 by 100 foot plots of land with macadamized roads, sidewalks, and utility connections already in place. Camp, who died in 1895, was a powerful New York financier who became active in real estate and specialized in improving large plots. His business address was 55 Liberty Street in New York, as seen on the sign at the foot of Bulls Ferry Road and Clifton Terrace.

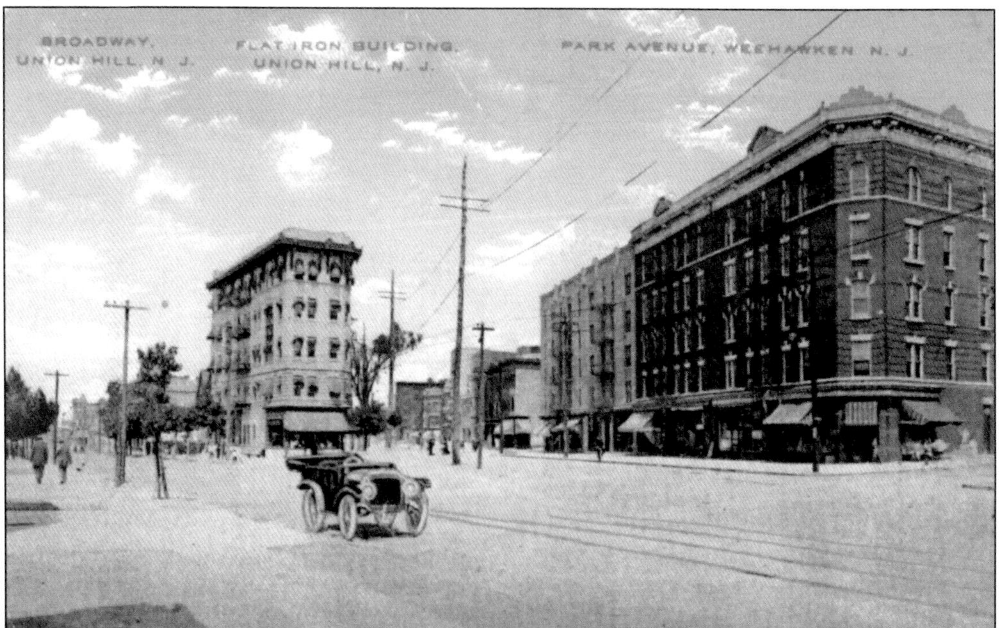

This early view of the junction of Park Avenue in Weehawken and Broadway in Union Hill does not look all that different today, aside from the new war memorial plaza just recently dedicated. The interesting triangular building (named for its similarity to the New York building on Fifth Avenue and Broadway) is somewhat of a landmark here too. (Al Berg.)

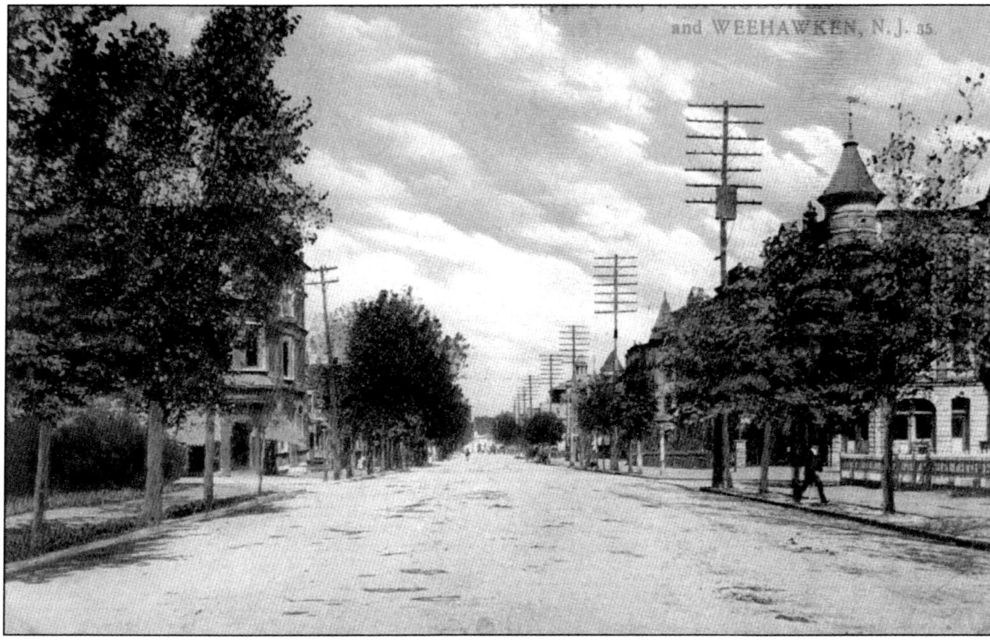

This early 1900s view of Palisade Avenue was taken just south of Shippen Street looking north. The west side of the street, now Union City, was then part of West Hoboken. When Weehawken became a township, a portion of West Hoboken that included areas from Gregory Avenue west to the east side of Palisade Avenue was joined to Weehawken. West Hoboken and Union were both created as separate townships from North Bergen in 1861. (Al Berg.)

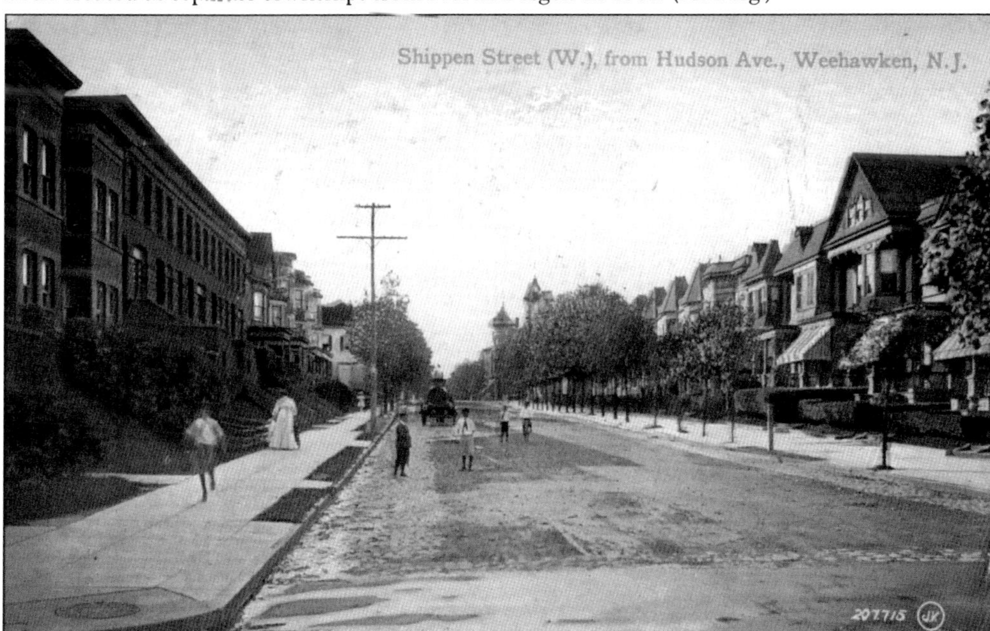

Shippen Street, named for William W. Shippen, president of the Hoboken Land and Improvement Company, was the one of the wider residential streets in the Heights section. Seen here in this c. 1900 postcard looking west toward Palisade Avenue is a partially paved street populated with children walking, running, and bicycle riding. (Al Berg.)

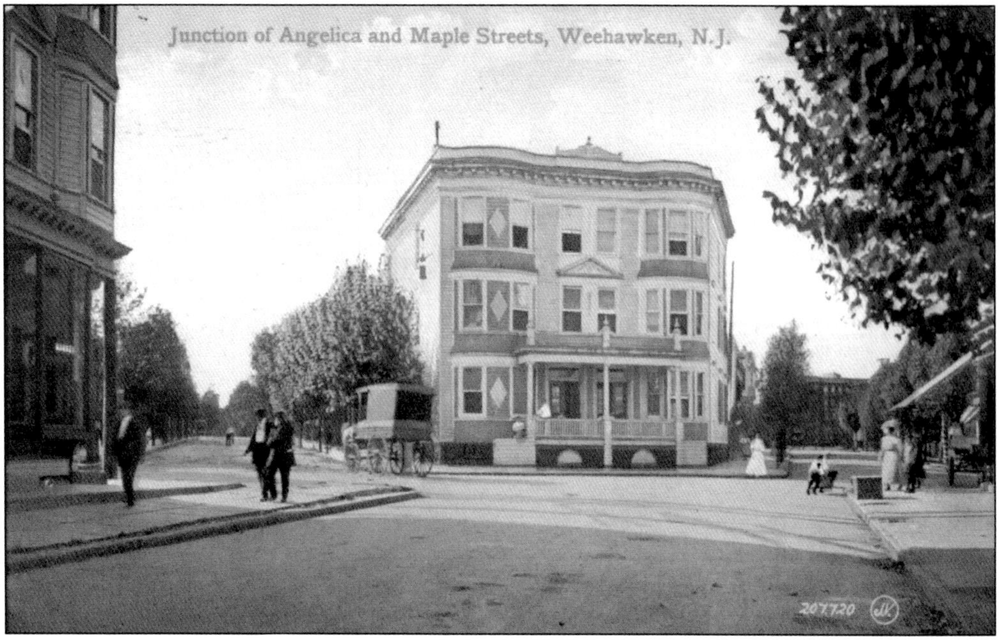

This view of the corners of Maple Street, Angelique Street, and Hudson Avenue is a wonderful glimpse into the slower pace of life in the Heights back in the early 1900s. A carriage makes its way west on Angelique Street and well-dressed ladies and gents are out for a stroll. All still existing though transformed are the corner market at left, the residential building at center, and a store on the northeast corner of Maple Street. (Al Berg.)

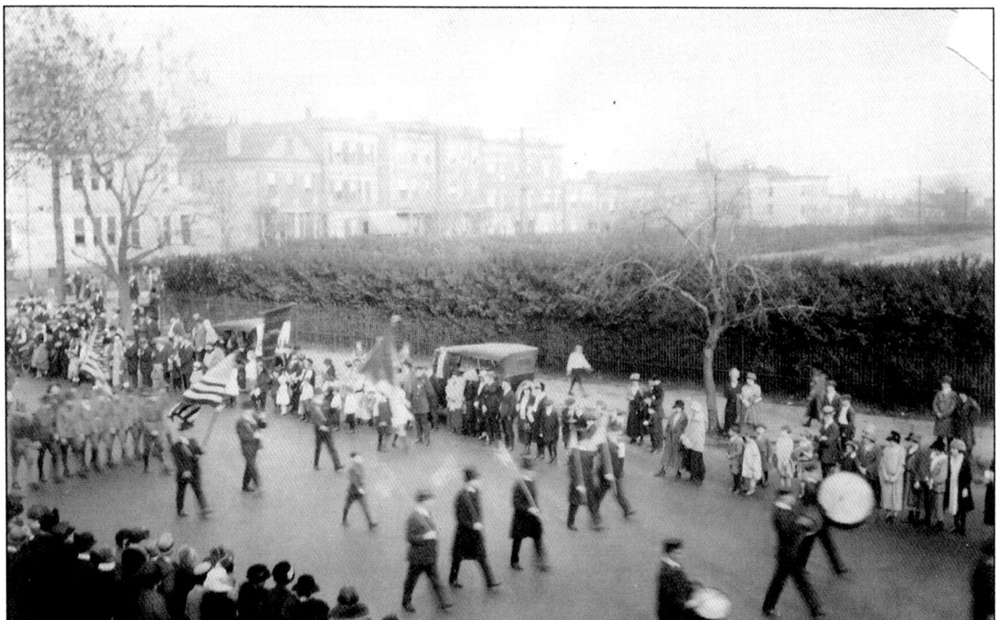

This undated photograph depicts a parade on Palisade Avenue just passing Highpoint Avenue and Hackensack Water Company's reservoir No. 2. Since there are World War I doughboys marching, no leaves on the trees, and women in coats, one might surmise that this is a celebration of Armistice Day on November 11, 1918. (Willie Demontreux.)

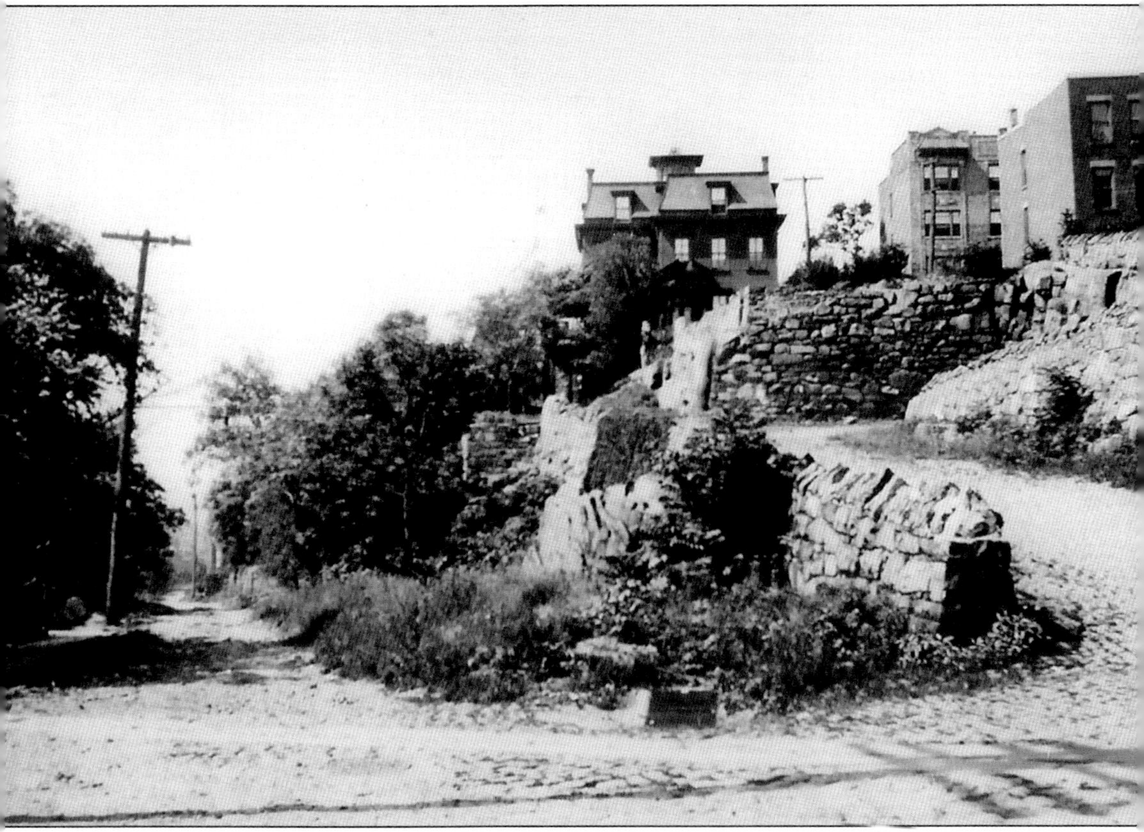

The Shippen Street horseshoe, a cobbled double-hairpin road connecting the steep grade change from Shippen Street to Hackensack Plank Road is seen here in the early part of the 20th century. The high road, as some locals call Hackensack Plank Road, was once a toll road leading from Hoboken to Hackensack. There are two sets of steps here: the first lead from Shippen Street to Hackensack Plank Road without walking the horseshoe, and across Hackensack Plank Road on the east side of the street is the second set that descend to Park Avenue just south of the old town hall. The Shippen Street double horseshoe was placed on the New Jersey and National Registers of Historic Places in 1997.

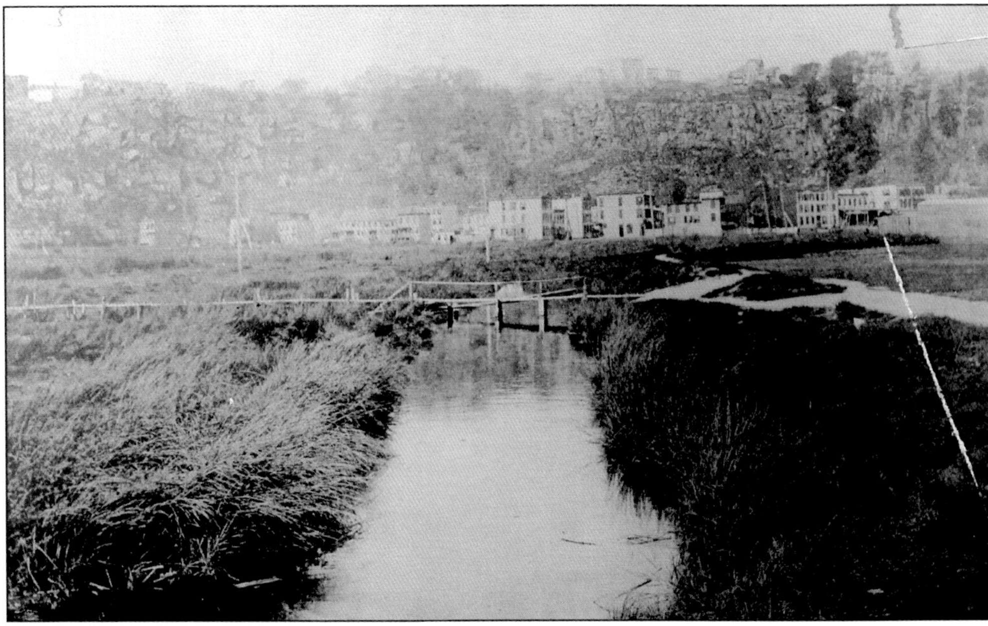

This view of lower Weehawken looking back towards the Shades shows a brook or creek that ran from the shore of the Hudson west towards the back of the downtown area. Though long gone, it marked the dividing line between Weehawken and Hoboken. The vegetation here looks similar to the marshy grasses of the Meadowlands a bit further west. The old footbridge in the photograph led from Weehawken across to Hoboken.

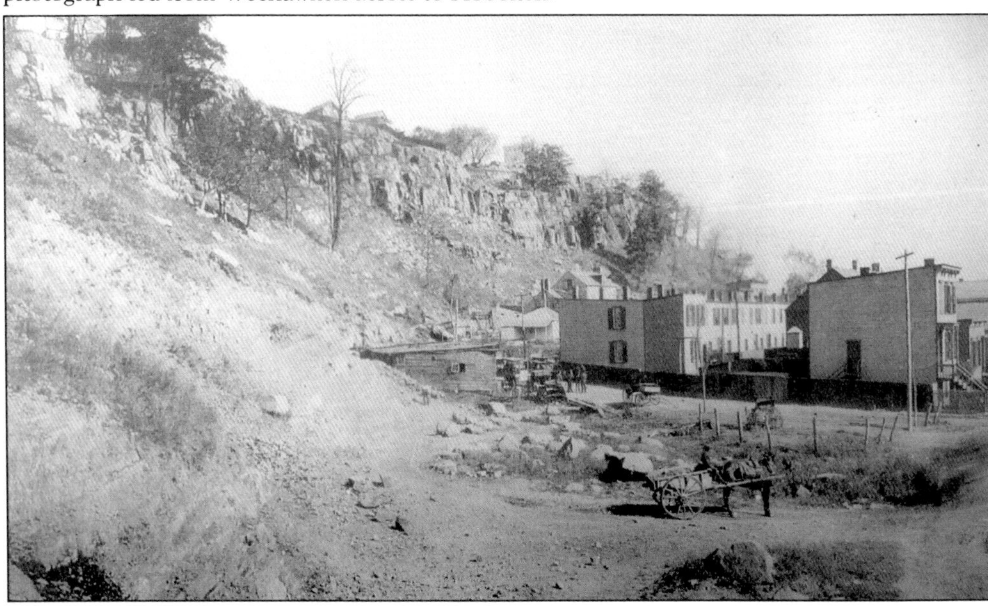

In 1879, the Shades, or downtown section of West Hoboken, was annexed to Weehawken, an area that included Nineteenth Street at the northern boundary, Eighteenth Street at the southern end, and from Willow Avenue through Hackensack Plank Road, Grand Street, and Amelia Street (later part of Nineteenth Street) at the western boundary. Shown in 1892 is the back end of the Shades at the foot of Chestnut Street and West Nineteenth Street with Pete Haye's stables in the center.

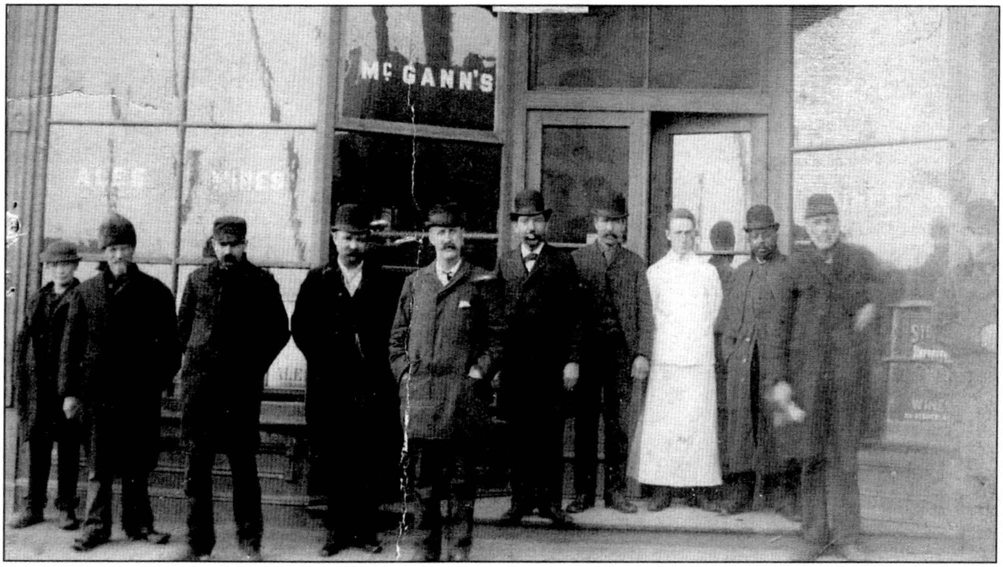

Patrick McGann was the proprietor of this saloon located at 1834 Willow Avenue, paying $100 a year for a tavern license. Pictured in 1895 are unidentified customers except for McGann, who is fifth from the left. The clientele was likely to be a rugged mix of waterfront dock workers and locals. From 1907 to 1921, McGann served as Weehawken's first regular uniformed police department chief.

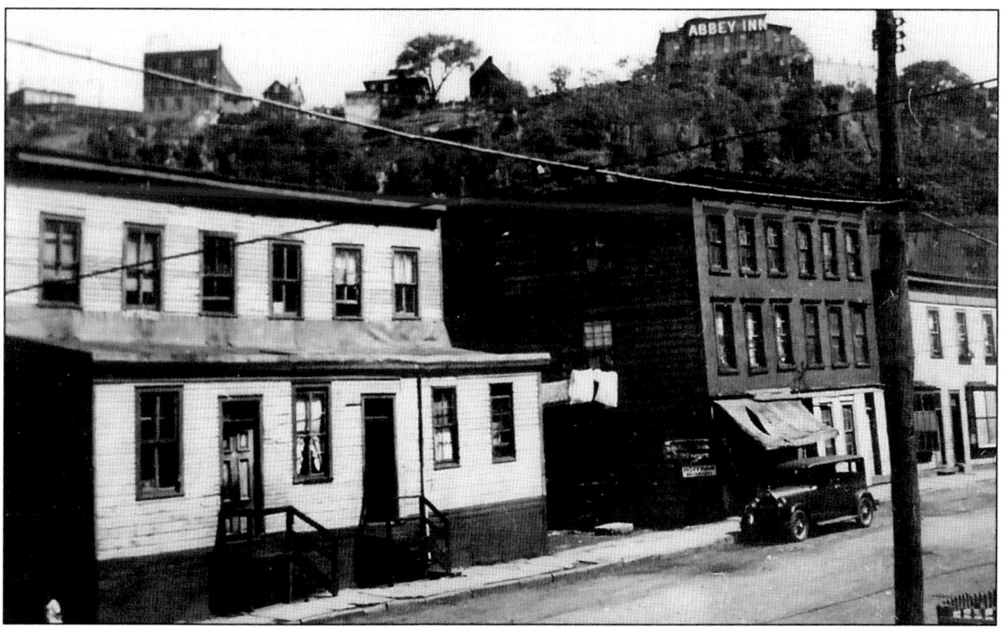

This 1930s photograph shows Hackensack Avenue looking north between West Eighteenth and West Nineteenth Streets. Perched on the cliff was the Abbey Inn, a Union City prohibition-era nightclub. The area was haven for gangsters and bootleggers due to its proximity to the waterfront and saw much illegal activity, including shootings, police raids, and even a plot to kill a Weehawken mayor. In 1931, the Abbey Inn was padlocked and the business closed. At left, walking out of the photograph is Geraldine Mickens, daughter of heavyweight African American fighter Gene Mickens, whose family lived downtown.

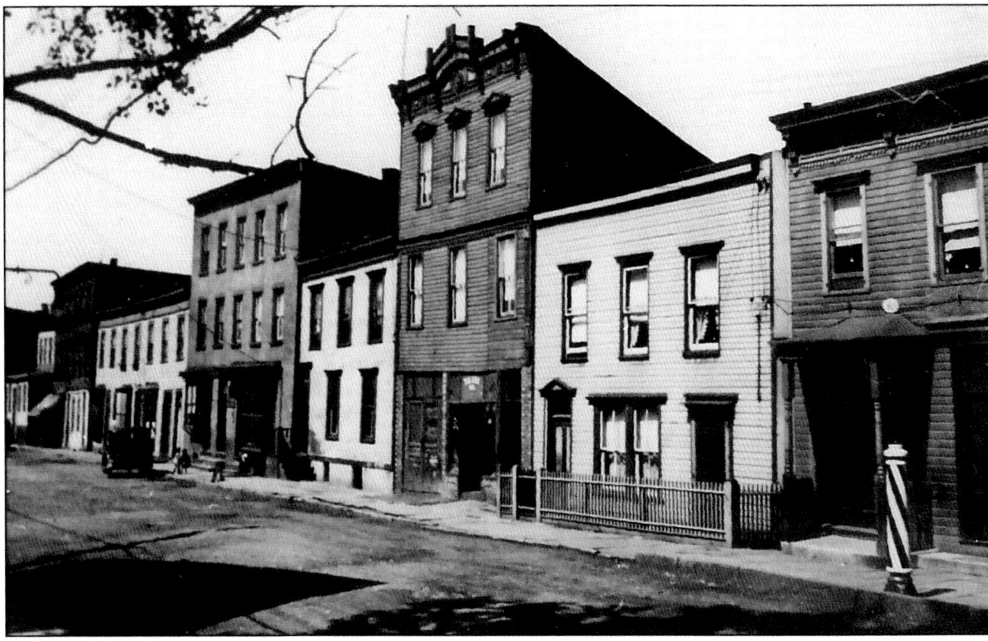

Hackensack Avenue was the main business block in the Shades. Pictured are several storefronts, including a barbershop with a pole in front in the foreground. According to an 1897 business directory, one Charles Carmici owned a barbershop at 25 Hackensack Avenue.

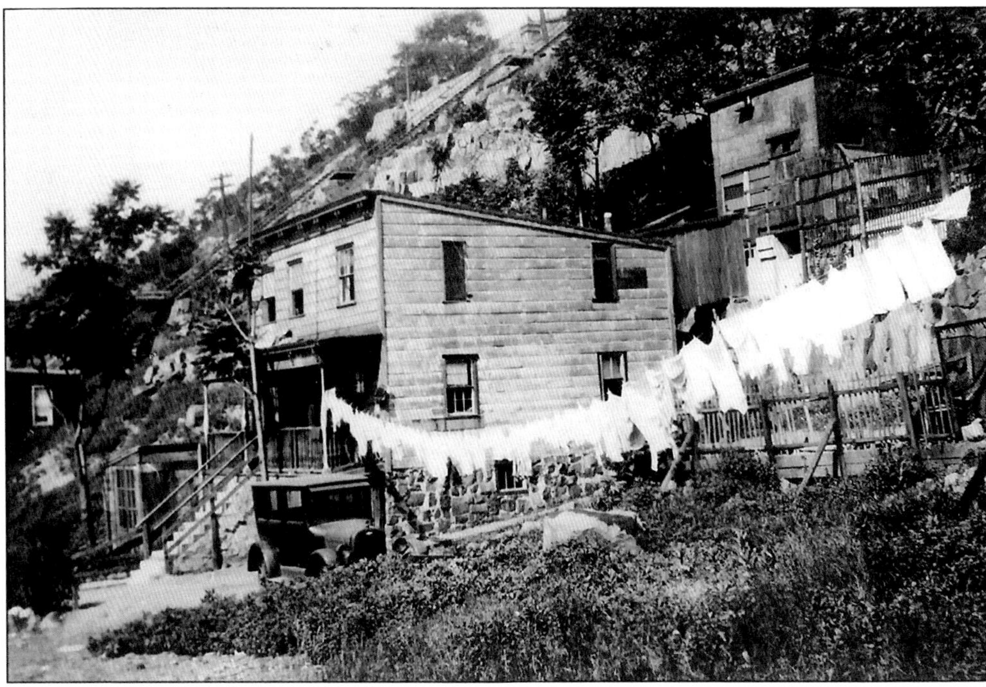

This home with a yard full of laundry drying on the line was located north of West Nineteenth Street along the west side of Hackensack Plank Road. The 100 steps (there were many more than 100) leading up to Mountain Avenue in West Hoboken are seen a little south of the property.

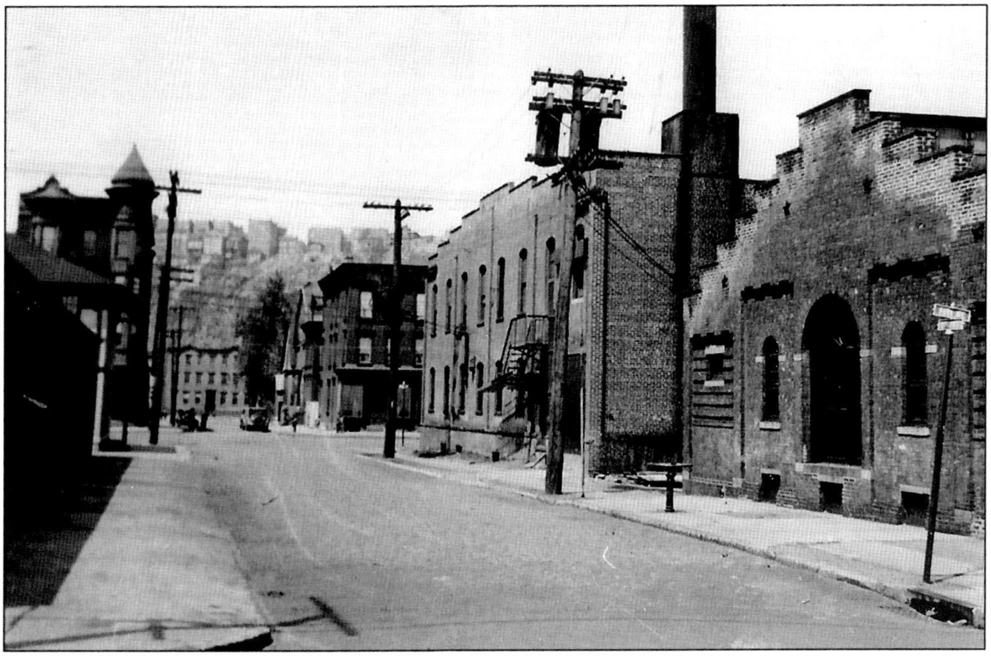

This view of Eighteenth Street looks west towards the hillside, crossing Park Avenue (see street sign at right) and Willow Avenue before either bridge was erected. At right were two factory buildings; the first is now gone. On the southwest corner of Willow Avenue is the Queen Anne turret of an apartment building called the Herme, which still stands.

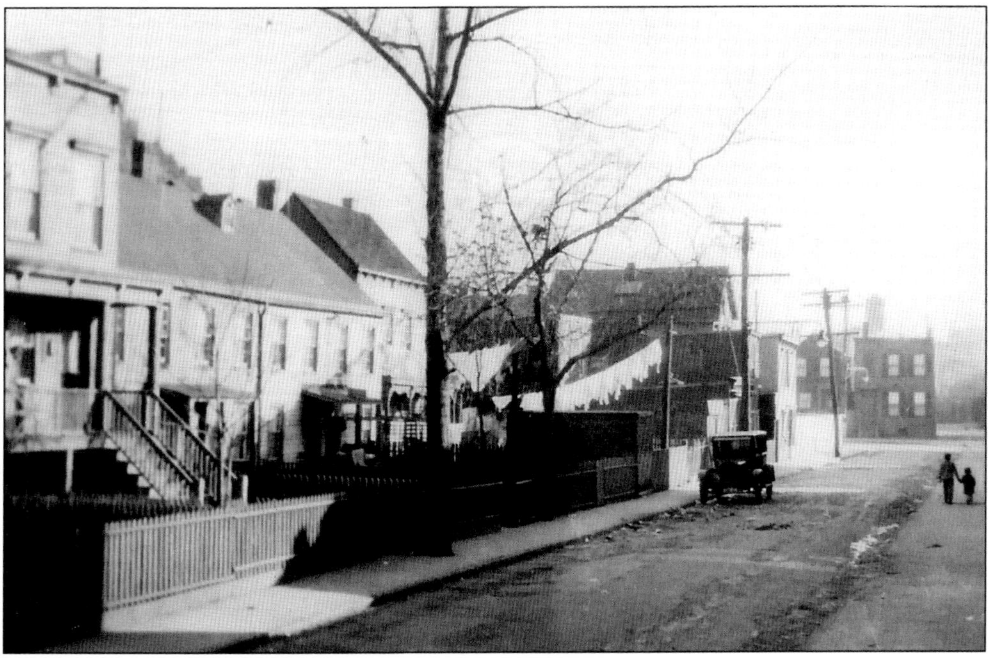

Chestnut Street was the greenest street in the Shades because it had front yards instead of rear yards. Looking east towards Grand Street is a row of homes, with a laundry, a vintage car, and a few pedestrians. In earlier days, there were several bars located on this short street. The block does not look very different today.

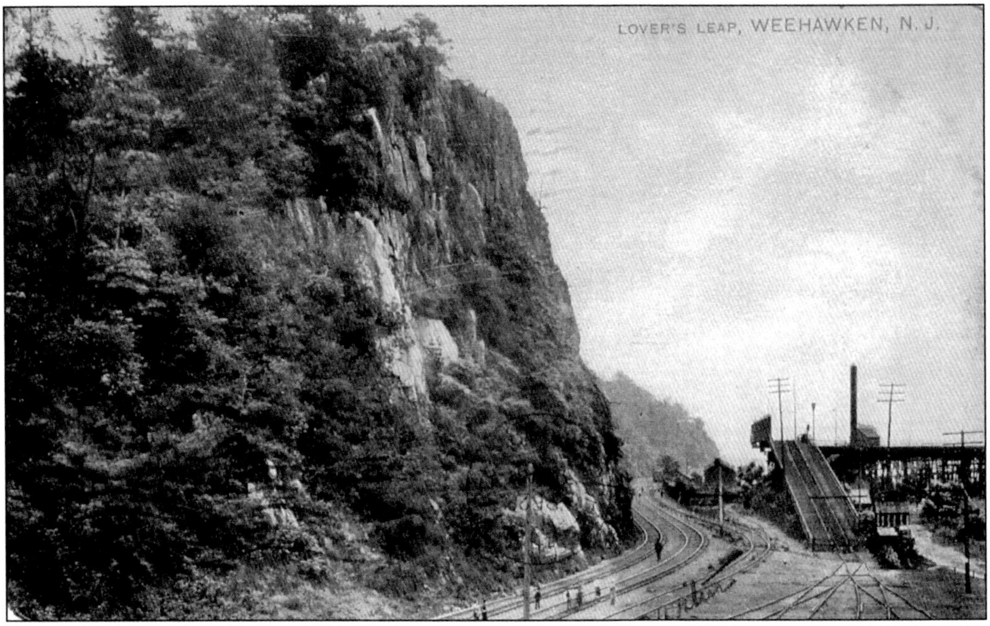

The end of King's bluff was known as Lover's Leap. The train ramp at right, part of the coal trestle, was located approximately opposite where the Lincoln Tunnel ventilation buildings stand. The Delaware and Hudson Canal Company's coal trestle permitted the transfer of coal to and from ships and barges arriving from the Morris or Erie Canals filled with Pennsylvania coal. (Ellen Robb Gaulkin.)

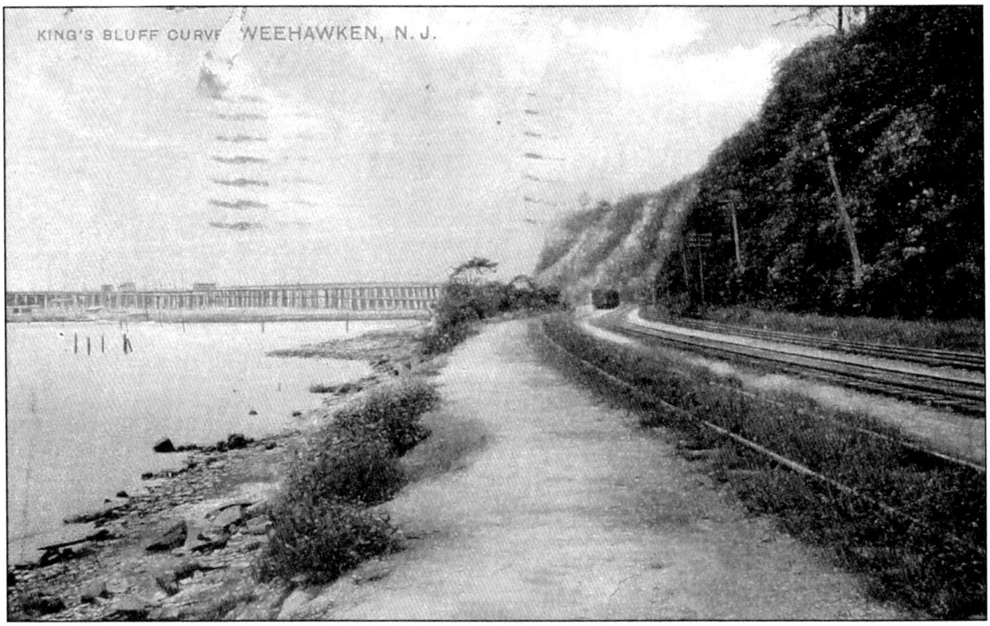

The railroads moved into Weehawken shortly after the end of the Civil War, with the New York, Lake Erie and Western Railroad starting up in 1868. The Delaware and Hudson Canal Company, situated between the Erie and the West Shore Railroad lines, served both as well as barges, ships, tugs, and ferries. The coal trestle seen in the distance was a part of its coal depot, the largest in the United States at one time. (Charlesworth family.)

Five

THE BODY POLITIC

Upon its incorporation by the New Jersey legislature on March 15, 1859, the township of Weehawken, organized under the township committee form of local government, set into motion the mechanisms to manage the collective needs of its citizenry—a police department to keep the peace, a fire department to protect property, schools to educate children, rules to manage communal infrastructure, and, to provide for all this, a method for collecting taxes.

Over the years, Weehawken's inhabitants organized their own churches, social clubs, and business opportunities, as townspeople do everywhere. They marched in parades, celebrated special events and anniversaries, built monuments, and proudly and lovingly recorded these community happenings.

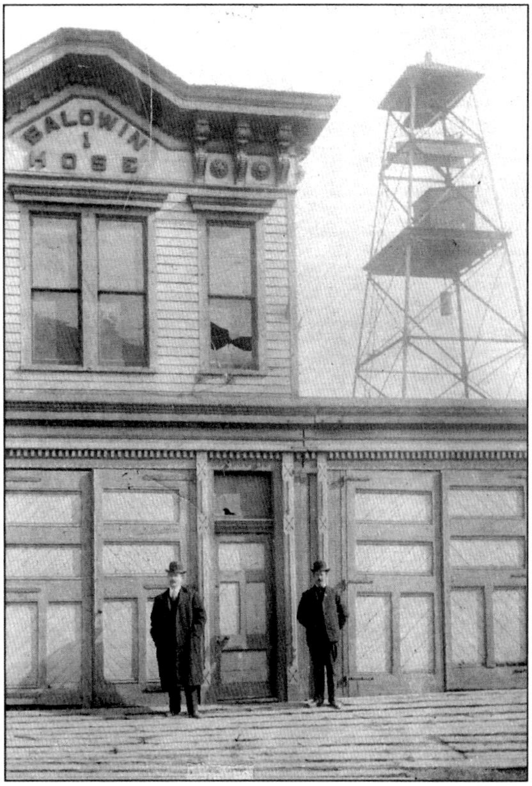

On October 5, 1883, the first fire company was organized in Weehawken, called the Baldwin Hose Company No. 1. The company was named for Aaron Baldwin, president of the National Stockyard Company. Through Baldwin's generosity, the company acquired its first piece of apparatus, a hand-drawn hose cart, purchased second hand. The frame building above was the company's first home on what was old Hudson Boulevard East downtown. The bell tower on the roof dates the photograph to sometime after 1898 when all Weehawken firehouses were equipped with this more modern device for summoning volunteer firefighters. Below, the new Baldwin firehouse, located on Willow Avenue below Nineteenth Street, is decked out in full bunting for a patriotic event around 1910. The Baldwin firehouse was replaced in the mid-1800s by the North Hudson Regional Fire and Rescue Department building, located between Willow Avenue and Boulevard East north of Nineteenth Street, the site of the old Lincoln School.

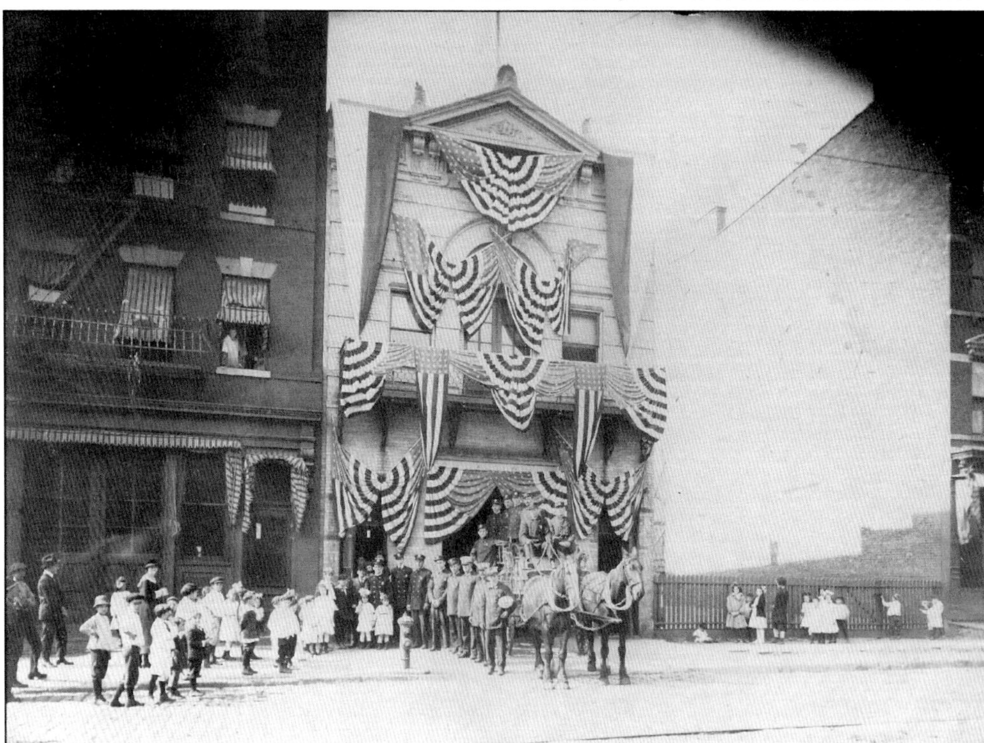

This little volunteer is George J. Walthers, well prepared with a hand-drawn hose cart and fireman's hat, coat, and boots. Young Walthers later became a full-fledged member of the Weehawken fire department and served as chief from 1951 until his death in 1953. He is pictured in front of the Palisade Hose Company on Jane Street around 1900.

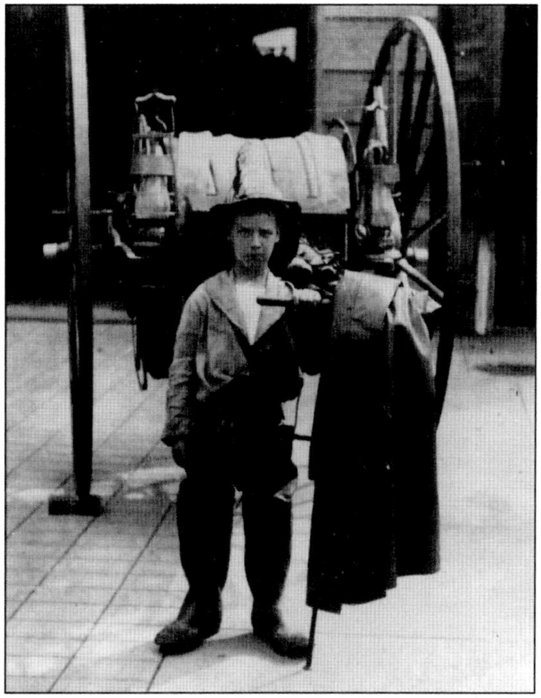

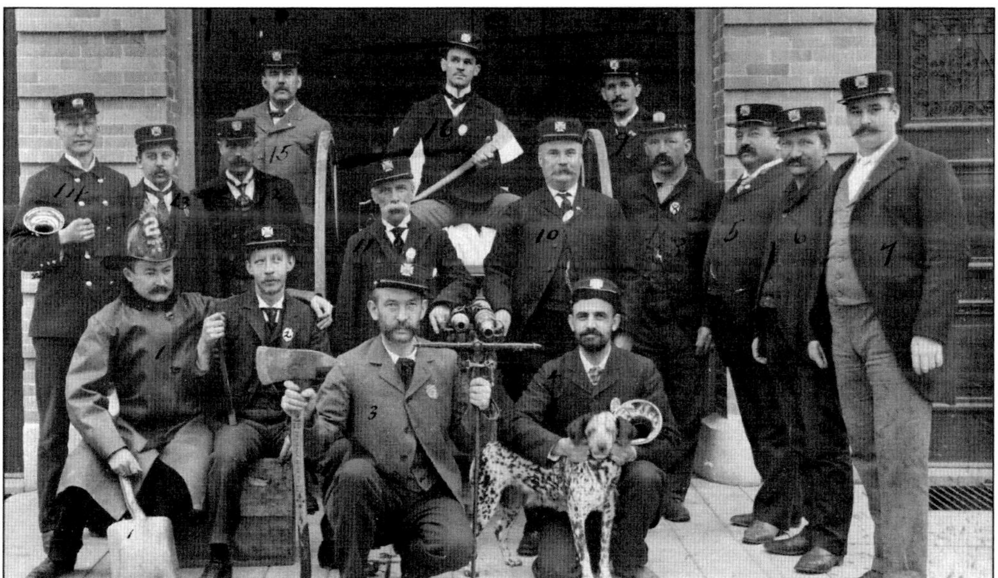

Twelve years after the Baldwin Hose Company was established, the Palisade Hose Company No. 2 was organized on December 7, 1895, in the Heights section of the township. The company is pictured here early after formation with their firefighting equipment and loyal friend. The names, handwritten in the lower margin, correspond to the numbers on the photograph. Pictured are, from left to right, (first row) H. Strauk (1); J. Ruren (2); ? Grundt (3); and ? Lestayer (4); (second row) ? Von Pelts (14); ? Acerman (13); ? Heardman (12); ? Blackhurst (11); ? Louche (10); ? Schaeffer (8); ? Frech (5); ? Kaieser (6); and F. G. Borgmann Jr. (7); (third row) ? Rerrick (15); Pessic Verarittas (16); and ? Oader (9). The dalmatian is not identified.

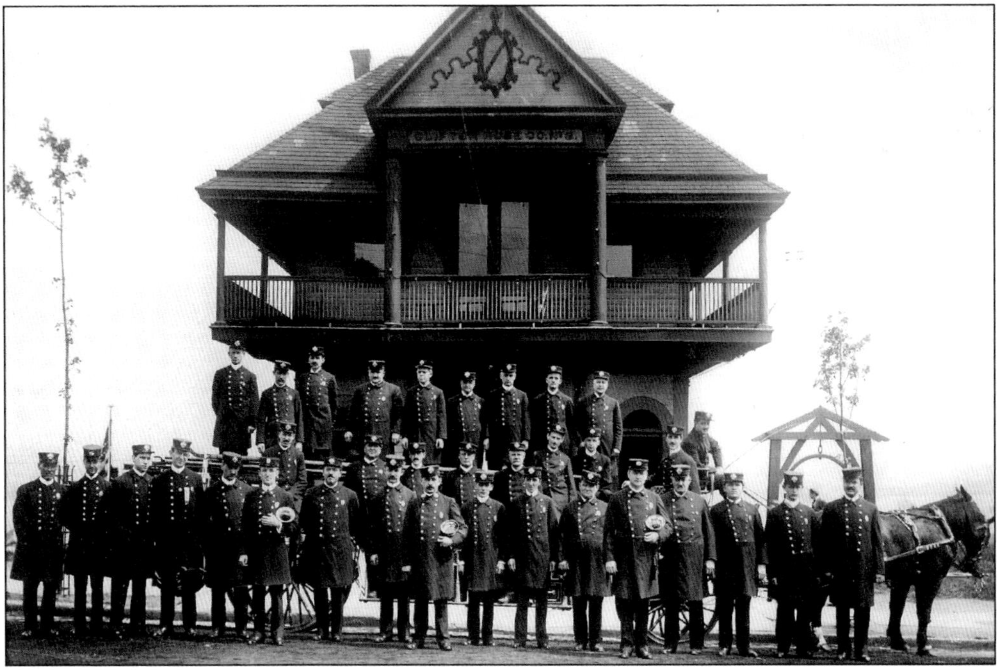

Just two years after the organization of the second company, the Clifton Hose Company No. 3 was formed in 1887 to serve the developing north end of the township. The company, above, is out in full force in the early 1890s in front of its headquarters on Boulevard East at Forty-nineth Street in what is now Old Glory Park. Note the construction at right behind the horse. In the early days, the volunteer firemen were summoned to headquarters by hammering on a large steel ring made from the outer edge of a locomotive wheel. In 1898, bell towers were added to each firehouse, and shortly after that, the township began to install telegraph fire alarm boxes throughout town. In 1912, the company moved to an updated house at 4610 Park Avenue, which is still in use by the regional department. Below, the Clifton Hose Company rises above the Palisades. (Above, Willie Demontreux; below, Al Berg.)

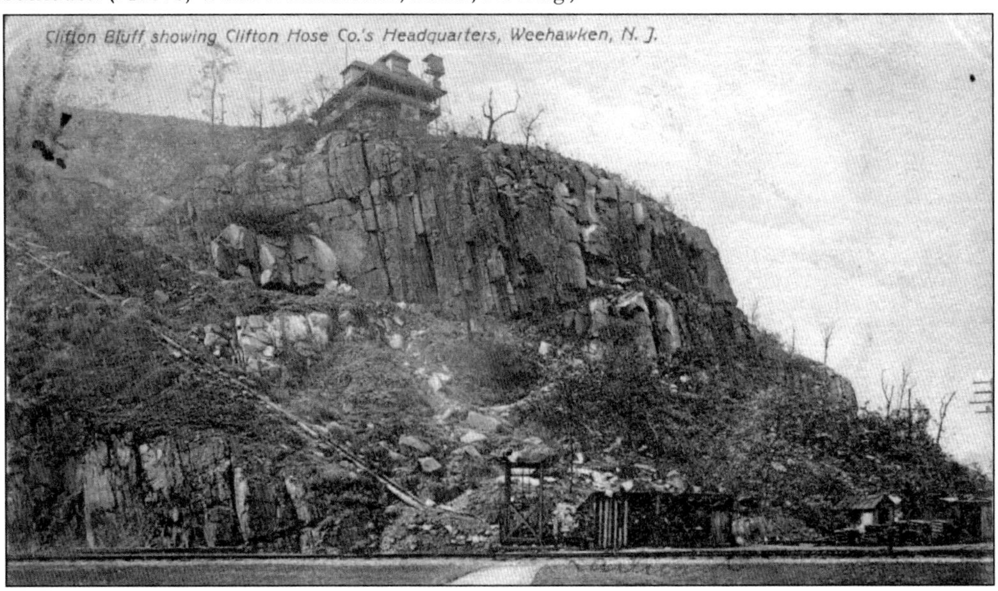

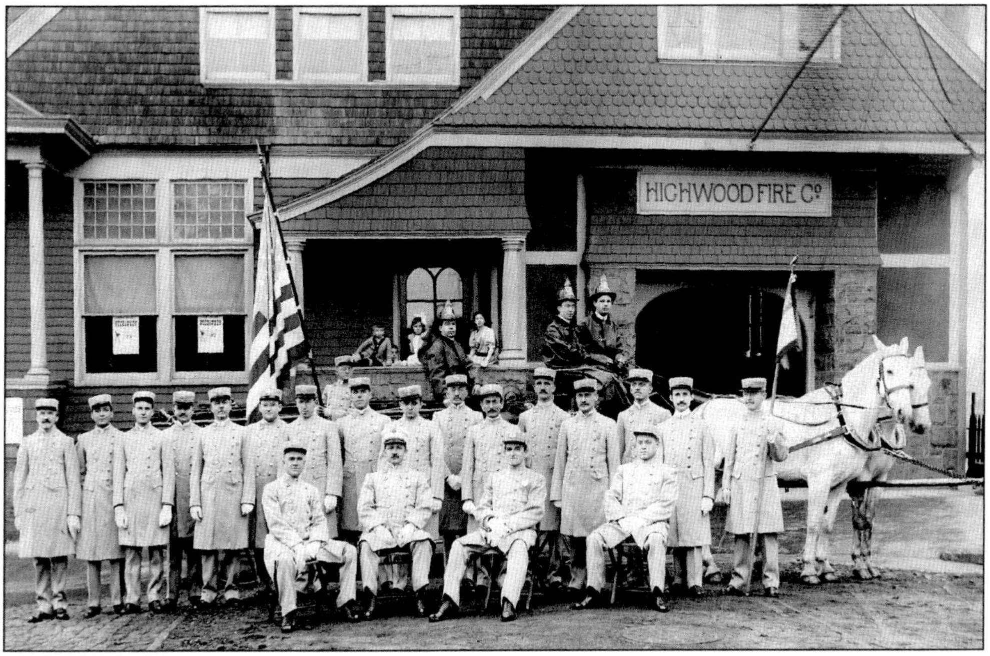

The Highwood Hose Company No. 4, the fourth and final fire company in Weehawken, was formed on February 2, 1900. The handsome shingle-style headquarters was located in the newly developed Highwood Park residential section of the township at 52 Duer Place. The company, shown above in 1912, remained in service through the early 1960s, at which time the building was sold and renovated into private homes. The original bell from its tower is now installed near the soldiers and sailors monument on Boulevard East in honor of Weehawken's deceased fire department members. Below, early fire department volunteers pose formally in typical late-19th-century style. The varying color uniforms and button and badge configuration indicate which firehouse the member represented. The ornate silver horn in the photograph was used traditionally as a megaphone to warn the public of an approaching fire wagon.

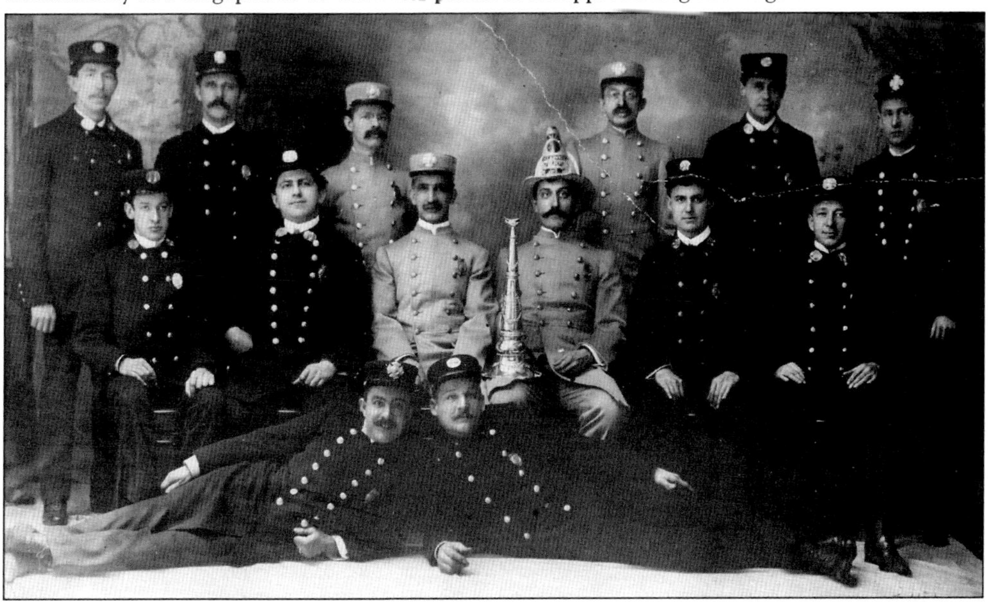

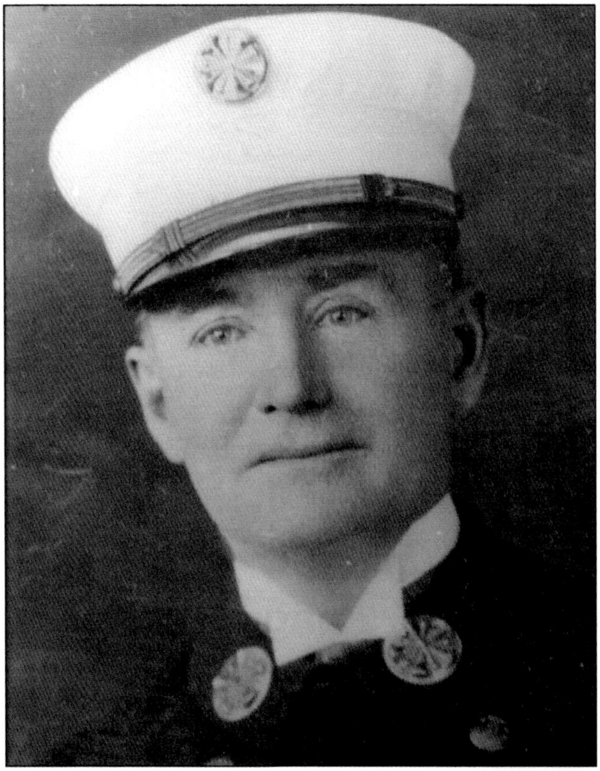

In 1912, the Weehawken Fire Department began the transition from a volunteer department toward a paid department, beginning with three paid members. In 1926, the department was reorganized to a fully paid professional force, and the volunteers were disbanded. William O'Neill, above, who started out as a volunteer and was one of the first round of paid members, was appointed the first chief of the newly organized professional department and served until his retirement in 1951.

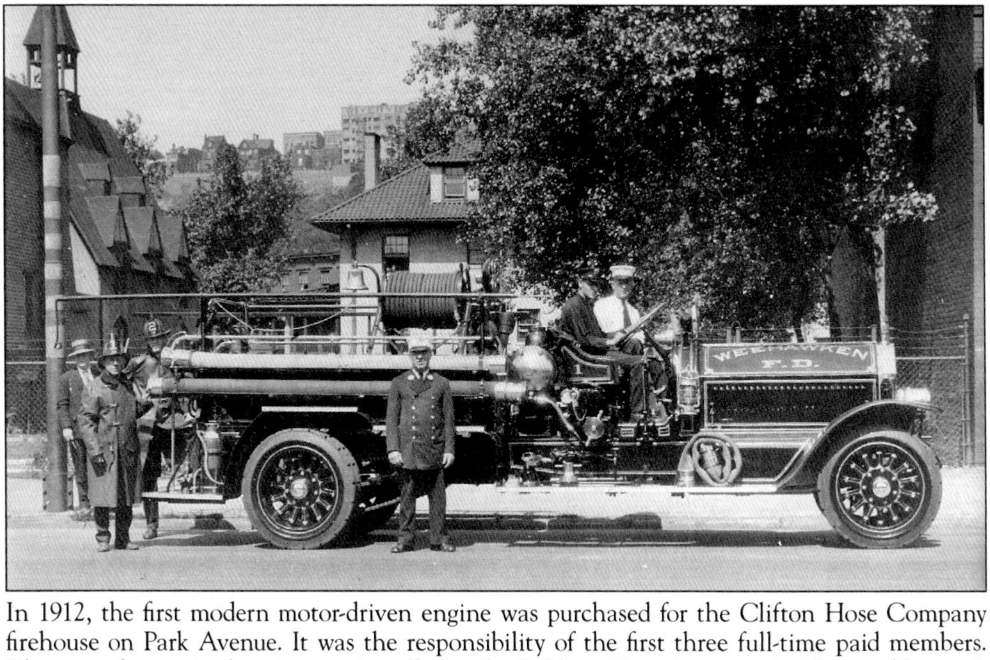

In 1912, the first modern motor-driven engine was purchased for the Clifton Hose Company firehouse on Park Avenue. It was the responsibility of the first three full-time paid members. The second motorized engine was installed at the Baldwin Hose Company in 1919, and by year's end, the department was completely equipped with motor-driven apparatus. In 1924, the first aerial truck was purchased. This is an early pumper from the Baldwin Hose Company parked downtown in front of St. Lawrence Church in 1927.

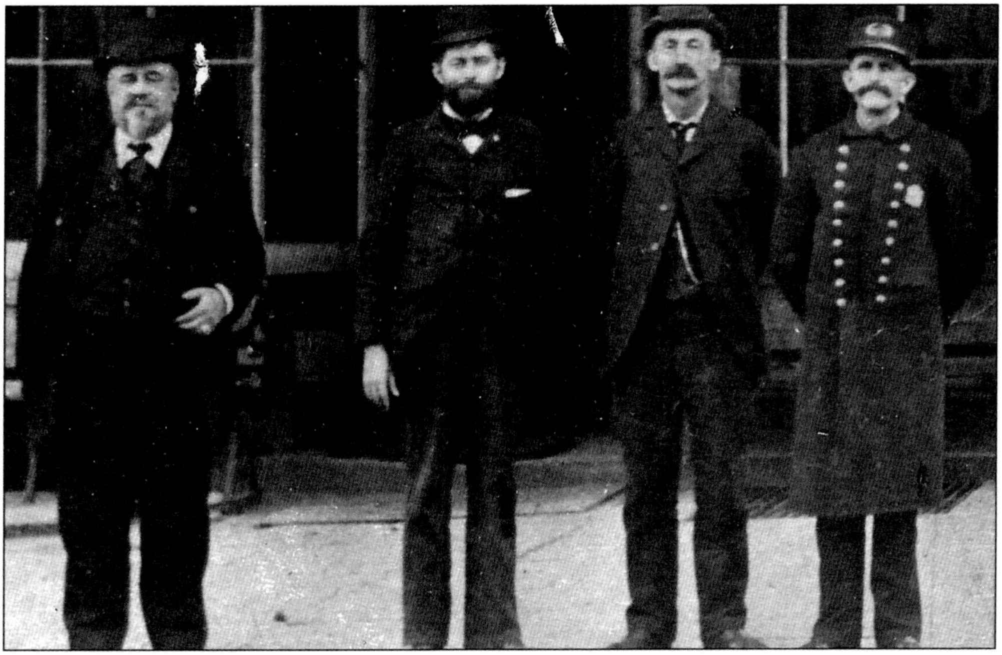

This 1895 photograph includes police and government officials. From left to right are Mayor Simon Kelly, Judge John Simon, committeeman Andrew J. Davis, and Capt. A. Charles Hessner. Kelly, a former police chief, was never out of office from 1870, when he started his public service as poormaster, until he died in 1900.

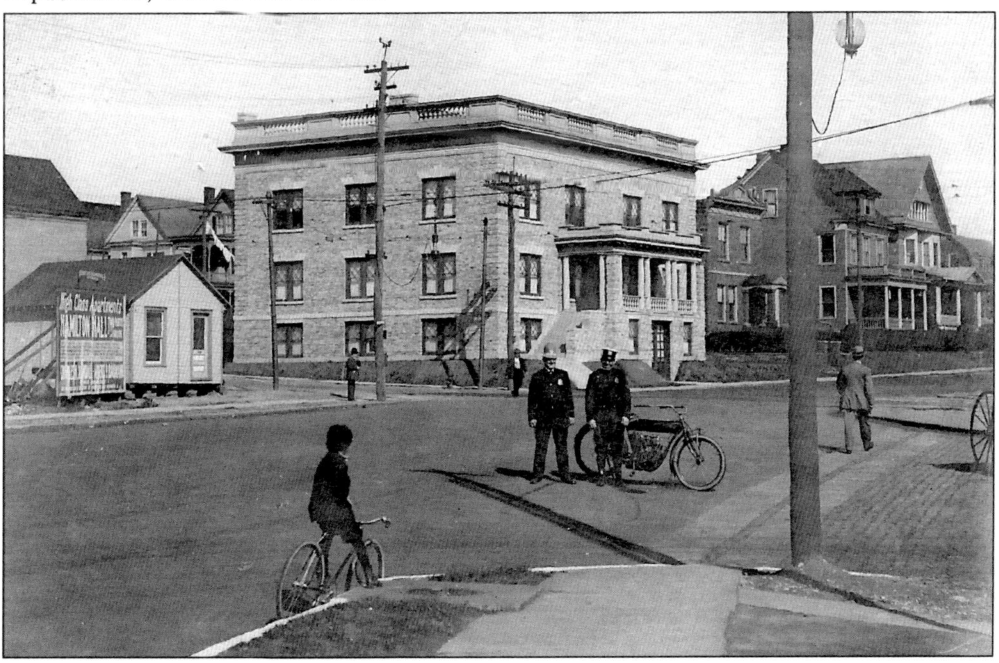

This early 1900s photograph shows Forty-eighth Street and Boulevard East and the intersection of Pershing Road. Pictured are patrolman Sydney Clute and Weehawken police and boulevard officer Patrick Dolan, who later became a chief of the Hudson County Police Department. Note the sign across the street with its advertisement of Hamilton Hall's "High Class Apartments."

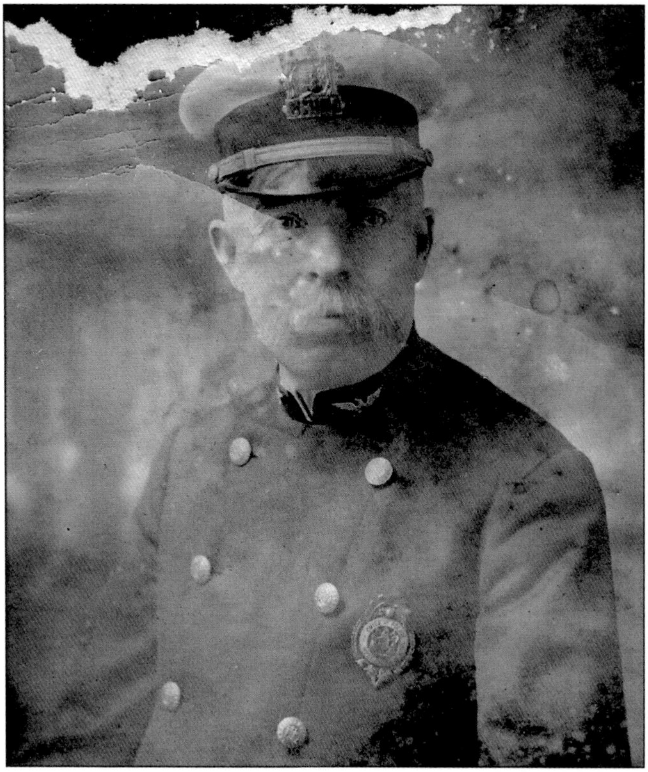

Patrick McGann served as police chief of Weehawken from 1907 to 1921. He was also a member of the Weehawken Board of Heath for several years and ran a popular saloon named for himself in the Shades. When he died in 1921, August Klassen was promoted to chief of police. (Billy Rapacki.)

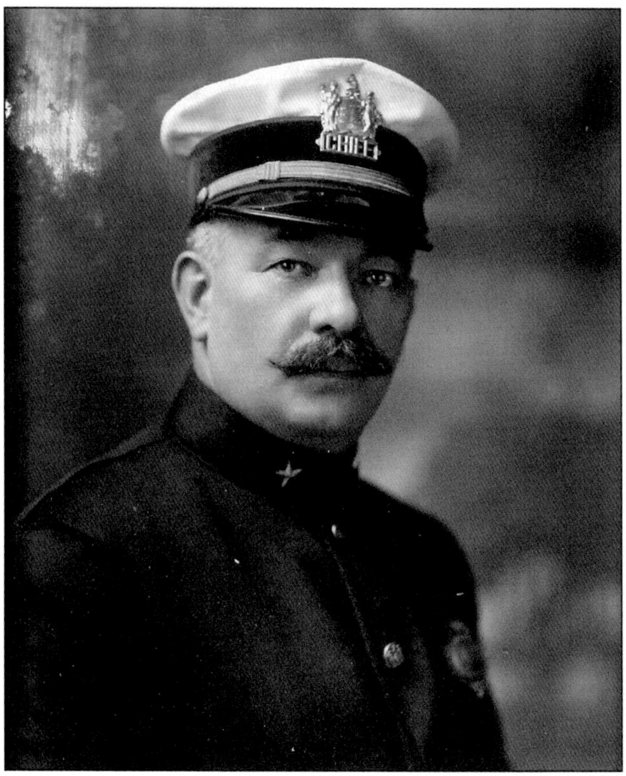

Succeeding McGann, Klassen served as police chief from 1921 to 1939. Born in Germany, he came to New York as a child, moved to Weehawken in 1899, and joined the police department. During the mid-1920s, the chief and his department were occupied with preventing the theft and transport of liquor from docked ships and other bootlegging crime along the waterfront. Klassen was active in police organizations, serving as president of the North Hudson Police Mutual Aid Association for many years. (Billy Rapacki.)

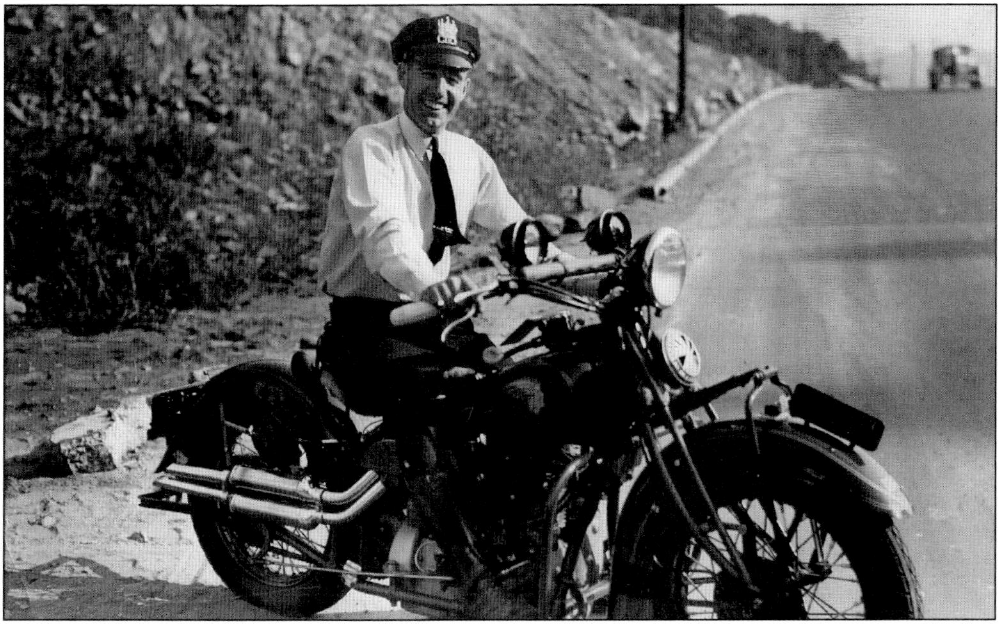

This is Capt. Lawrence (Larry) A. Hessner on August 11, 1937, one of the first motorcycle cops. He joined the force in 1924, the same year his father, Capt. A. Charles Hessner, retired from the force. Having graduated from the FBI National Academy in Washington, D.C., and becoming lieutenant in 1946, Lawrence went on to head Weehawken's detective bureau and served for 41 years until his mandatory retirement at age 65. (Virginia Hessner.)

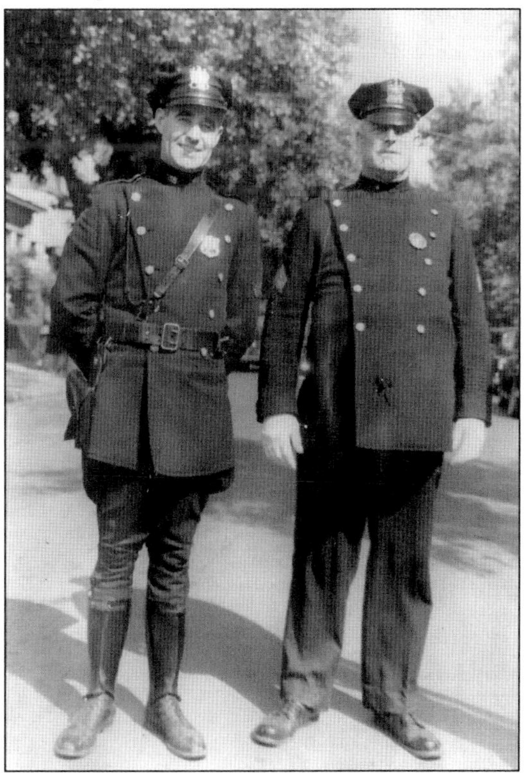

Brothers Capt. Lawrence A. Hessner (left) and Sgt. Charles Hessner served in the Weehawken Police Department for a combined total of 79 years. Charles retired from the department in 1945, and Lawrence retired in 1965. Including their father, A. Charles, the Hessners collectively gave 111 years of duty to the township of Weehawken. (Virginia Hessner.)

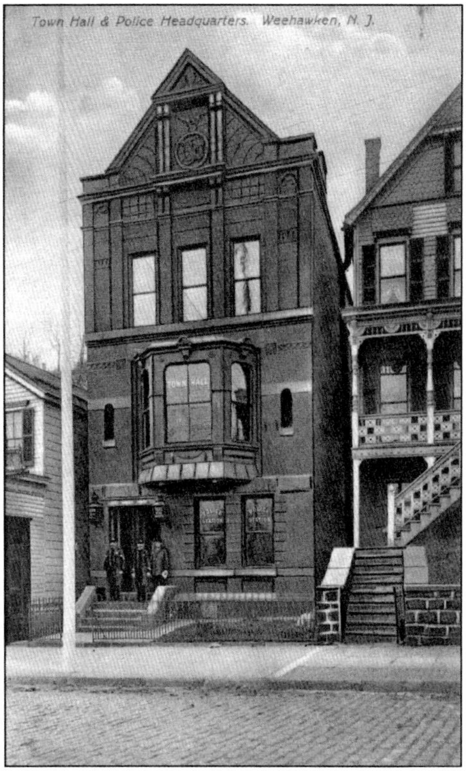

The old town hall, constructed in 1890 and still standing, is located about halfway up the hill from the foot of Nineteenth Street and Bulls Ferry Road (Park Avenue) on the west side of the street. The three-story brick building housed the police station on the bottom floor, including jail cells in the rear and government offices on the upper two levels. The date of the building appears on the decorative brick fascia at the top. In 1928, government and police headquarters moved up the block to the new town hall at 400 Park Avenue. (Al Berg.)

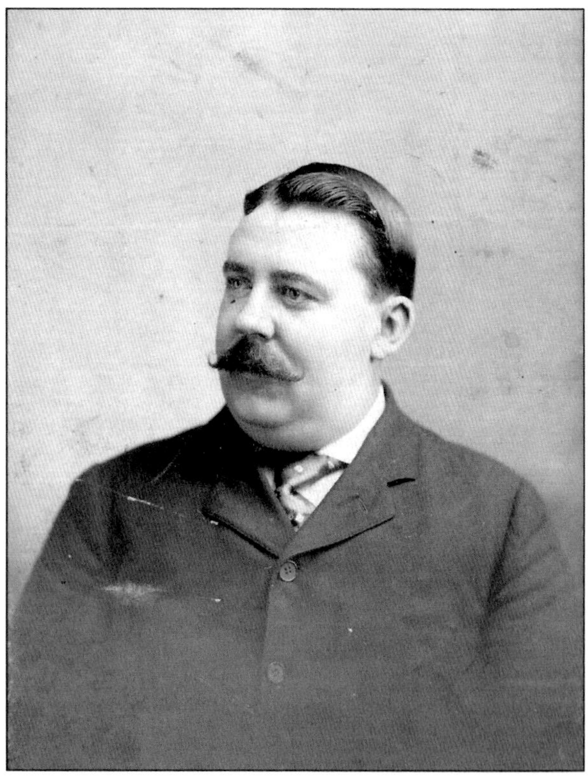

Thomas Carroll was born, raised, and schooled in Hoboken and for some years had his own plumbing business. Carroll was an active Republican and took part in local politics, serving as police clerk of Weehawken for six years. He also served as secretary of Baldwin Hose Company No. 1, exempt from firefighting duties. In 1891, he was elected to public office as township clerk, a position he served in for 34 years.

Simon Kelly, known as "King of Weehawken" was born in Ireland in 1848 and was raised in Hoboken. He held many public offices in Weehawken, beginning with poormaster. He served as chief of police, president of the school board, freeholder, township council member, and held two nonconsecutive terms as mayor, beginning in 1895. Kelly was also one of the founders of St. Lawrence Parish. His roadhouse, located at Boulevard East and Clifton Road, was often used as headquarters for the Hudson County Democratic Committee, of which he was an active member.

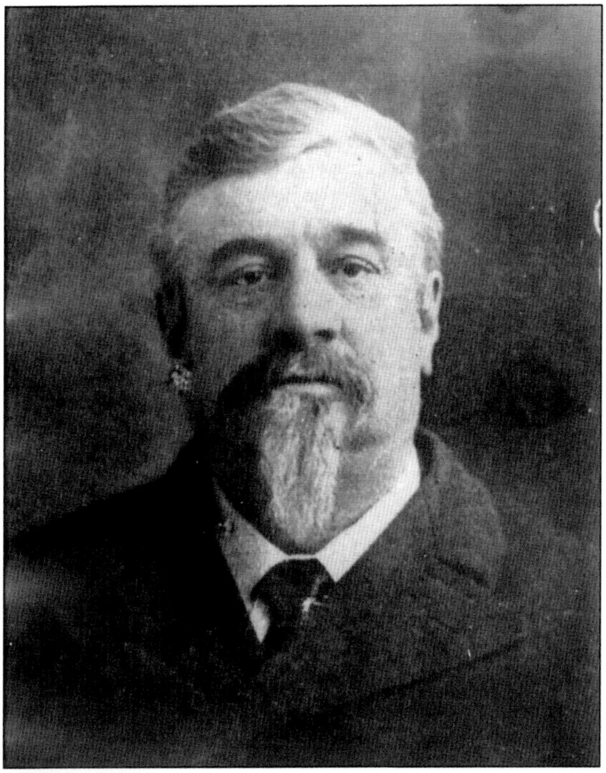

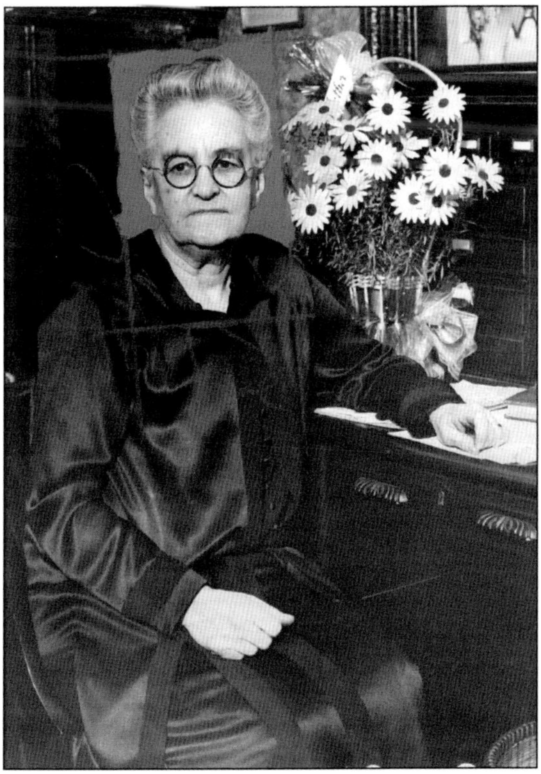

When the township committee could not agree on a successor after Mayor Emile W. Grauert died in office in April 1931, they appointed 72-year-old Clara Grauert to serve out her husband's term, which she did until January 1, 1932. She was elderly and excused herself from the township meetings, appointing committeeman Martin Haas to preside in her place. She did officiate at weddings, the part of the job she enjoyed most, according to a December 1931 interview with the *New York Times*. (Al Berg.)

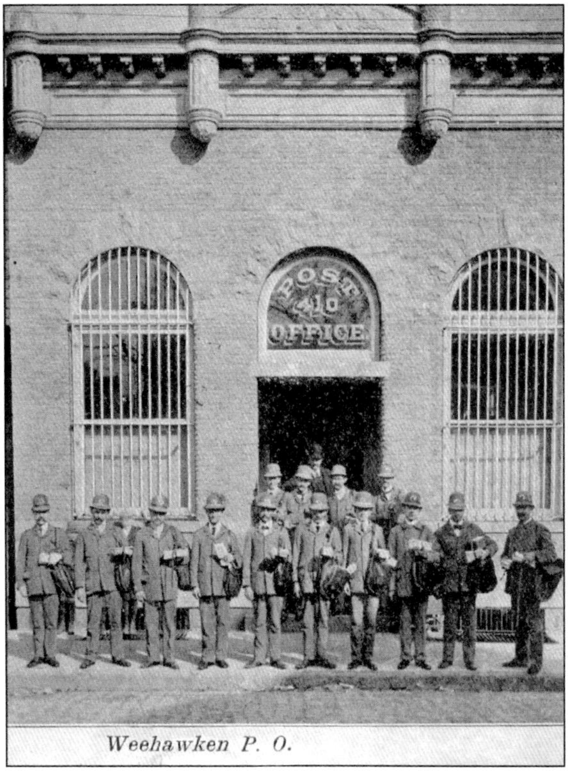

The official Weehawken Post Office was for many years located in Union Hill at 410 Lewis Street, (today's Thirty-eighth Street). Pictured around 1903 from left to right are (first row) L. P. Smith, F. Fuehrein, W. M. Orr, G. D. Spill, O. Wittreich, A. Popp, J. B. McConnell, J. G. Weiss, F. A. Bott, and E. A. W. R. Kaising; (second row) A. Schoenfeld, F. G. Thurnan, William O. Armbruster (postmaster), A. E. Roem, and W. H. Tangeman. On July 14, 1946, the Weehawken branch of the post office officially opened on Park Avenue. (Steve Dorio.)

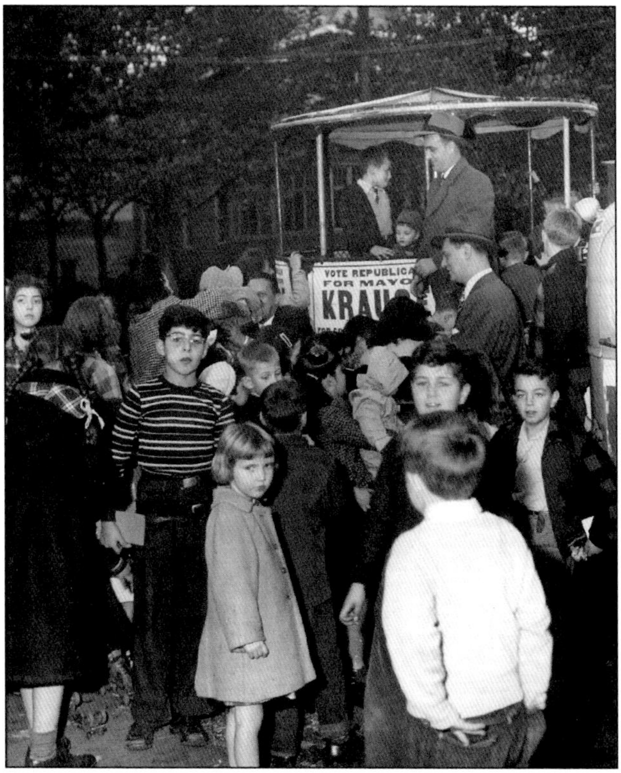

This photograph captures a political rally at the intersection of Clifton Terrace and Potter Place in the mid-1950s. Mayor Charles F. Krause Jr. is standing to the left of the sign, kissing a baby. He served as mayor of Weehawken from 1951 to 1966, defending the rights of the township versus the port authority in regard to construction of the third tube of the Lincoln Tunnel.

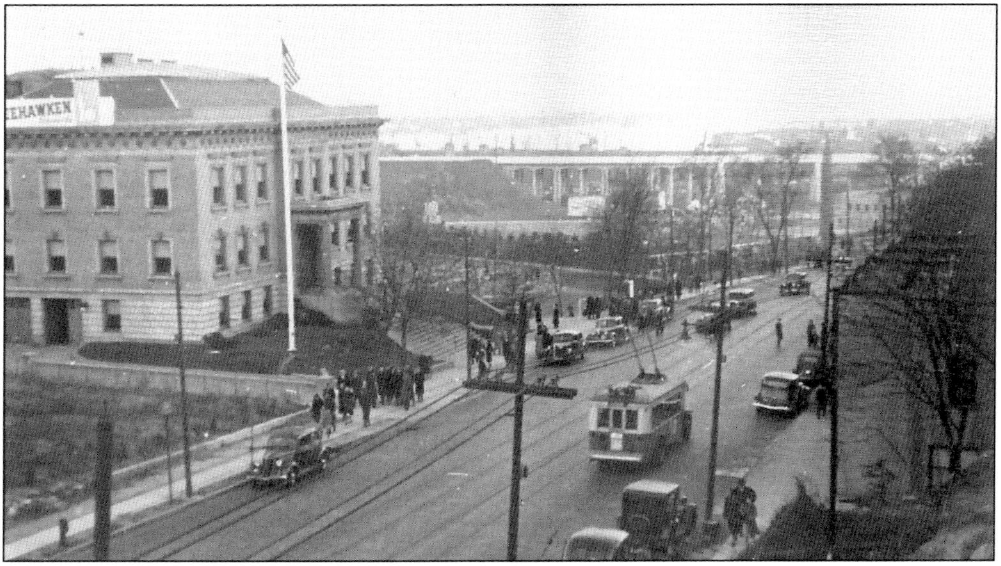

On December 26, 1928, the government moved from the cramped spaces at 309 Park Avenue to a spacious and modern town hall at 400 Park Avenue, just up the block. Workmen carried the records from one location to the other. This photograph was likely taken on October 21, 1938, at the dedication of the new township recreational facility just behind town hall built by the Port of New York Authority. On Park Avenue, trolleys were replaced by trolleybuses. The Weehawken sign with the trylon and perisphere logo was promoting the upcoming 1939 New York World's Fair.

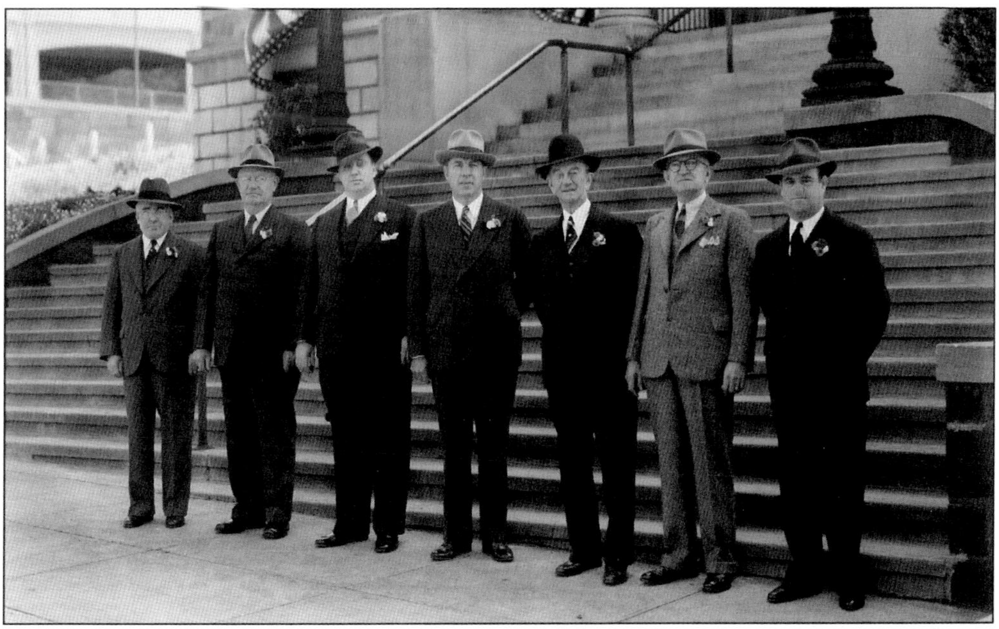

The township committee, standing in front of town hall, marks a patriotic celebration of some kind, possibly the opening of the helix, which occurred on October 16, 1938. Pictured from left to right are committeeman Thomas A. Donlan, committeeman Henry H. Nagel, committeeman Frederick Bergmann Jr., Mayor John G. Meister, committeeman George H. Hilge, committeeman John H. Schuster, and unidentified.

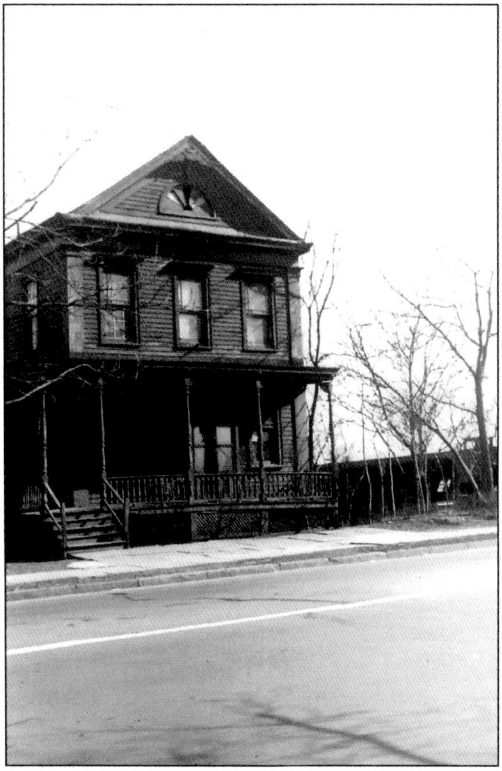

At the first meeting of the township council in 1859, $100 was appropriated for school purposes, and Joshua J. Benson was elected superintendent of public schools. The first Weehawken schoolhouse was a two story, three-room frame building located on Boulevard East south of Baldwin Avenue. Emily Wiggins was the first principal and school teacher. Her salary per year, noted in an 1874 township expenditure journal, was $500. By 1890, a population increase necessitated the building of the Lincoln School.

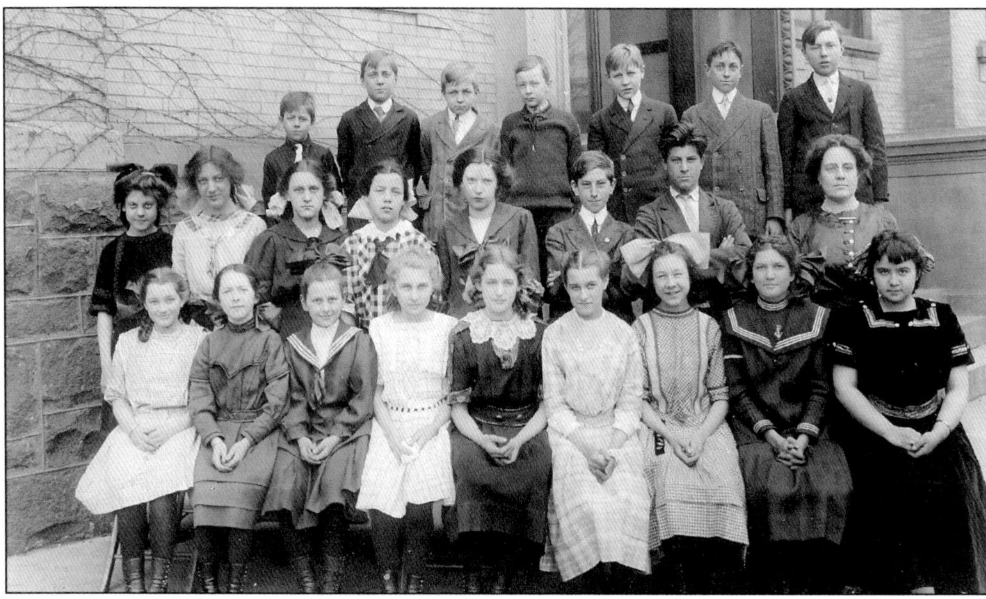

This sixth-grade class was photographed in front of the Lincoln School around 1915. The one identifiable child is Grace Purcell, seventh from the left in the first row. The school, located between Boulevard East and Willow Avenue, was built in 1890 and replaced the original wooden schoolhouse. The building was sold to the Port of New York Authority for Lincoln Tunnel construction but was returned in negotiations over the third tunnel tube. Classes continued until the early 1960s after which the building was condemned and finally demolished.

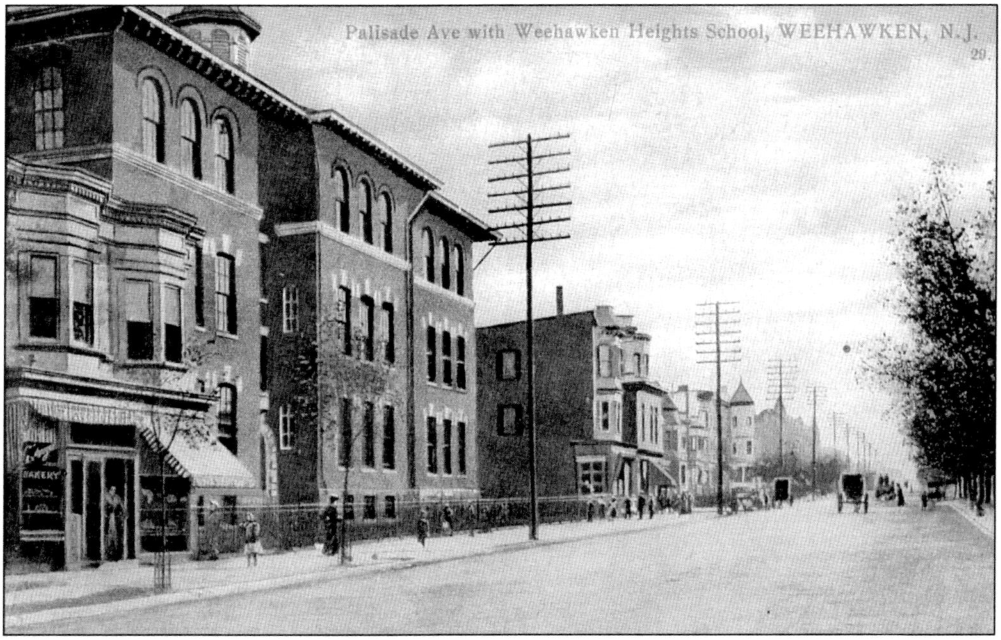

This early-20th-century postcard above pictures the old Webster School within the context of Palisade Avenue, the main business thoroughfare dividing Weehawken Heights from Union City. The original two-story brick Webster School fronted Angelique Street and consisted of four rooms. In the view below, some of the original part of the school to which the impressive Gothic-style addition was attached is visible. This building was razed in 1939 to make way for a new Webster School, dedicated on October 15, 1940. The school now services the Heights area, from pre-kindergarten through second grade. (Above, Barbara Hansen; below, Al Berg.)

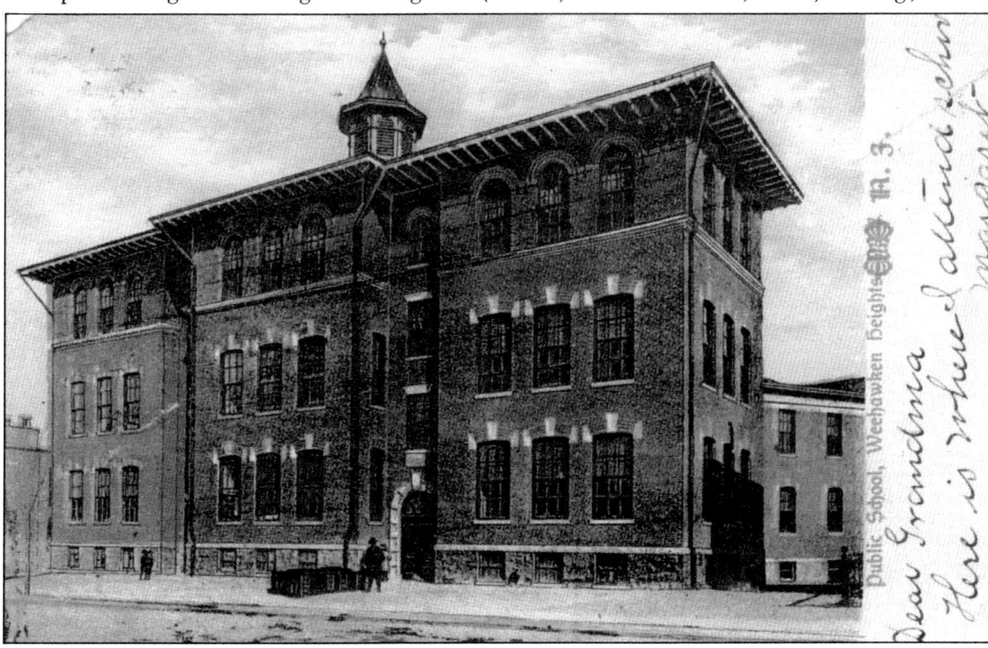

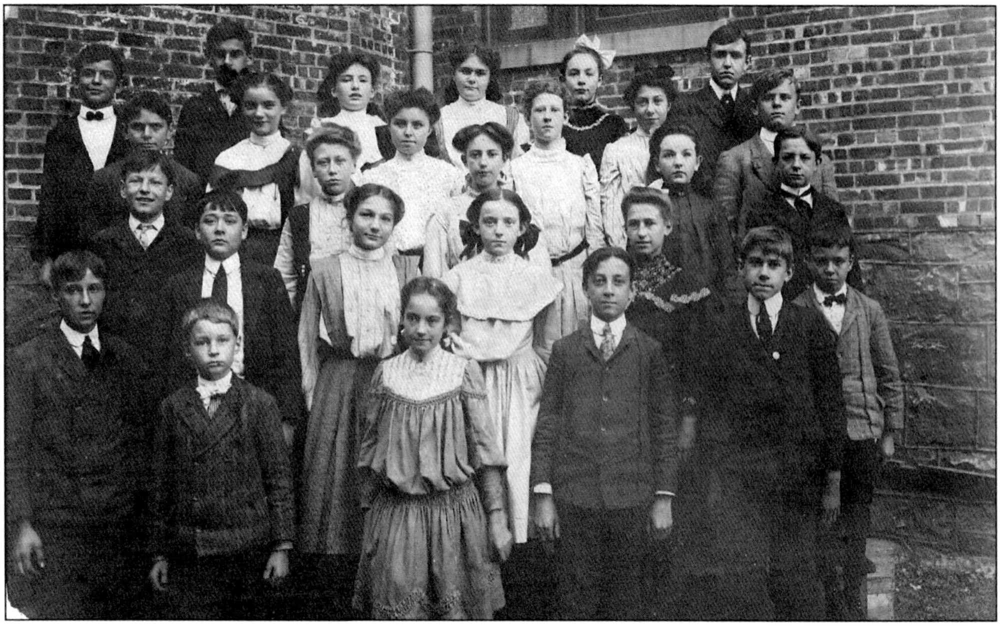

The first Webster School, named for Daniel Webster, who owned property nearby at one time, was built in 1896 to meet the growing needs of the Heights area. In 1899, an additional six rooms were added. Due to further population increases, the school doubled its size to 20 rooms in 1905, with a brick addition on Palisade Avenue connecting to the older section. This eighth-grade class from around 1907 poses in the rear of the building.

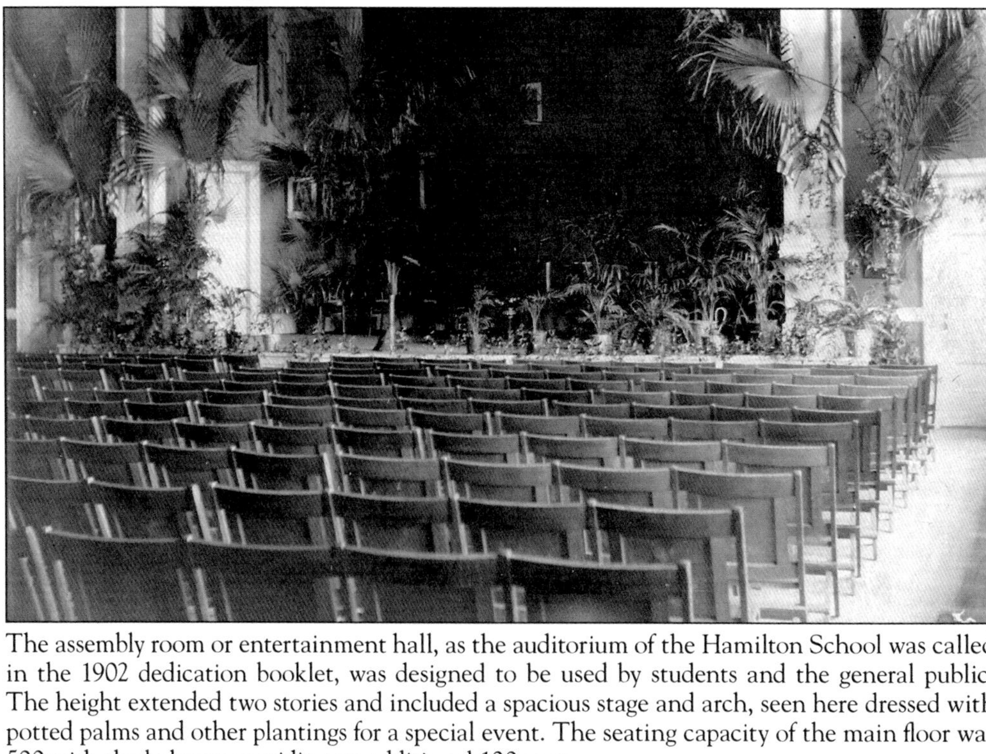

The assembly room or entertainment hall, as the auditorium of the Hamilton School was called in the 1902 dedication booklet, was designed to be used by students and the general public. The height extended two stories and included a spacious stage and arch, seen here dressed with potted palms and other plantings for a special event. The seating capacity of the main floor was 500 with the balcony providing an additional 100 seats.

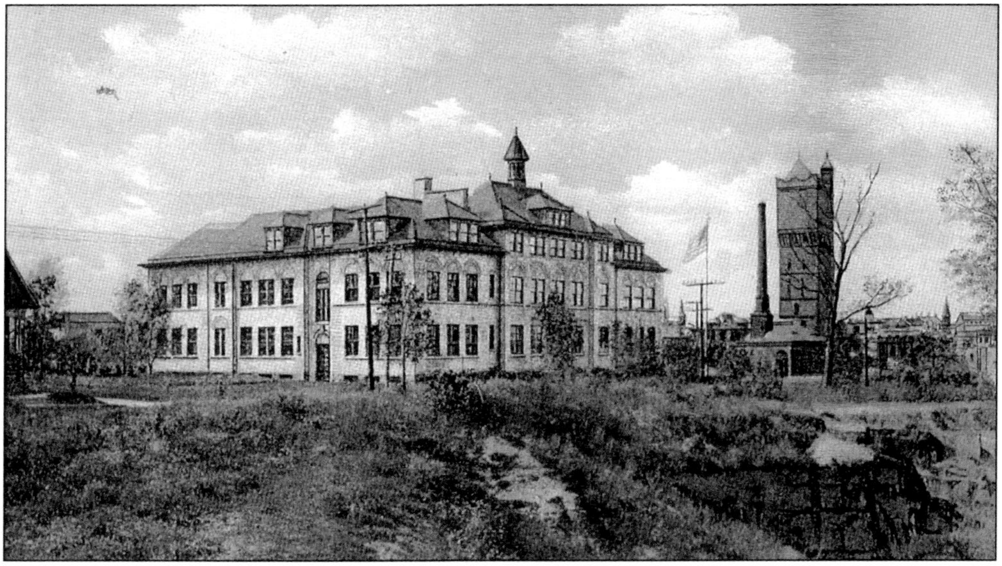

Excavations for a new high school began on March 4, 1901. Weehawken High School (later Hamilton School), designed to house elementary and high school students, was dedicated on March 6, 1902. The image above shows the school looking southwest towards the water tower. The main floor consisted of four classrooms plus two kindergarten rooms and an auditorium. The second floor had eight classrooms. The third floor held seven classrooms, and the gymnasium was in the basement. (Willie Demontreux.)

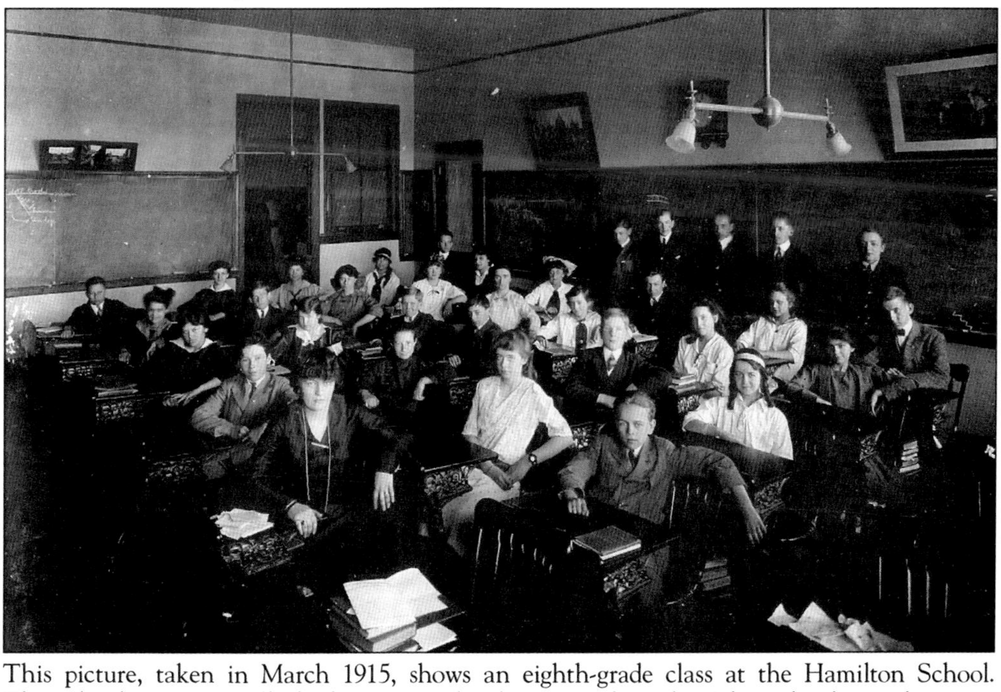

This picture, taken in March 1915, shows an eighth-grade class at the Hamilton School. The school was originally built to serve kindergarten through 12th-grade classes, however, circumstances were such that students wishing to continue past the eighth grade were required to attend high school in neighboring communities until the Woodrow Wilson High School was built in 1926.

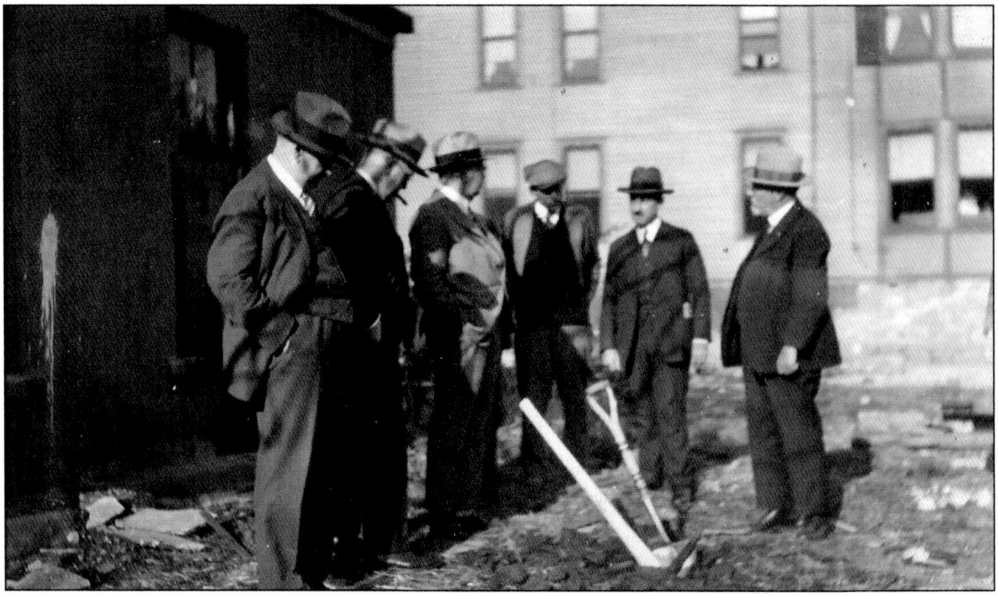

Ground was broken for the new Roosevelt School on October 14, 1927, at the corner of Louisa Place and First Street (now Cooper Place). All pictured are unidentified except for Mayor Emile W. Grauert (far right), who served three nonconsecutive terms between 1909 and 1931 for a total of 21 years. The photograph was taken by William Weir, the school's architect.

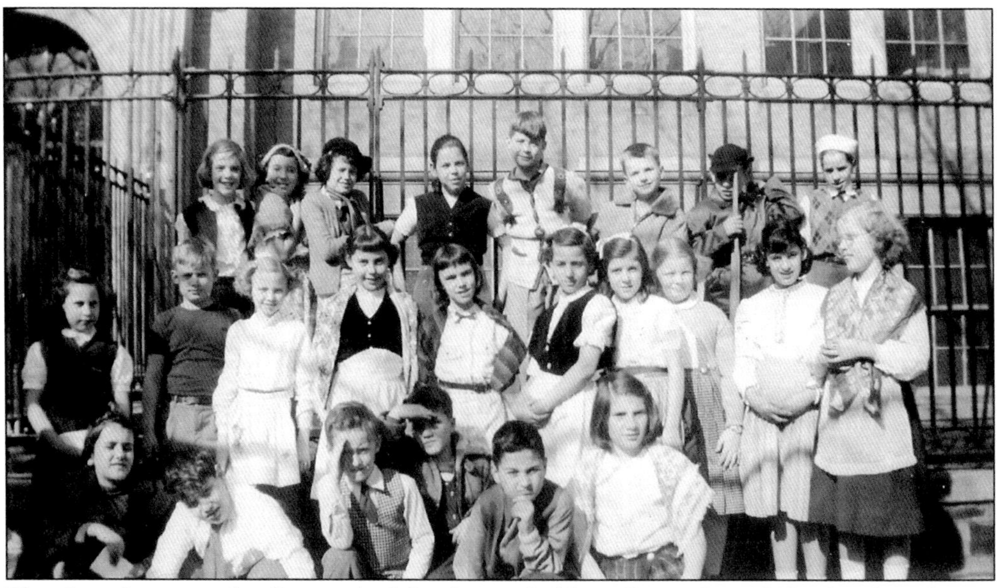

The first classes at the Roosevelt School were held in September 1928 after less than a year's construction. It opened as an elementary school, but by January 1930, it also housed the seventh- and eighth-grade students of the township. This informal fourth-grade class photograph was taken in front of the Roosevelt School in 1952. More recently, the school was converted to a middle school, serving grades three through six. (Cheryl Burns Mansfield.)

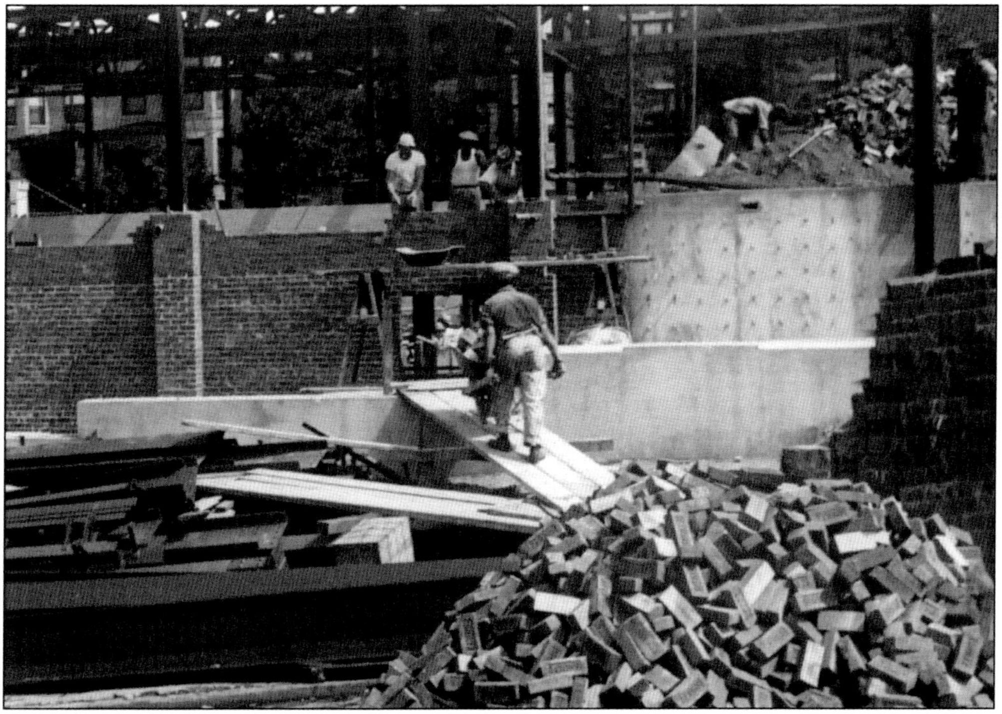

In 1938, Weehawken citizens voted in a special election to raise funds to replace several schools in the township. Money was made available from the Public Works Administration to help replace this school, the Lincoln School, and the Webster School and to make renovations to the Roosevelt and Woodrow Wilson Schools. The new high school was built on the old school site, beginning in 1939. This construction view looks north towards Liberty Place from Eldorado Place. The new school was dedicated in October 1940. (Below, Steve Dorio.)

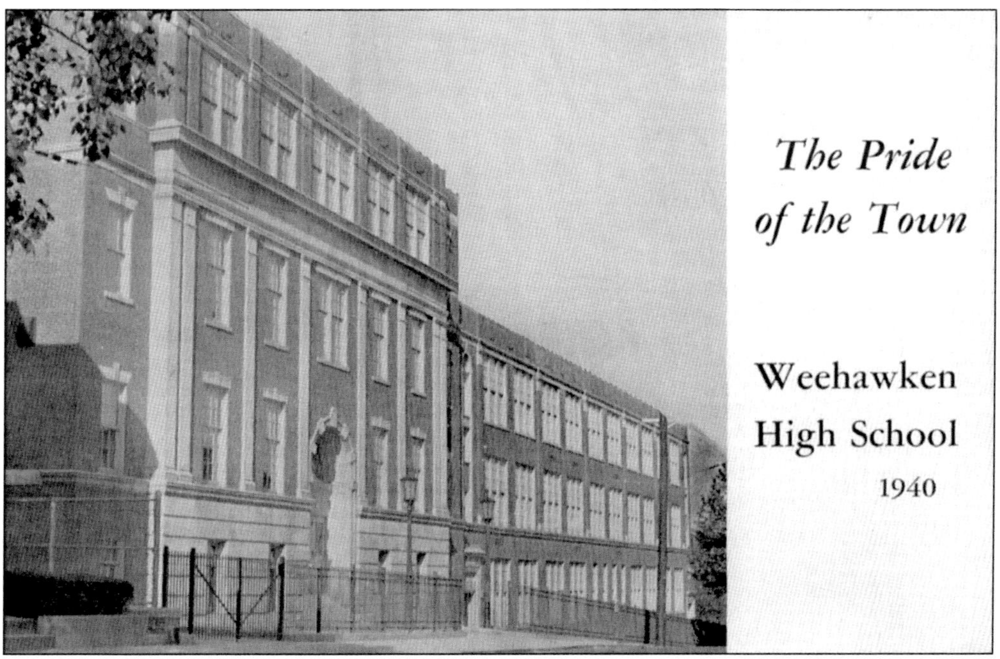

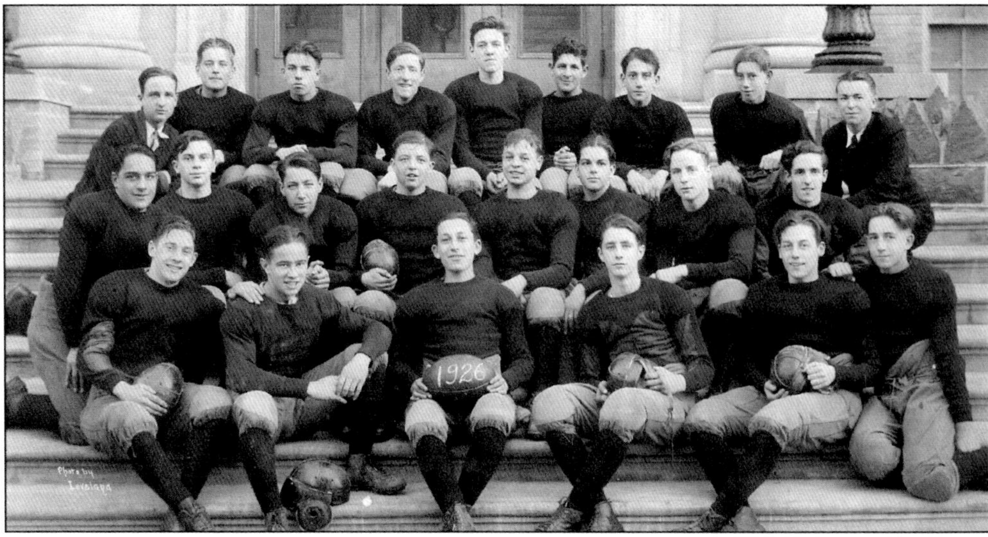

This 1928 photograph of the varsity football team on the front steps of Woodrow Wilson High School pictures Weehawken's first lettermen. The football is marked 1926 to indicate the school's first year of high school sports. From left to right are (first row) Charles O'Neil, Xavier Federer, Alex Levine, Joseph Miles, Daniel Hickey, and Herbert Roth; (second row) Victor Tiscornia, Stanley Sprinz, Paul Korn, Ernest Demontreux, George Hero, Joseph Costanzo, William Rowe, and Robert Brown; (third row) Walter McMahon, C. Lippert, Robert Cleeren, Walter Clews, George Apfel, Leo Treuhaft, Lawrence Wolfberg, ? Prange, and James MacCurran. (Willie Demontreux.)

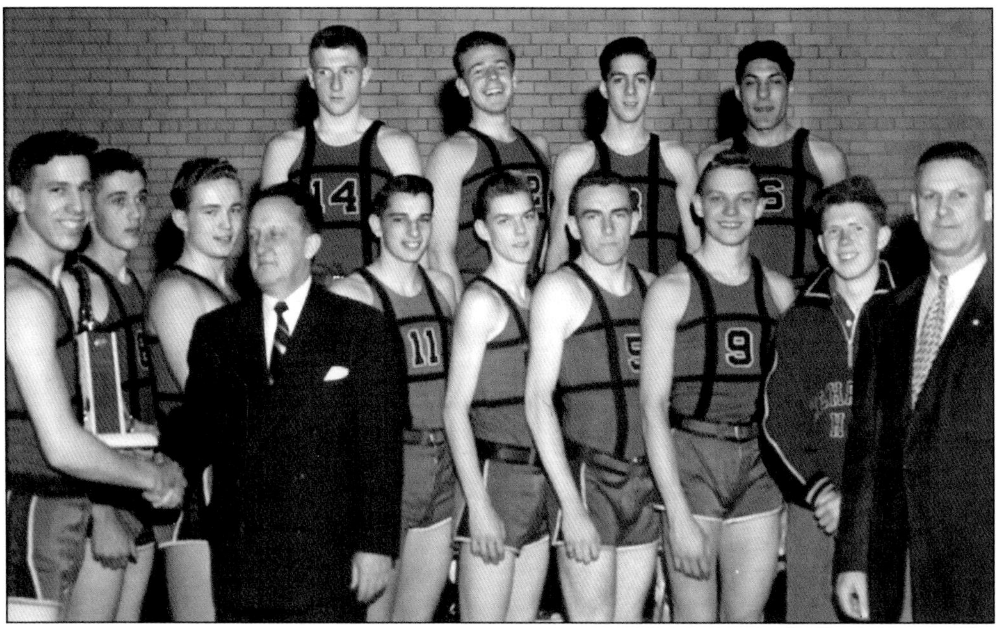

The Weehawken varsity basketball team won the Group II state championship in 1953. Pictured from left to right are (first row) Steven Madreperla with the trophy, William Prior, Robert Wieboldt, Mayor Charles F. Krause Jr., Charles Cavadini, Robert Graham, Ronald Gorman, Steve Afferica, manager John Looney Jr., and coach Lester Purvere; (second row) Donald Adler, Arnold Zunz, Joseph Puglisi, and Joseph Pesciotta.

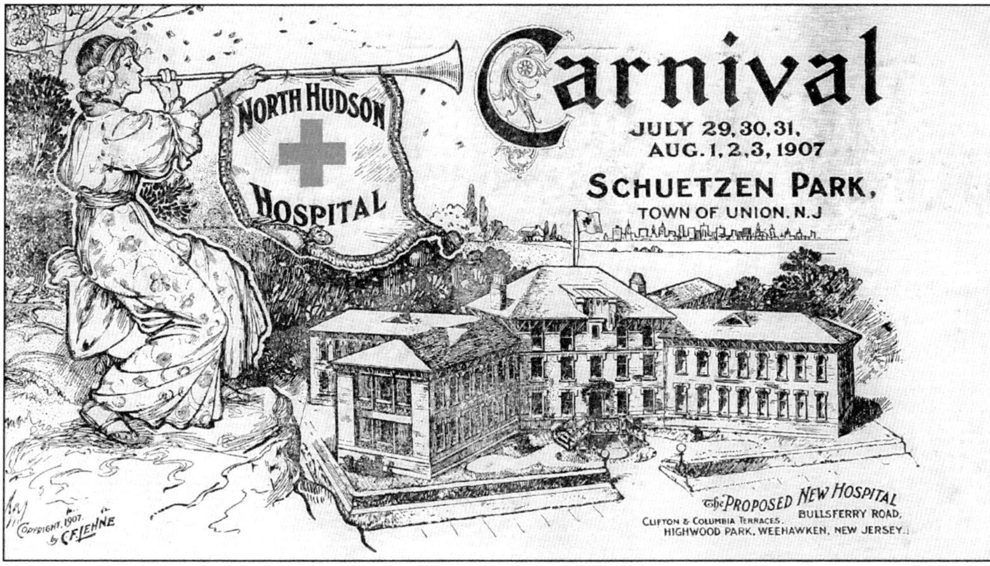

This postcard announces a carnival to be held from July 29 through August 3, 1907, at Schuetzen Park in Union (today's Union City) to raise money to build the new North Hudson Hospital. The new hospital was to be built on Bulls Ferry Road to replace the woefully inadequate and outmoded original North Hudson Hospital building, located on New York Avenue near Forty-fourth Street in Union City. (Steve Dorio.)

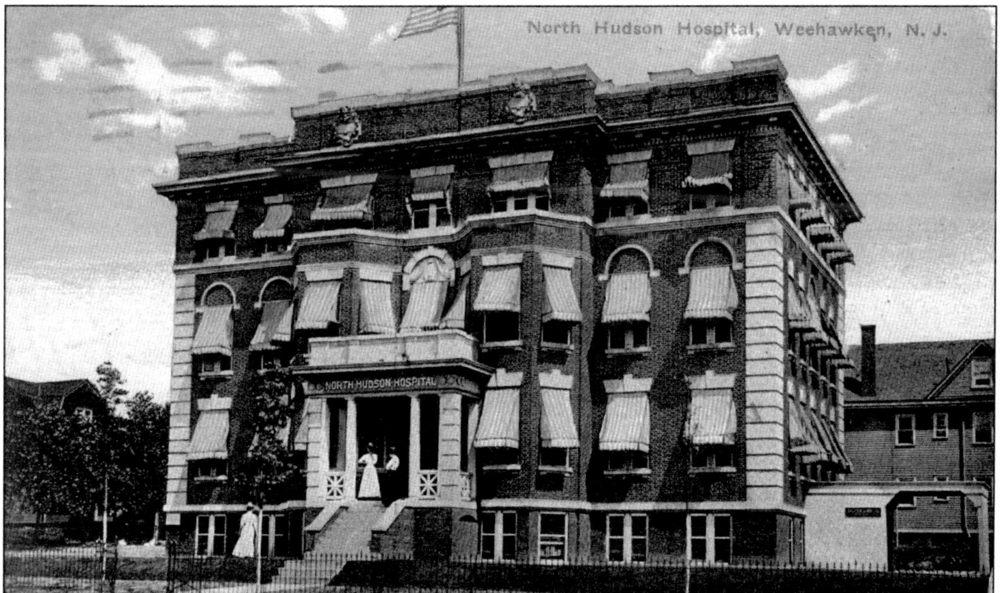

When North Hudson Hospital opened around 1900, it was a modest wood-frame building. After 1905, monies were sought through fund-raising means like the carnival (above) to build a larger and more up-to-date facility. In 1910 and 1911, a brick building was constructed, consisting of three floors and a basement. In 1913 and 1914, it was enlarged to meet the growing needs of the community and was further expanded in 1927 to keep up with the population. The hospital closed its doors in 1978, and patients were moved to the new Palisades General Hospital in North Bergen. (Al Berg.)

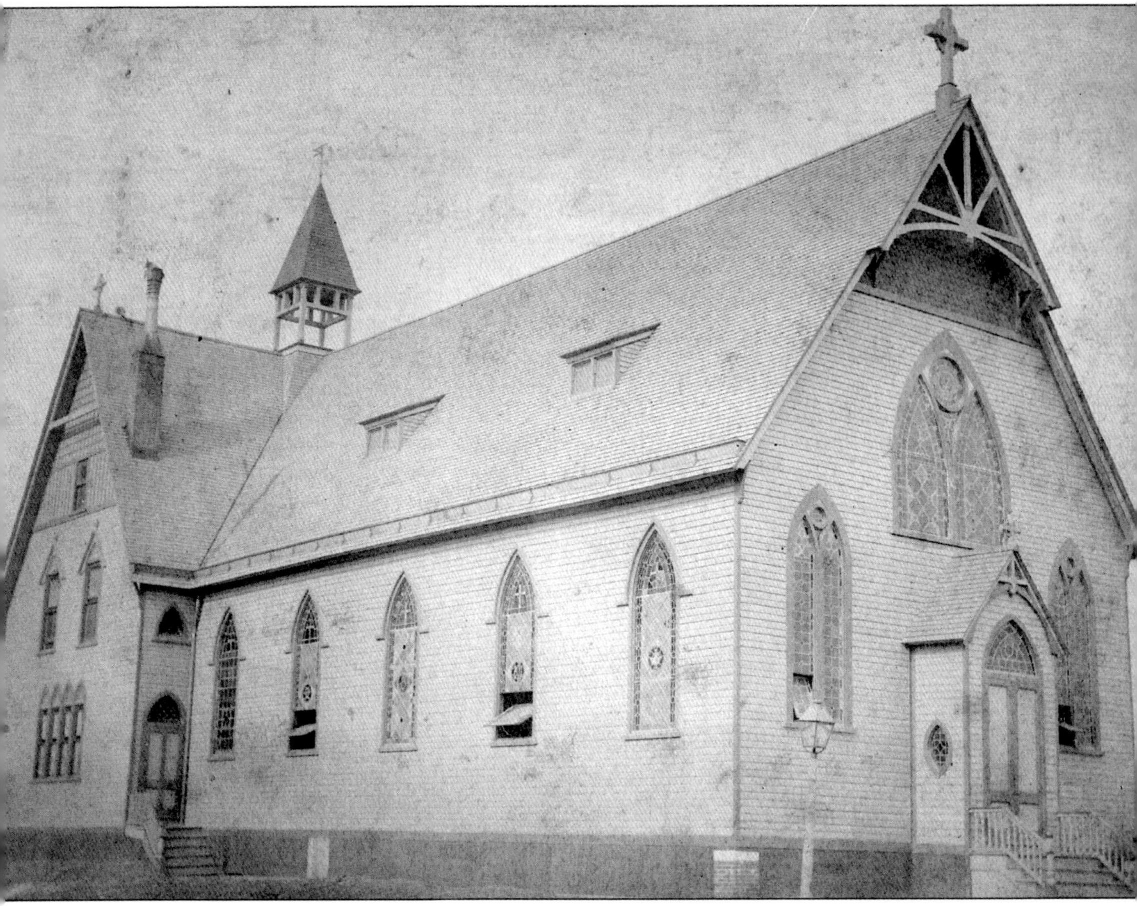

The first Weehawken mass was celebrated in a Bulls Ferry Road storefront by visiting priest Father Lawrence in 1883. With an influx of Irish, German, and Italian immigrants, the first ward downtown population had swelled, creating a need for a Catholic church in Weehawken. Before that time, Catholics traveled to West Hoboken, Hoboken, or elsewhere to attend mass. The St. Lawrence Parish was founded in 1886, with Simon Kelly and Michael Hannan as the first trustees. That December, Rev. John Murphy was appointed the first pastor, and on March 20, 1887, the cornerstone of St. Lawrence Church was laid. The church was dedicated in August, when this photograph was taken. In 1894, the St. Lawrence Parochial School was built; it closed in 1934 and was torn down in 1956. The original church building was also demolished to make way for the present-day St. Lawrence Church, built in 1966.

The Methodist Episcopal Church, a wood-frame building located at 27–29 West Nineteenth Street was erected in 1913. Rev. A. L. DeWire (inset) was the pastor in 1921, the year of this image. The church closed in 1958, and in August 1960, a rock slide on the Palisades caused two 18 to 20 ton boulders to crash down the cliffs into the rear yard of the church. Soon after, the damaged building was demolished. The empty lot, fronted by its original iron fence, remains. (Al Berg.)

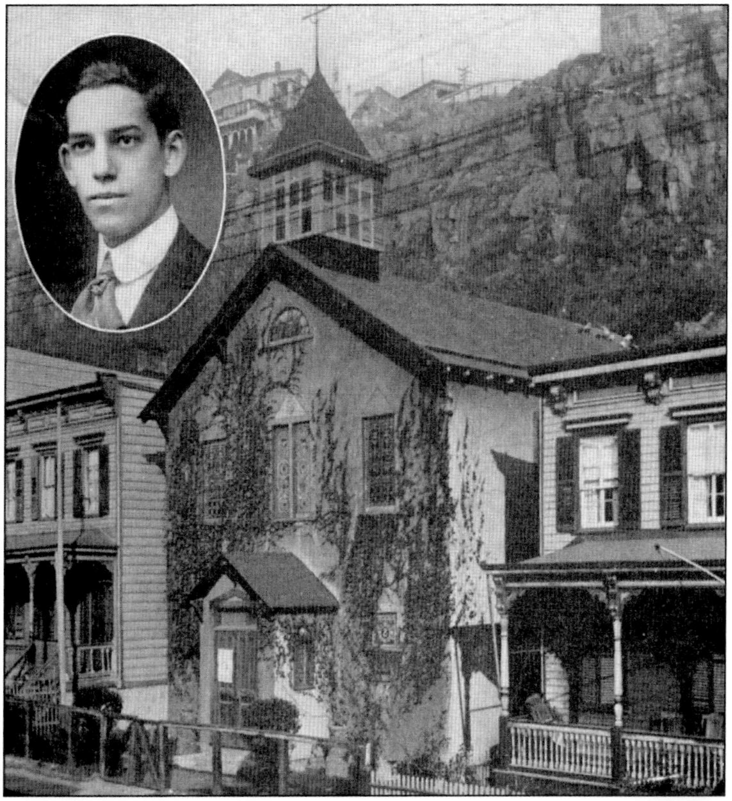

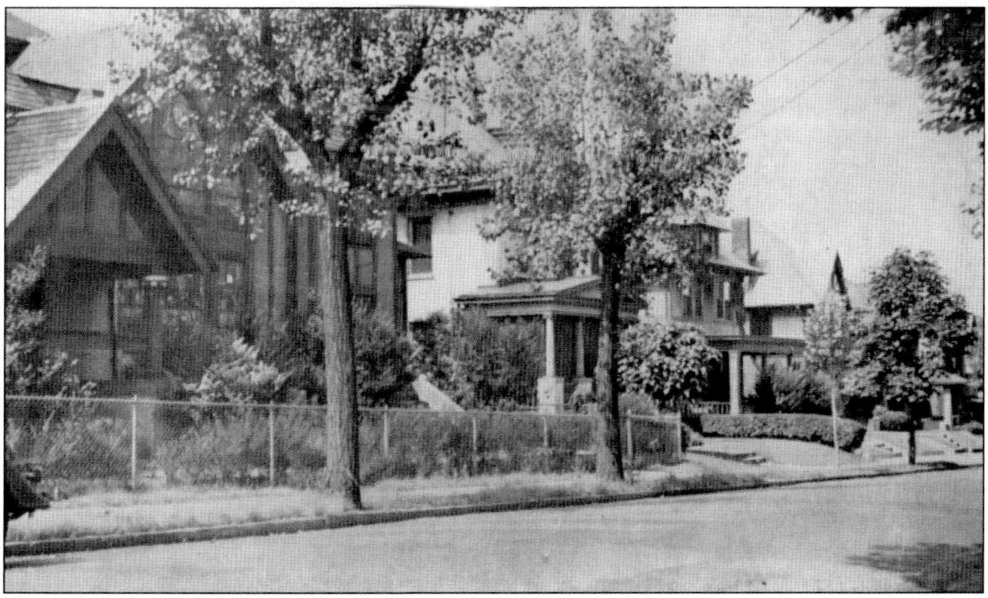

The Park Methodist Episcopal Church was organized in 1901 under the leadership of Rev. George W. Osmun, and early services were held in a converted carpenter shop on Liberty Place. The new Tudor-style building located at the corner of Clifton Terrace and Potter Place, built after a purchase of four lots from the Camp estate, was dedicated on June 20, 1909. In 1959, a new sanctuary was added to the church building. (Al Berg.)

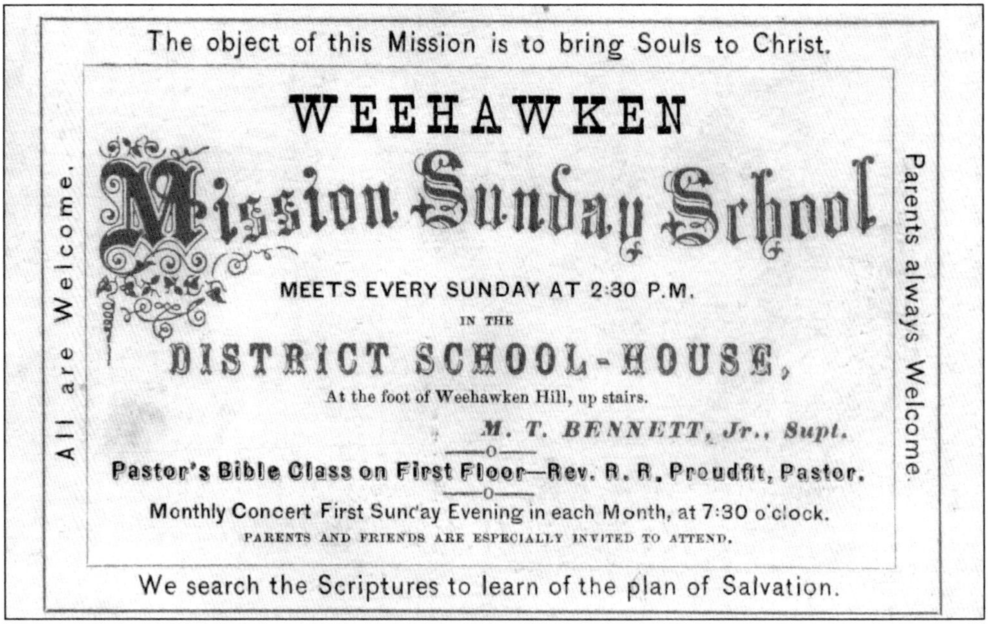

The object of this Mission is to bring Souls to Christ.

WEEHAWKEN

Mission Sunday School

MEETS EVERY SUNDAY AT 2:30 P.M.

IN THE

DISTRICT SCHOOL-HOUSE,

At the foot of Weehawken Hill, up stairs.

M. T. BENNETT, Jr., Supt.

—o—

Pastor's Bible Class on First Floor—Rev. R. R. Proudfit, Pastor.

—o—

Monthly Concert First Sunday Evening in each Month, at 7:30 o'clock.

PARENTS AND FRIENDS ARE ESPECIALLY INVITED TO ATTEND.

We search the Scriptures to learn of the plan of Salvation.

All are Welcome.

Parents always Welcome.

The Weehawken Presbyterian Church was founded in 1868. The wooden structure, located on the west side of Bulls Ferry Road about halfway up from the foot of Nineteenth Street, was dedicated in May 1871 with Rev. Robert Proudfit serving as the first pastor. This undated business card advertises Sunday school bible classes as well as a monthly Sunday evening concert. (Al Berg.)

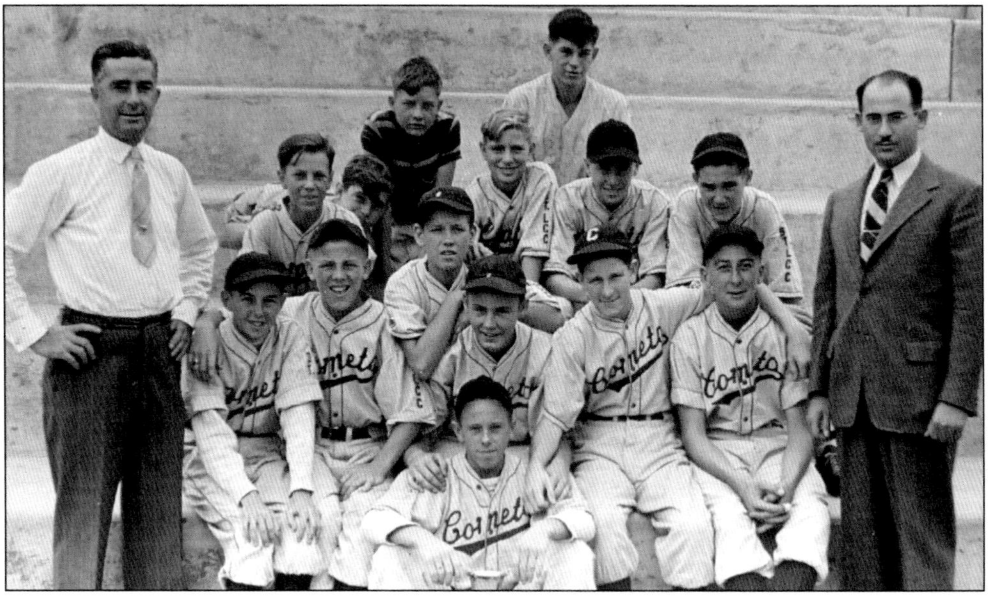

The Comets was a team organized from the Boy's Club of St. Lawrence Catholic Church. Pictured are John Canavari, Richard Schleicher, James O'Donnell, John Nagurka, William Faistl, Raymond Kannon, Thomas Rovito, Kenneth Anderson, William Nagurka, Francis McBride, George Kane, Raymond Cummings, Francis Loftus, and Robert Conway. This 1941 photograph was inscribed and sent "to Father Flannigan" of Boy's Town. In the 1980s, Boy's Town sent it back to Weehawken when clearing out its files.

The soldiers and sailors monument commemorating the fallen of World War I was erected in 1930 as part of the construction of Hamilton Plaza and Hamilton Park on Boulevard East. The bronze figures were designed by John Rapetti (1862–1936), a sculptor and resident of Weehawken. Several years later, he created the replacement bust for the Hamilton memorial at the south end of the park. (Al Berg.)

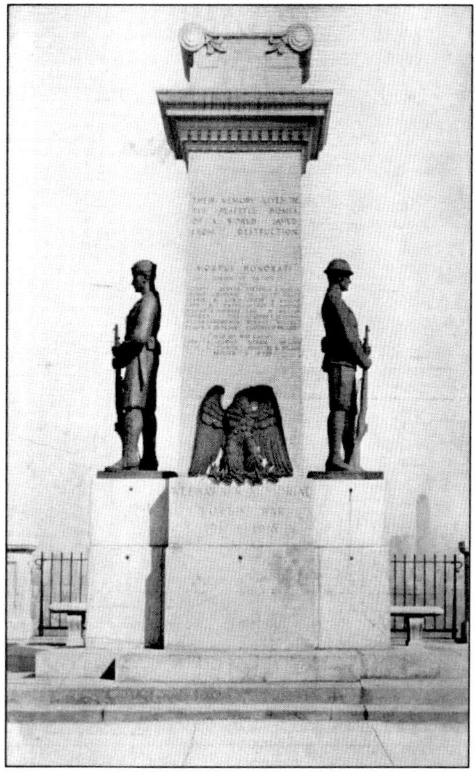

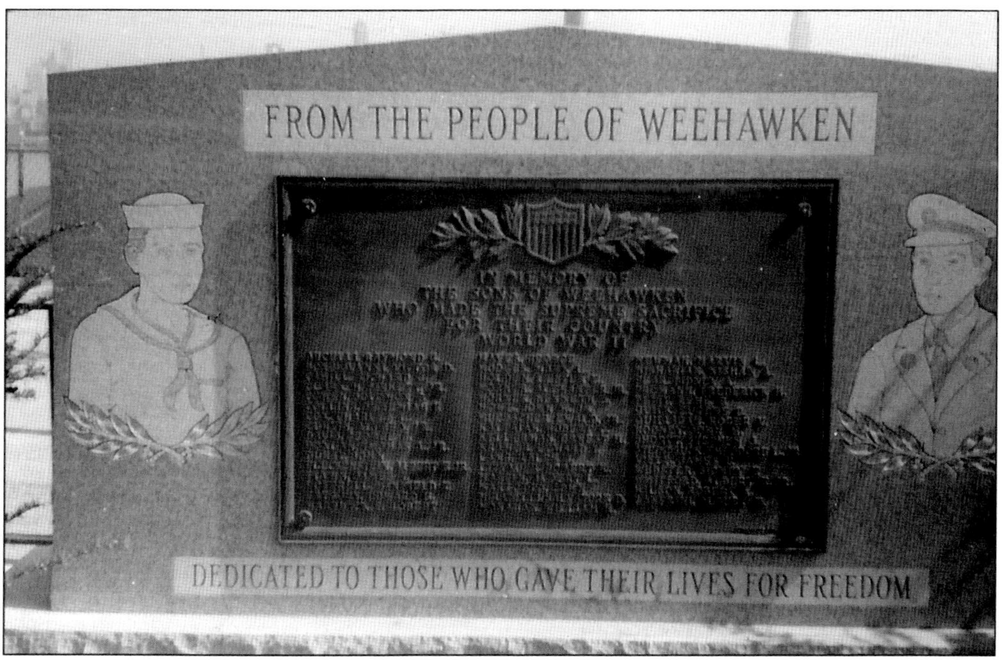

This monument commemorates the 47 Weehawken men who served and died during World War II. The monument, now at Hamilton Plaza to the left of the World War I soldiers and sailors monument, was originally located at Old Glory Park. At some point, the bronze plaque seen in this vintage photograph was stolen.

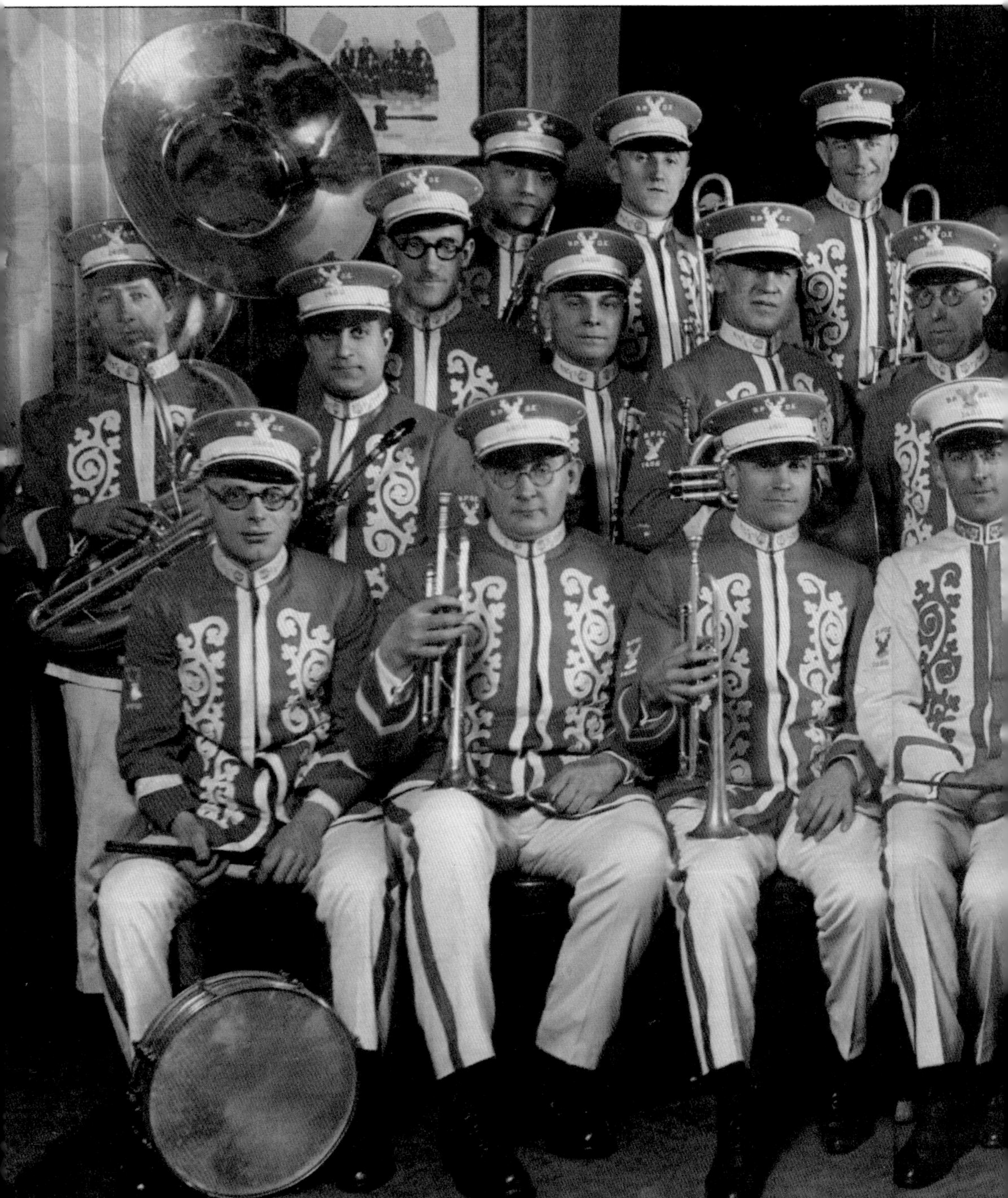

Weehawken Elks Lodge No. 1456 was instituted on June 11, 1922, with a group of 75 charter members. The women's arm, the Ladies Benevolent Guild, was founded around the same time. The Elks building, purchased in 1923, was part of the estate of Henry G. Schmidt and looks out on a "million dollar" view across the Hudson River. The Elks have been active performing philanthropic works in and around the community, especially in support of Camp Moore,

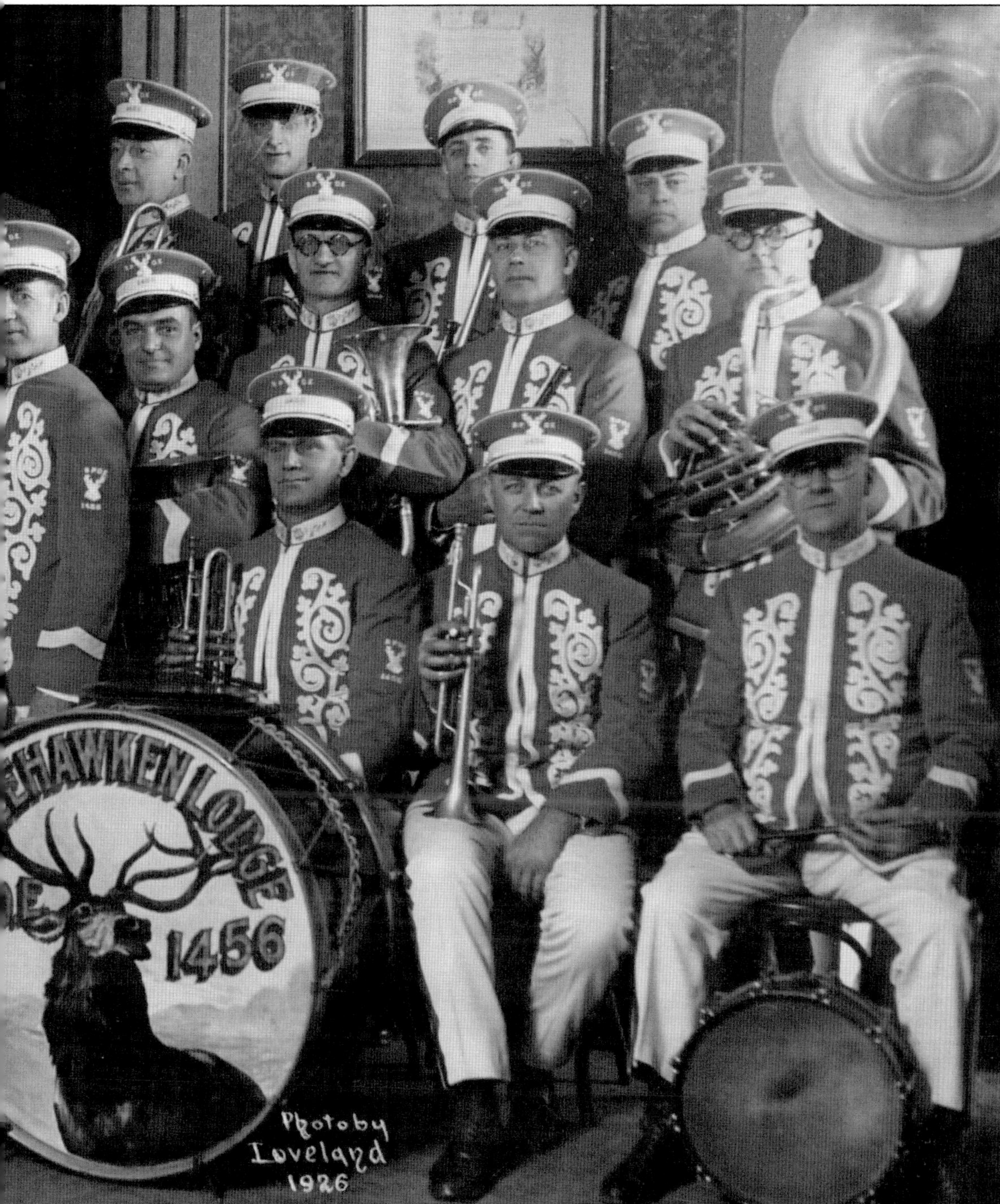

designed for special needs children and in support of United States veterans and their families. This 1926 professional photograph of the Weehawken Elks Band was taken to show off band members in their new uniforms in preparation for a special performance on April 9, 1926. William A. McCann was the director of the band that frequently recorded concerts on radio station WOR. (Joseph Cimino.)

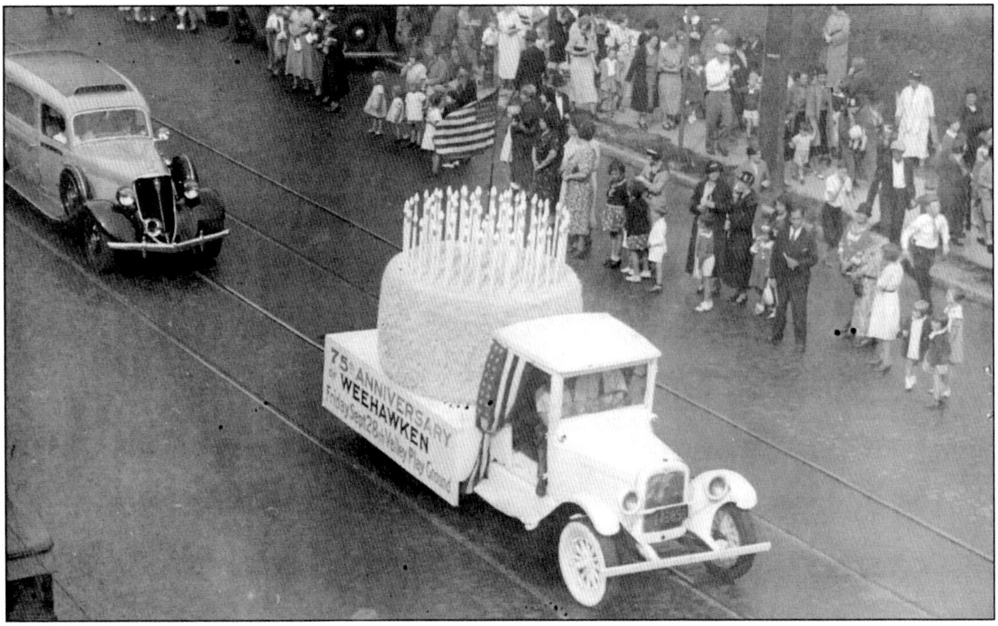

On September 28, 1934, Weehawken Township celebrated its 75th anniversary with a parade along Park Avenue that ended at the valley playground (soon to be demolished to make way for the new Midtown-Hudson Tunnel). The celebration continued that evening with a band concert and speeches by Mayor John G. Meister and Gov. A. Harry Moore, and it ended with a fireworks display.

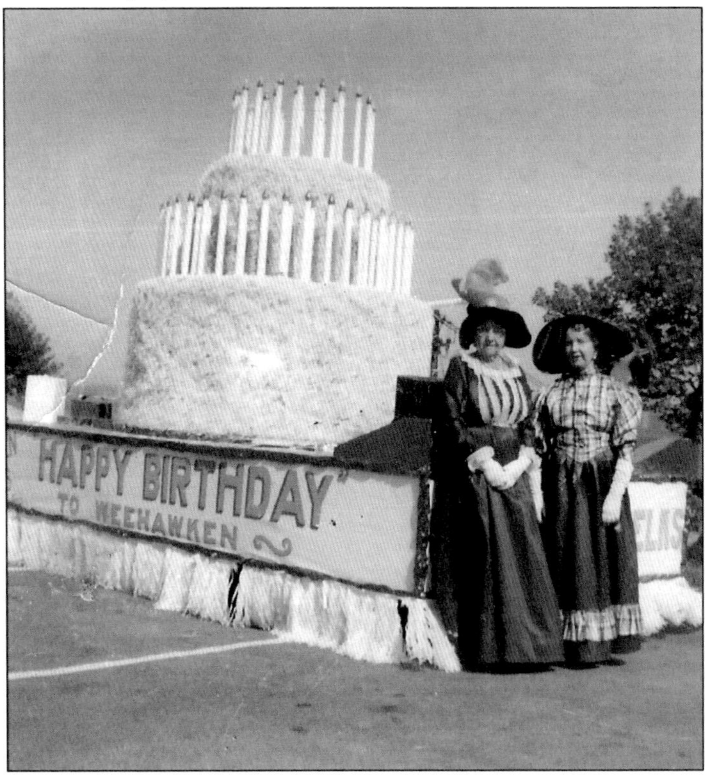

The parade to mark the celebration of Weehawken's centennial was held on Saturday September 19, 1959, after a week's worth of activities. Other events included orchestra performances at the stadium, the crowing of the centennial king and queen, band concerts, an art exhibit, and sports demonstrations. Pictured next to the Weehawken Elks Club birthday float are Elks Benevolent Guild members Marguerite C. Demontreux (left) and an unidentified woman. (Willie Demontreux.)

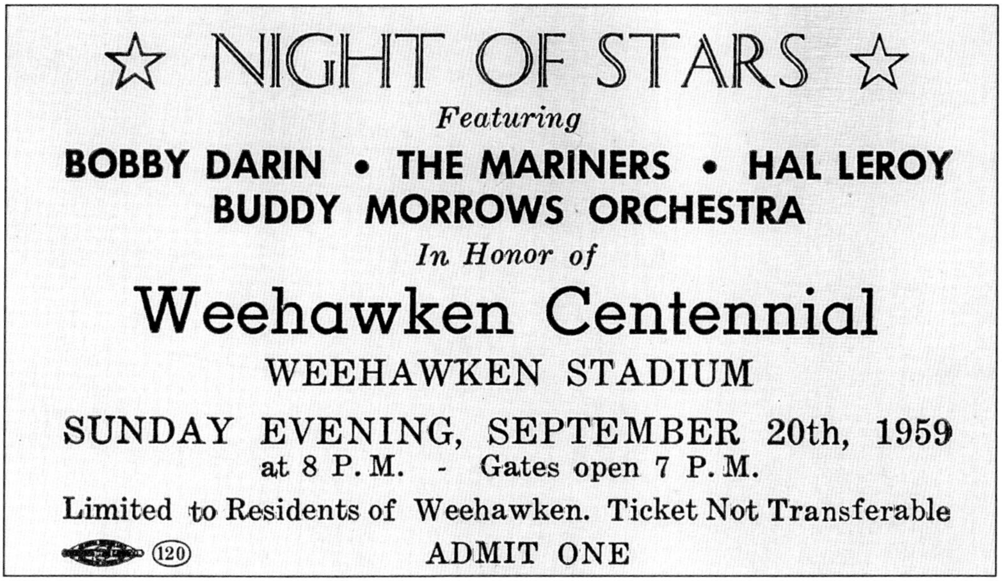

This ticket to Night of Stars capped Weehawken's centennial celebration week. The event was held at Weehawken Stadium and featured the sensational singing star Bobby Darin, whose hit "Mack the Knife" was at the top of the charts.

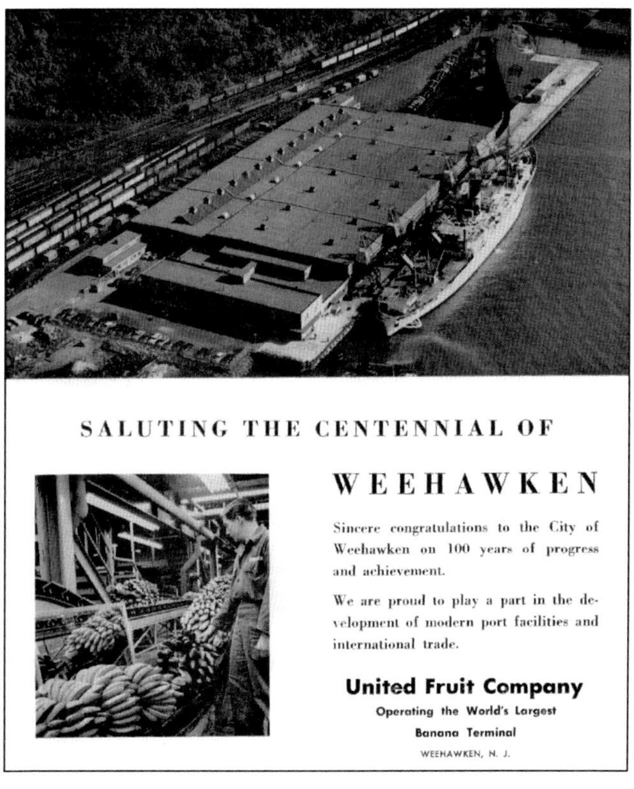

United Fruit Company's advertisement was featured in the *Weehawken Centennial Souvenir Journal*, a 63-page booklet published in conjunction with the centennial activities of 1959. The banana building and pier, with its low, flat profile, remained a landmark on Weehawken's waterfront for more than 50 years from its completion in 1952 until it was demolished in 2005 to make way for townhouses, a continuation of the waterfront walkway, and the township's new 16-acre waterfront recreational park.

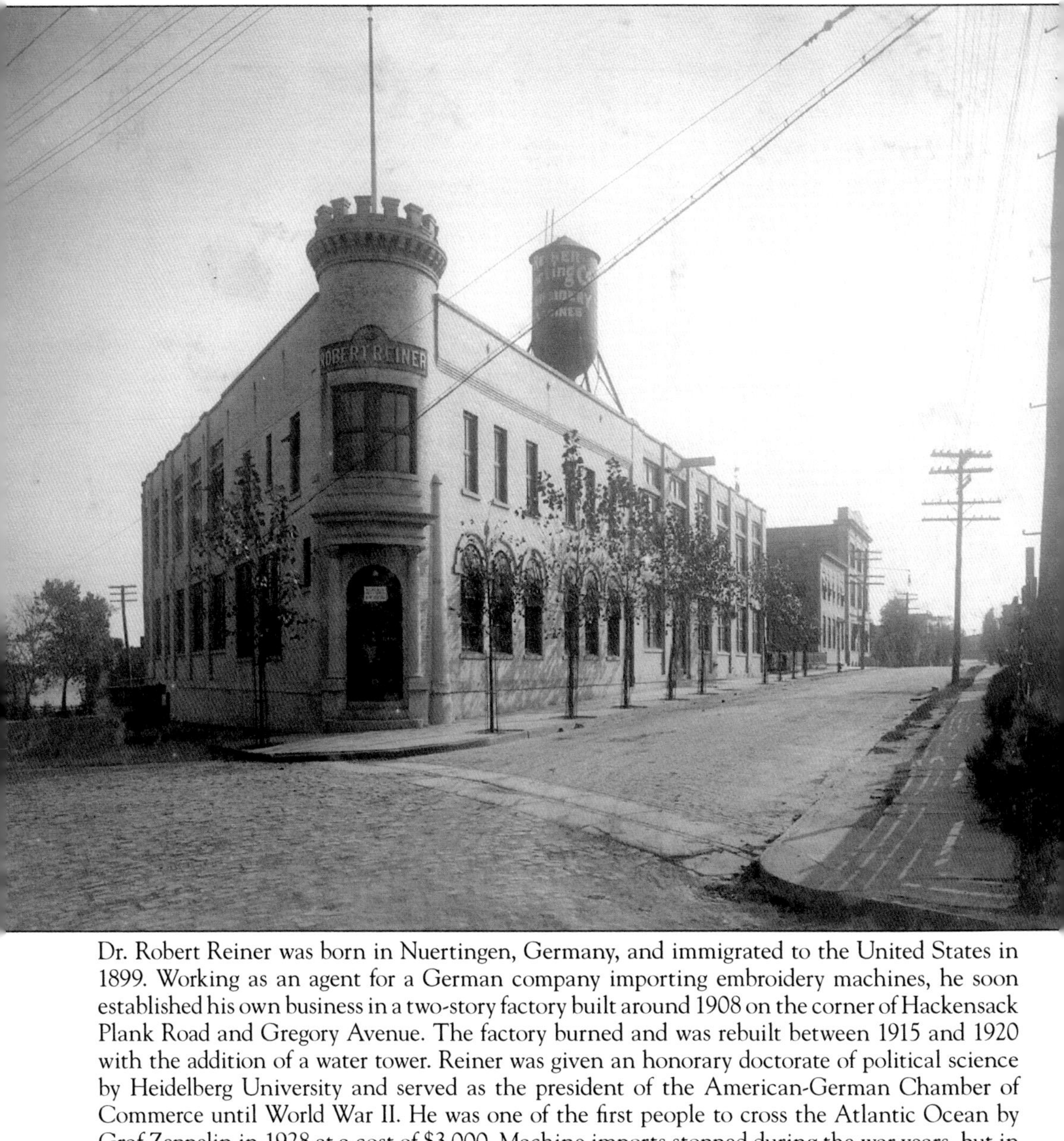

Dr. Robert Reiner was born in Nuertingen, Germany, and immigrated to the United States in 1899. Working as an agent for a German company importing embroidery machines, he soon established his own business in a two-story factory built around 1908 on the corner of Hackensack Plank Road and Gregory Avenue. The factory burned and was rebuilt between 1915 and 1920 with the addition of a water tower. Reiner was given an honorary doctorate of political science by Heidelberg University and served as the president of the American-German Chamber of Commerce until World War II. He was one of the first people to cross the Atlantic Ocean by Graf Zeppelin in 1928 at a cost of $3,000. Machine imports stopped during the war years, but in 1953, the company began manufacturing the first American-made Schiffli embroidery machines (meaning "little boat" in the Swiss dialect), named for the shape of the shuttle on the machine. Reiner was a great benefactor to his native city of Nuertingen throughout his life. (Marlene Brandt Riley.)

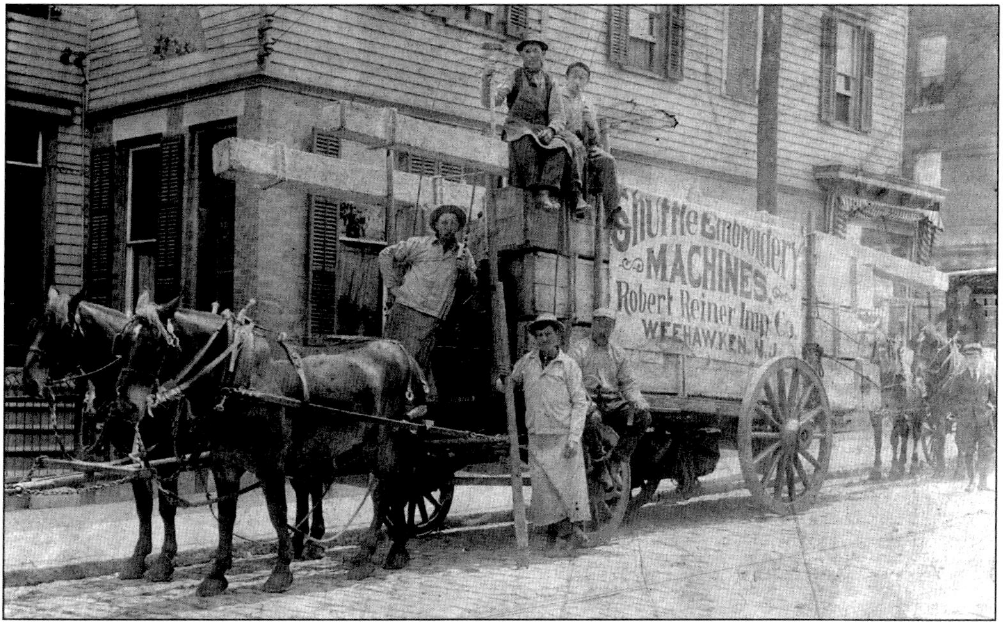

This horse-drawn wagon from about 1903 advertises the shuttle embroidery machines sold by the Robert Reiner Importing Company. Reiner started his company as an importer of German-made machinery, eventually producing his own in the 1950s. At one time, Hudson and Bergen Counties were the largest centers of embroidery and lace manufacture in the world, with Union City and West New York leading the way. (Marlene Brandt Riley.)

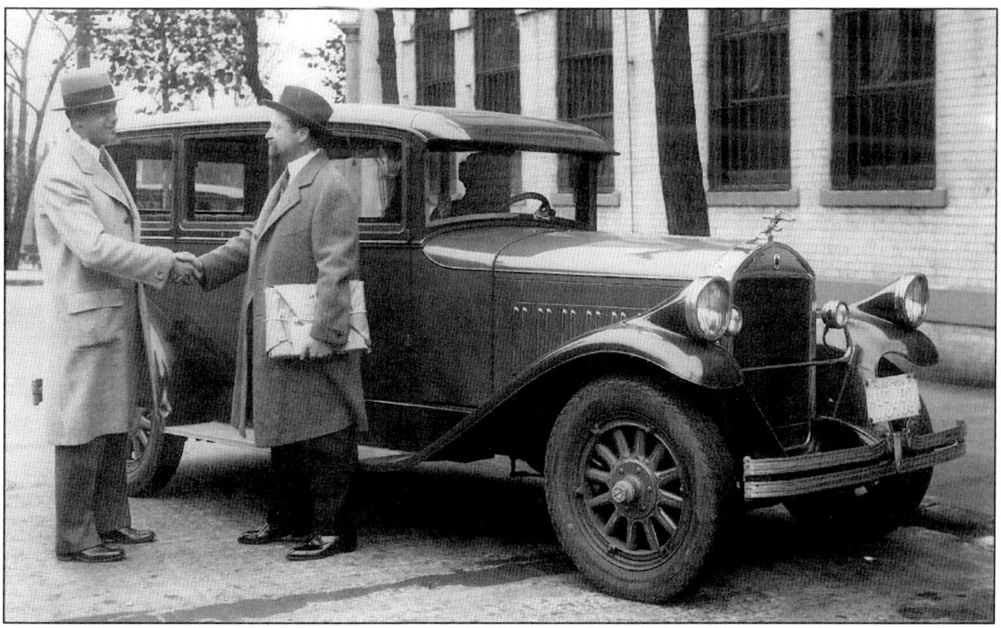

This photograph from 1923 shows Reiner (right) and Mr. Vollmann, his bookkeeper, outside the Robert Reiner Importing Company's demonstrating plant on Gregory Avenue. The company later became Robert Reiner, Incorporated. The men are standing in front of a Pierce-Arrow motorcar, which was driven by John (Reiner's driver). Several years ago, this factory building was converted to luxury lofts and became the Bella Vista Estates. (Marlene Brandt Riley.)

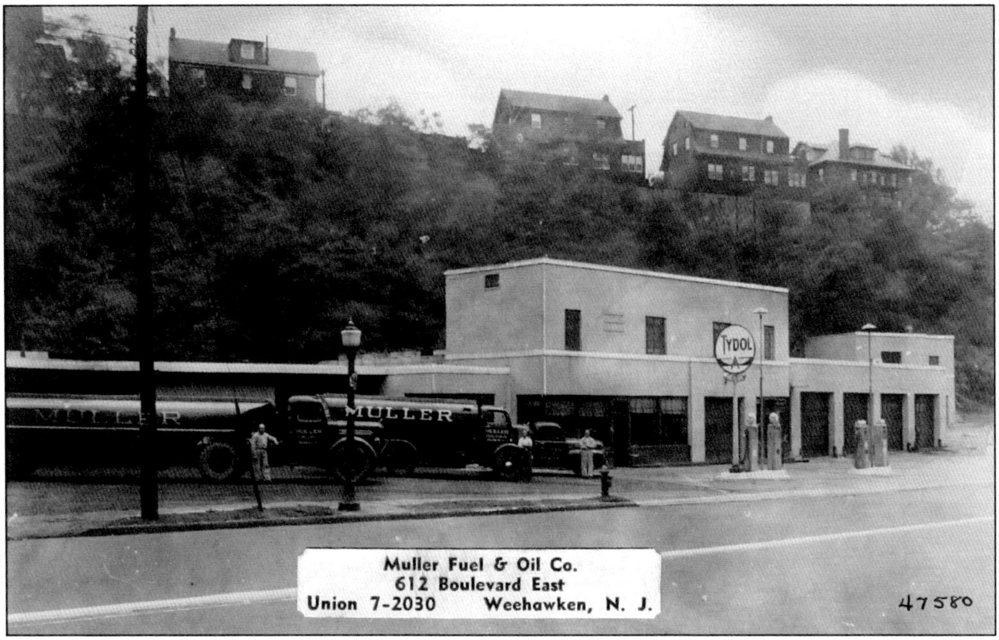

Henry Muller started his business in 1925 with a single truck but soon the company grew. The Muller Fuel and Oil Company delivered oil by way of its trucking fleet, sold gasoline at the pump, and sold industrial and domestic oil burners. Muller was also a successful real estate investor. (Al Berg.)

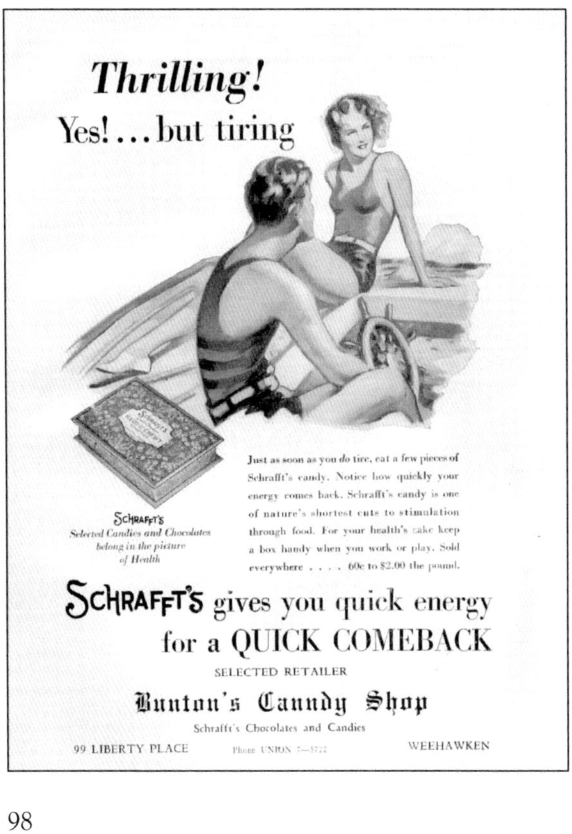

Alfred Bunton, confectioner, owned Bunton's Candy shop at 99 Liberty Place in Weehawken. This full-page advertisement came from the 1931 *Weehawken Zenith* yearbook. Who knew that candy was so healthy? In the 1950s, the store became Van's Ice Cream Parlor and Luncheonette, still selling candy, with the addition of Horton's Ice Cream. Note the spelling of "Canndy."

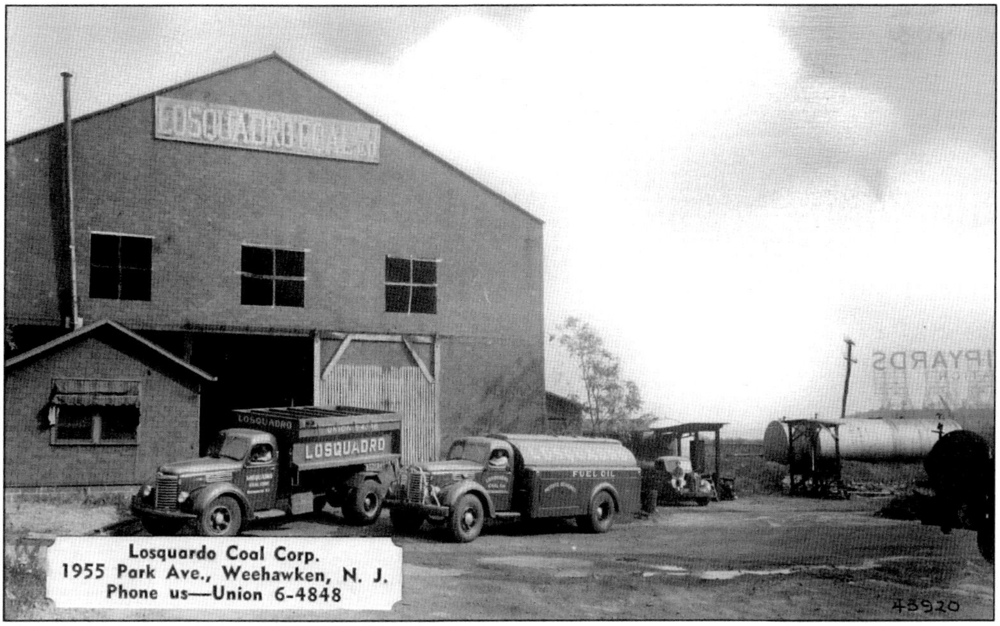

The Losquadro Coal Corporation, run by William Losquadro, was located on Park Avenue behind Dykes Lumber at Nineteenth Street and was in business until the 1980s. Along with coal and fuel oil delivery, it also installed and serviced oil burners. As coal use diminished, the company began delivering ice during the summer months and oil during the rest of the year. (Al Berg.)

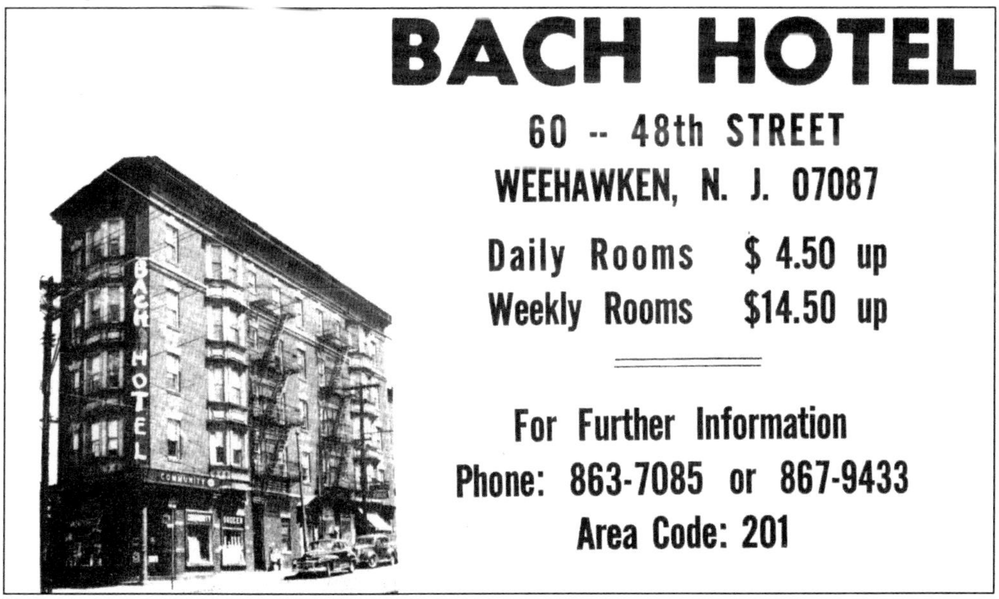

The Bach Hotel (now the Park Avenue Hotel) is located on the northeast corner of Park Avenue and Forty-eighth Street. An old-timer said that he used to bring contraband liquor through the West Shore Railroad tunnel and up into the hotel during the Prohibition days of the 1920s. The story was corroborated when surveys were made for the Hudson Bergen Light Rail, and it was found that one of five shafts along the tunnel, designed to vent the steam engines, did lie directly underneath the Bach, making it a convenient bootlegger's connection. (Al Berg.)

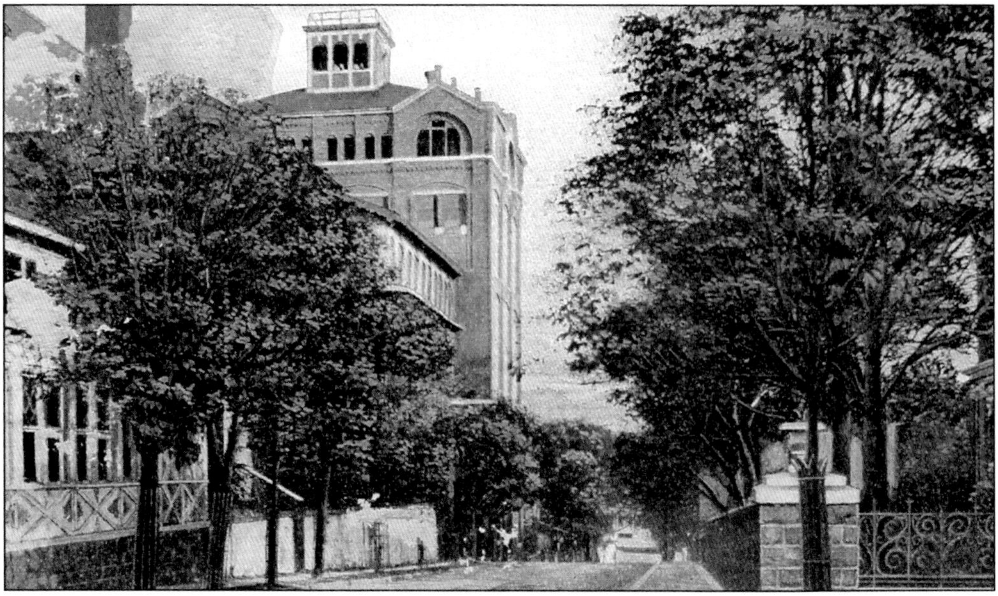

The Peter's Brewery, later the William Peter Brewing Company, was located in Union City on Weehawken Street, later called Peter Street. The brewery was owned and built by William Peter, whose successful venture developed into a large complex. The seven-story main brew house was built in 1887, eventually including a bottling department with a capacity of 60,000 barrels and the latest in modern machinery. The public beer room or saloon was located in the original section of the brew house and drew locals and New Yorkers alike. (Barbara Hansen.)

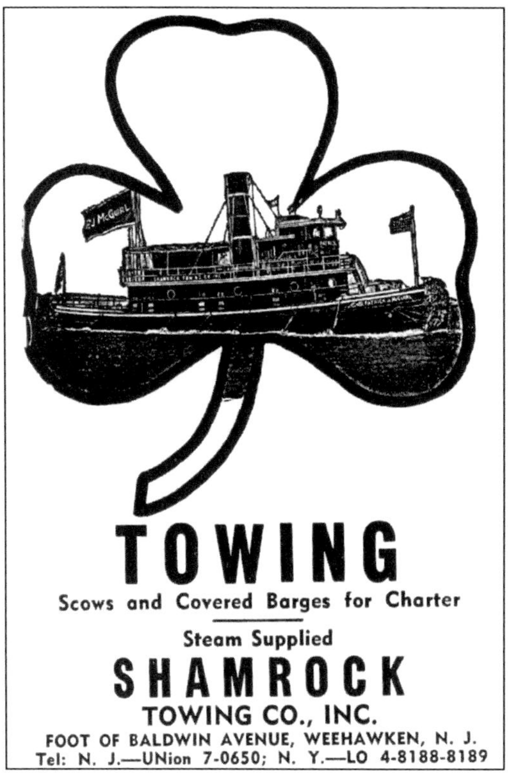

This is an advertisement for Shamrock Towing Company, which was founded in the New York Harbor in the 1870s by Capt. Patrick McGuirl. The president of the company was Robert J. McGuirl, whose initials are visible on the large flag on the tug. All tugs were named for a McGuirl family member. The family is still active in the tug, barge, and shipping business. (Al Berg.)

Six

THE TRANSPORTATION NETWORK

It is geography that defines Weehawken as a significant transportation hub. Its location opposite New York City necessitated the movement of goods and people across the Hudson River. However, it has long been a challenge to negotiate the 150-foot Palisades barrier on the west bank where Weehawken is located. The difficulties have been confronted over the years by all manner of engineering feats. In the 1880s, a tunnel was blasted through the Palisades to gain rail access to the west. In 1891, a huge passenger elevator on the waterfront was contrived to lift hundreds of people at a time from a ferry at river level to the top of the bluff for pleasure seekers' easy access to the popular Eldorado. Ferries holding pedestrian commuters, horse-drawn carriages, and eventually automobiles plied the river. Trolleys chugged passengers down Pershing Road to catch the ferry, and some commuters simply walked Pershing Road or the steps of the Grauert Causeway. Wooden stairs connected high and low neighborhoods throughout the township. A mechanized wagon lift carried horses, carts, and goods up the steep cliffs. To the community's credit, the innovations have been endless. There are more to come.

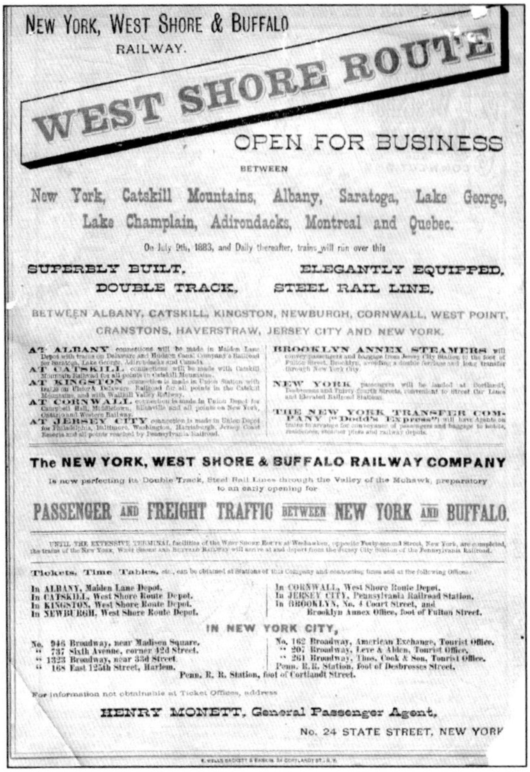

This advertisement, published by the New York, West Shore and Buffalo Railway Company, announces that new tracks traveling from New York were due to open on July 9, 1883, to improve train travel to parts as far north as Quebec. It also announces the start of the New York to Buffalo line, which will terminate in Weehawken as soon as the new West Shore Ferry terminal is completed.

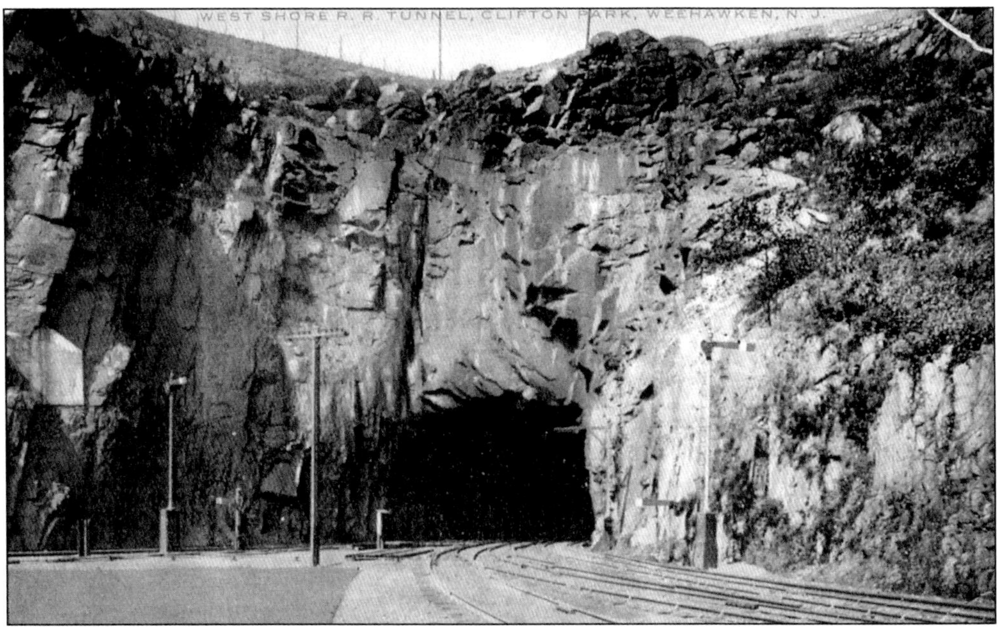

Construction by the New York, Ontario and Western Railway on the Weehawken tunnel began in 1882. The two-rail-wide tunnel with five airshafts ran nearly parallel to Forty-eighth Street and exited the Palisades in North Bergen just west of Tonnelle Avenue, now the site of the Hudson Bergen Light Rail station. The airshafts were designed to vent the engine fumes out of the tunnel and to bring in fresh air to the passengers. (Ellen Robb Gaulkin.)

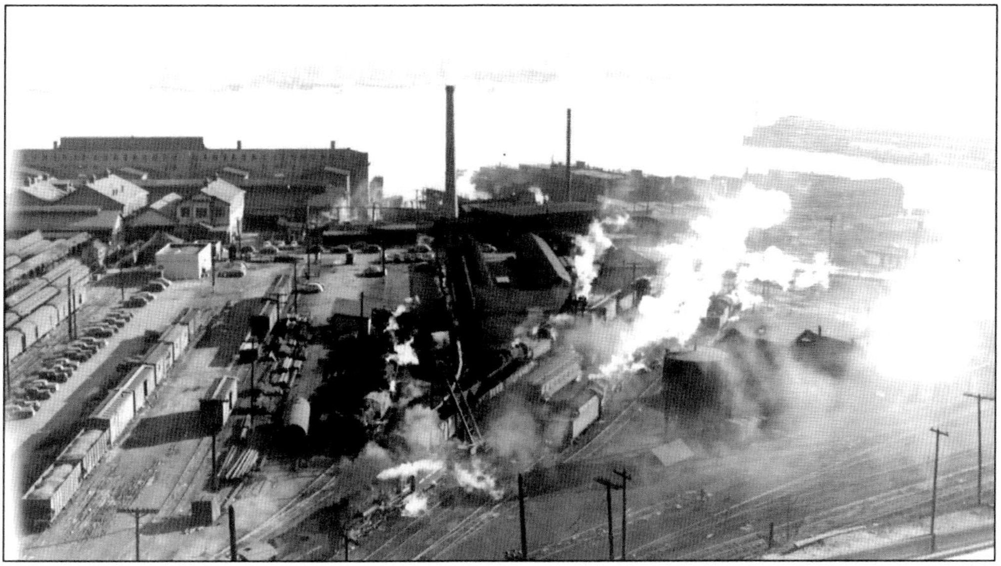

Pictured in this photograph from about 1940 are the steam-powered New York Central Railroad trains servicing a freight yard located near the foot of Pershing Road. From 1898 under West Shore Railroad's jurisdiction and then by the New York Central until the early 1950s, nine special milk trains from the Catskills passed through the yards, with one terminating in Weehawken.

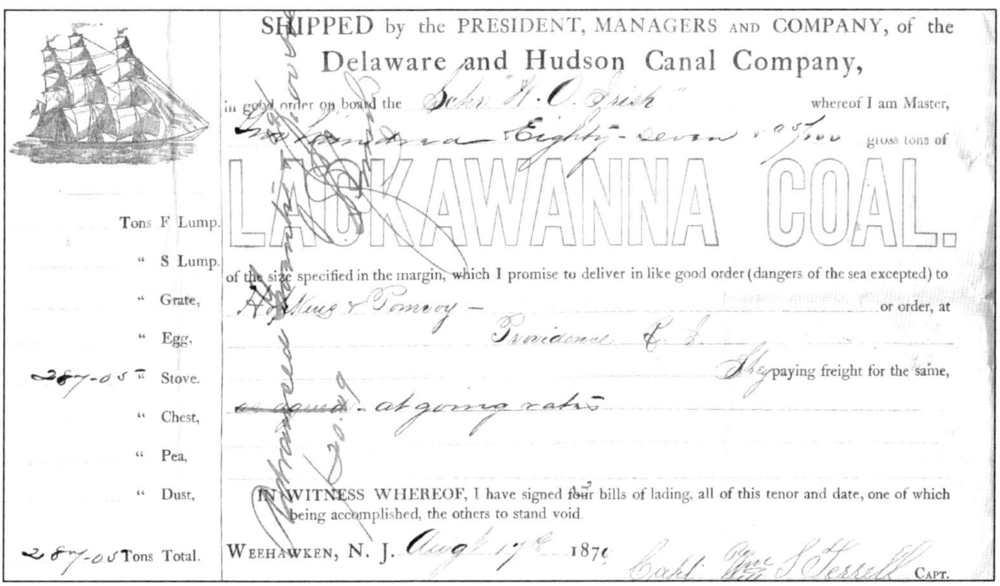

SHIPPED by the PRESIDENT, MANAGERS AND COMPANY, of the

Delaware and Hudson Canal Company,

in good order on board the Schr. "W. O. Irish" whereof I am Master,

Two hundred Eighty-seven 05/100 gross tons of

LACKAWANNA COAL.

of the size specified in the margin, which I promise to deliver in like good order (dangers of the sea excepted) to

Hopkins & Tomroy — or order, at

Providence R. I.

She paying freight for the same,

at going rates

IN WITNESS WHEREOF, I have signed four bills of lading, all of this tenor and date, one of which being accomplished, the others to stand void.

WEEHAWKEN, N. J. Aug 17th 1870 Capt. Wm. S. Terrell CAPT.

Tons F Lump.
" S Lump.
" Grate,
" Egg,
287-05 " Stove.
" Chest,
" Pea,
" Dust,
287-05 Tons Total.

This receipt dated August 17, 1870, shows that 287 tons of Lackawanna stove coal was shipped from Weehawken to Providence, Rhode Island, on the schooner *W. O. Irish* via the Delaware and Hudson Canal Company. The company, in business from 1823 to 1899, had its headquarters just north of Baldwin Avenue, occupying the present-day site of the township's waterfront park. (Al Berg.)

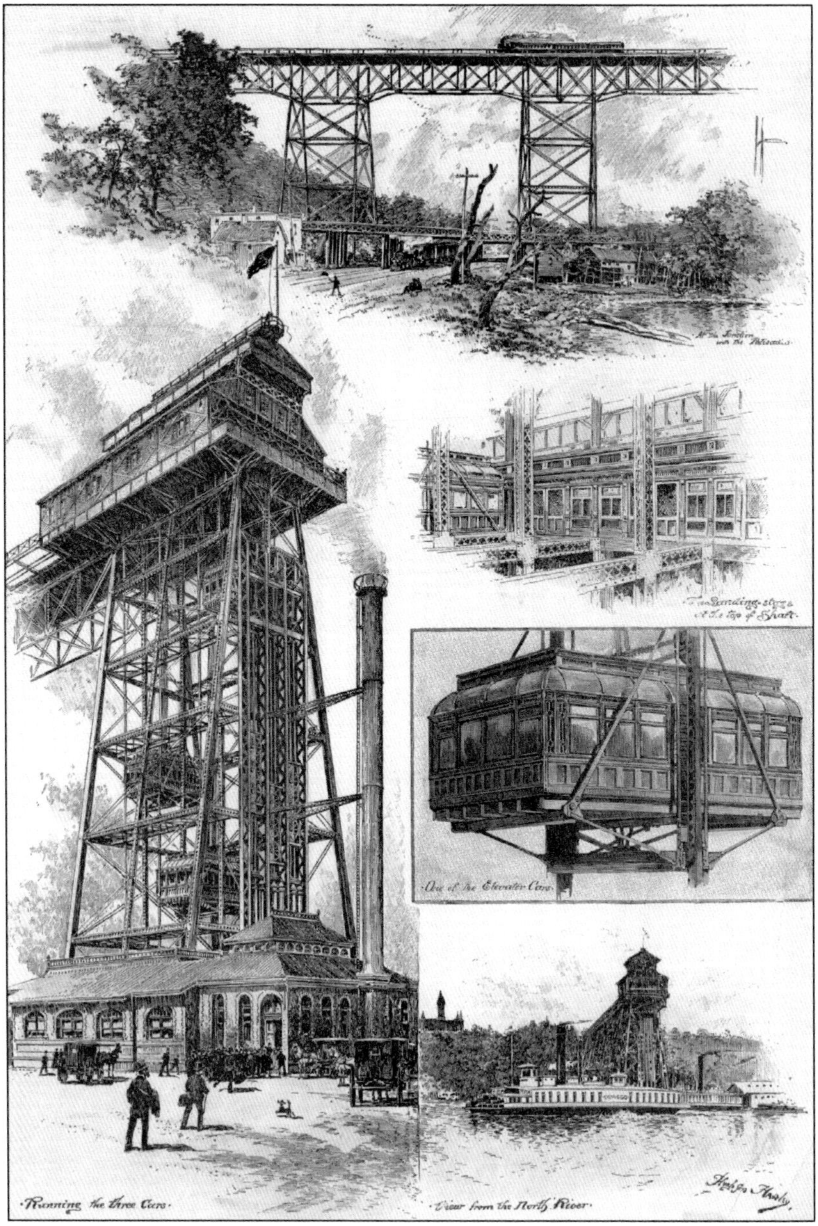

The giant passenger elevator, completed in October 1891 and opened to the public in April 1892, was the brainchild of John Hillric Bonn, president of the North Hudson County Railway Company. At a cost of $850,000, the elevator, tower, and viaduct system provided quick and convenient access for the crowds from New York coming to Eldorado and those continuing on to the Guttenberg racetrack. Passengers traveled in style; the cars were richly appointed in mahogany and fitted with comfortable wicker chairs. Each car could carry 400 people from the ferry slip up nearly 200 feet to the railroad station at the top in less than a minute. From there, the train carried passengers across a 900-foot-long trestle that passed through a cut in the Palisades to the train station at Bulls Ferry Road. Despite the capability of transporting 60,000 visitors daily, the elevator was only in operation for about three years, closing in June 1895. This illustration is from an 1891 *Harper's Weekly* issue.

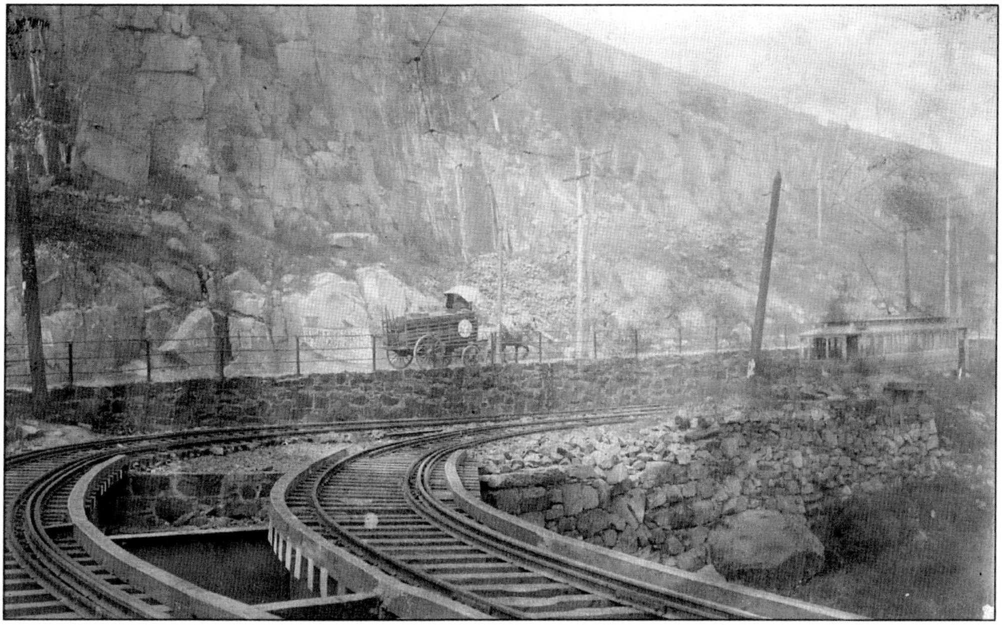

In June 1895, an electrified trolley service was instituted by the North Hudson County Railway Company starting at the Weehawken Ferry terminal. The cars traveled up the Palisades, running parallel to Clifton Road (later Pershing Road), crossed the boulevard at Fourth Street (today's Forty-eighth Street) and continued west to Bulls Ferry Road and Bergenline Avenue.

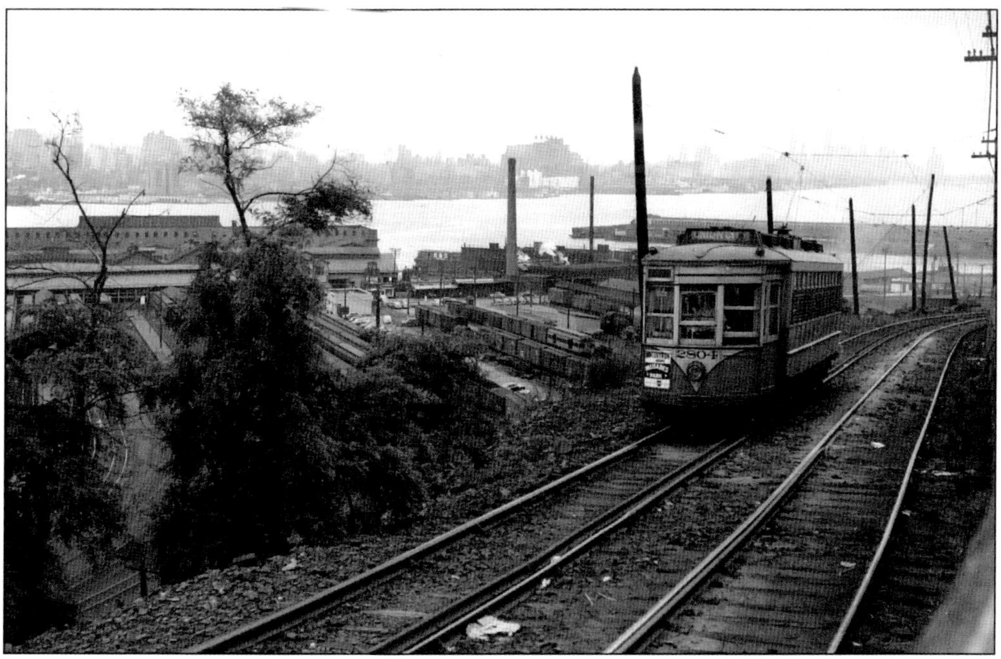

In this late-1940s photograph, public service trolley No. 2804 marked Union City makes its way towards the top of the Palisades. The trolley lines ran just east of Pershing Road, precariously close to the drop off of the cliff. The last trolley car in north Hudson left the West Shore station on August 7, 1949. (Al Berg.)

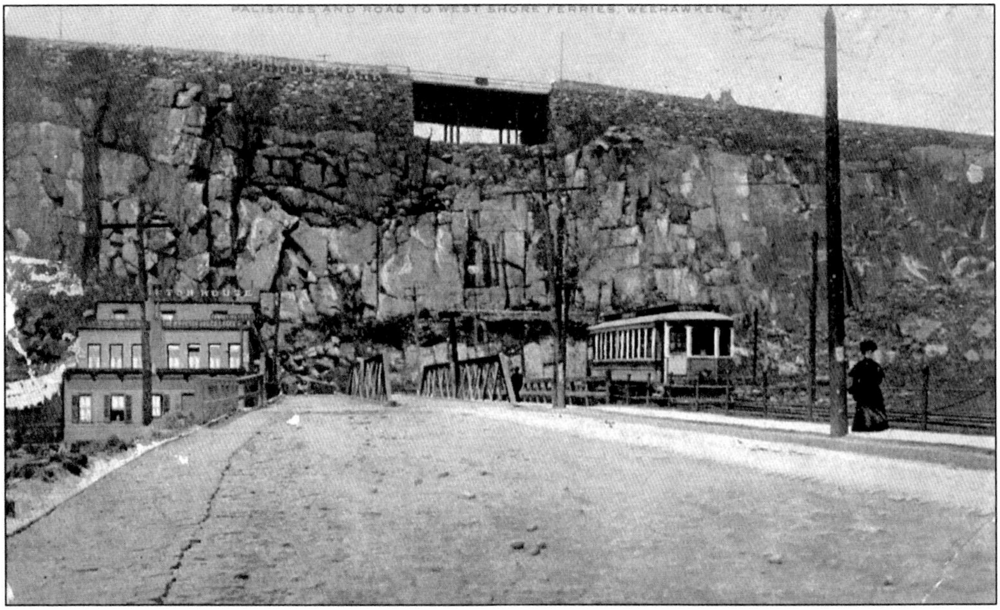

Looking up from Clifton Road, a trolley is en route to the ferry traveling over a trestle bridge that allowed trains to pass underneath. On the left is an old-time roadhouse, called Clifton House. At the top of the Palisades is the old railroad cut through which the trains from the elevator passed along the trestle to stop at Eldorado. Just left of the cut are the words "Highwood Park" painted on the retaining wall. (Lauren Sherman.)

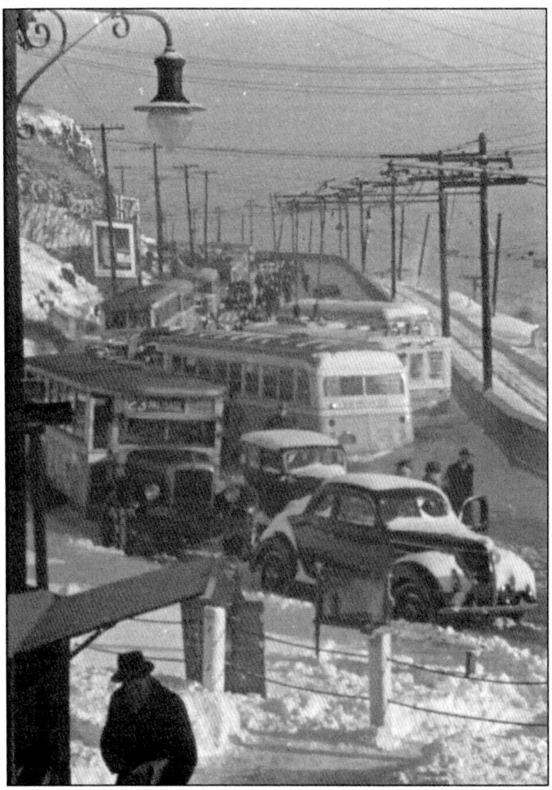

During the peak ferry travel years of the 1920s and 1930s, it was not uncommon to experience traffic delays of several hours on the Pershing Road hill, with an array of buses and cars all vying for position along the narrow roadway. If someone was prominent or famous, patrolman Edward Kirk might pass that person through the line, as he did for Pres. Calvin Coolidge and prizefighter Jack Dempsey. This late 1930s photograph shows what the addition of a snowstorm could do to snarl traffic even further.

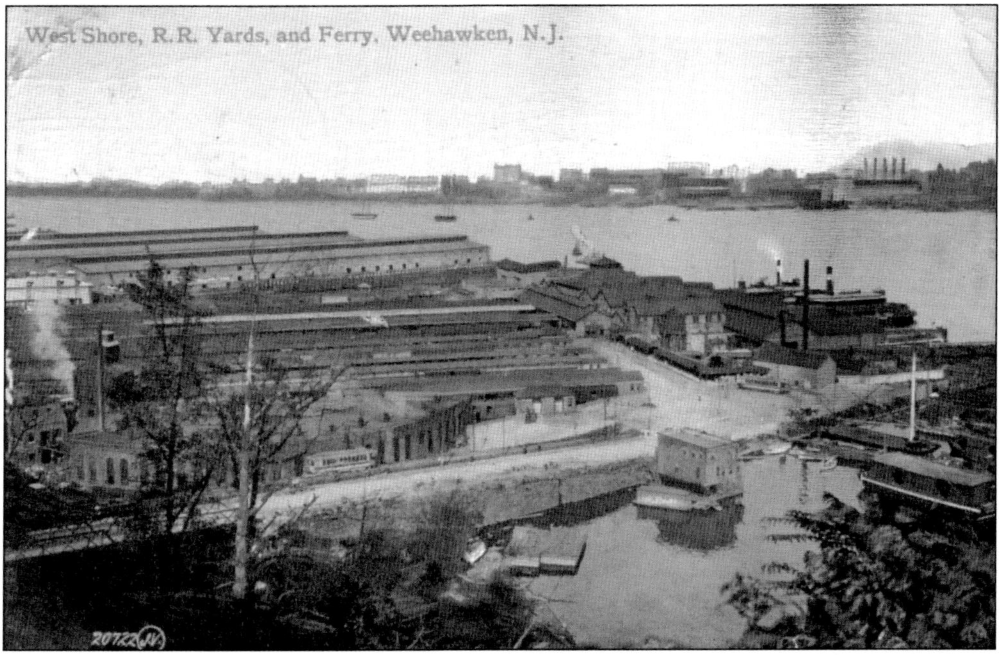

This view of the ferry terminal and West Shore Railroad train platforms is from around 1910. Pershing Road leads from left to right across the photograph with a trolley descending. The building behind the trolley is a railroad roundhouse, which stored engines for repair or rerouted them to alternate tracks. The small cove in the foreground was home to a ragtag mix of barges, small craft, and a floating restaurant. Below, about 40 years later, not much has changed, except that most of Union Dry Dock's property now rests on landfill, an expansion of waterfront acreage completed shortly before 1930. The site of the ferry terminal with its five ferry boats in their slips was a rare occurrence. Behind the terminal are three long storage piers that belonged to the West Shore Railroad, and at far left is Pier 7. (Above, Al Berg.)

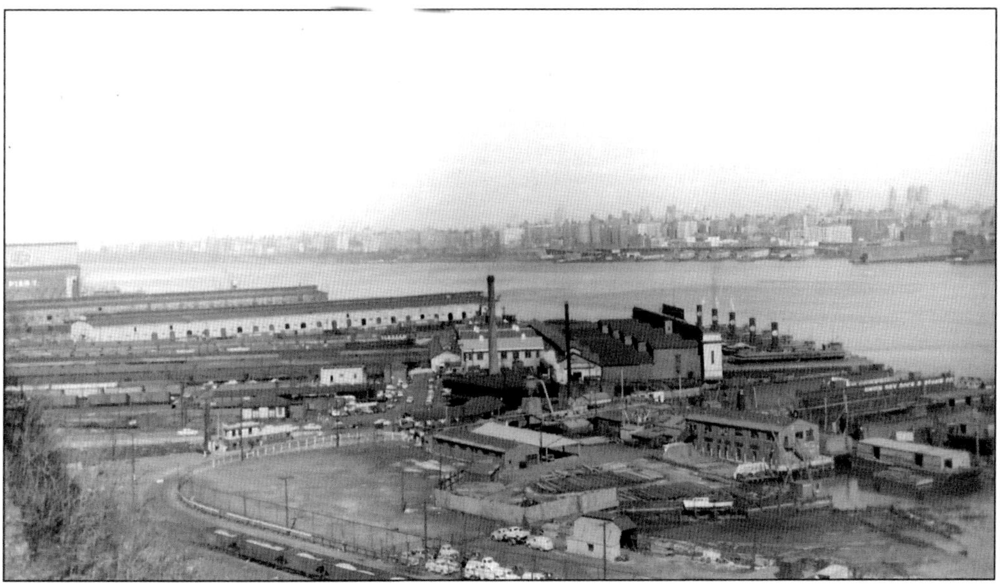

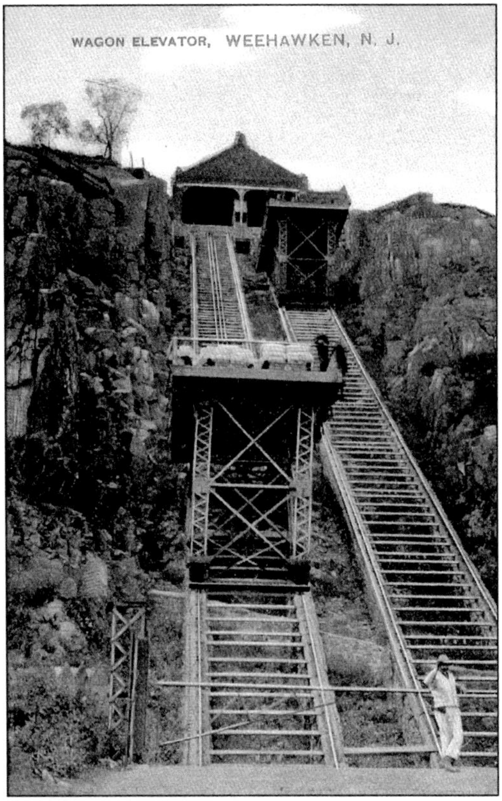

The wagon lift took passengers, wagons, and horsecars from lower Weehawken to Weehawken Street in West Hoboken. Built in 1874 by John H. Bonn's railroad company, it was located beneath the present site of Troy Towers. Part of its track is still visible. Cars that were 20 feet wide, 40 feet long, and capable of carrying a load of 50,000 pounds could climb the span in one minute by means of a 300-horsepower electric motor. (Lauren Sherman.)

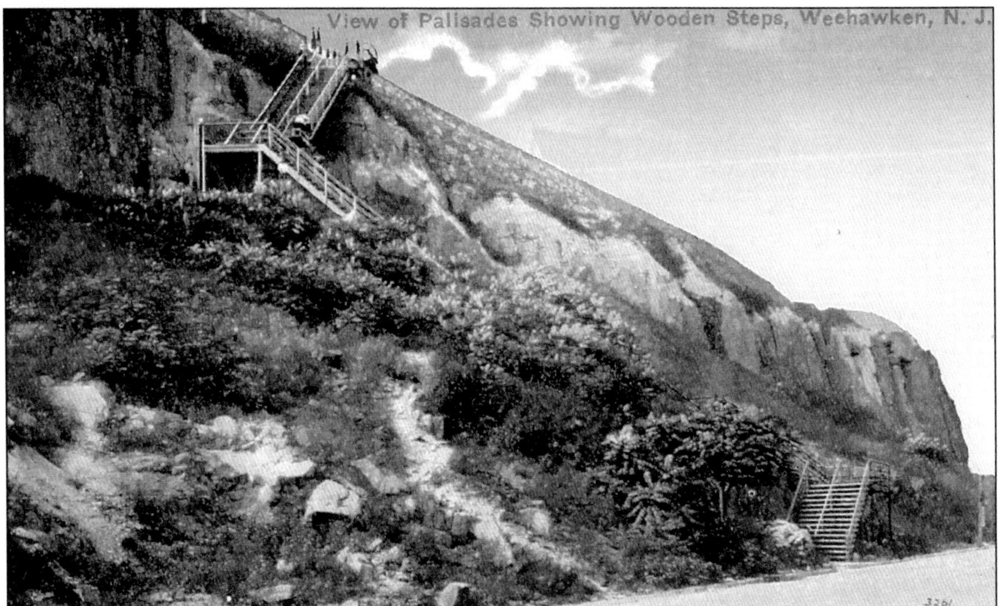

This set of wooden stairs at Boulevard East and Columbia Terrace is just one of nine sets of steps throughout the township aiding pedestrians to access the various parts of town in the preautomobile days of the 19th and early 20th centuries. In addition to stairs, there were two other conveyances, namely the giant elevator and the wagon lift. (Lauren Sherman.)

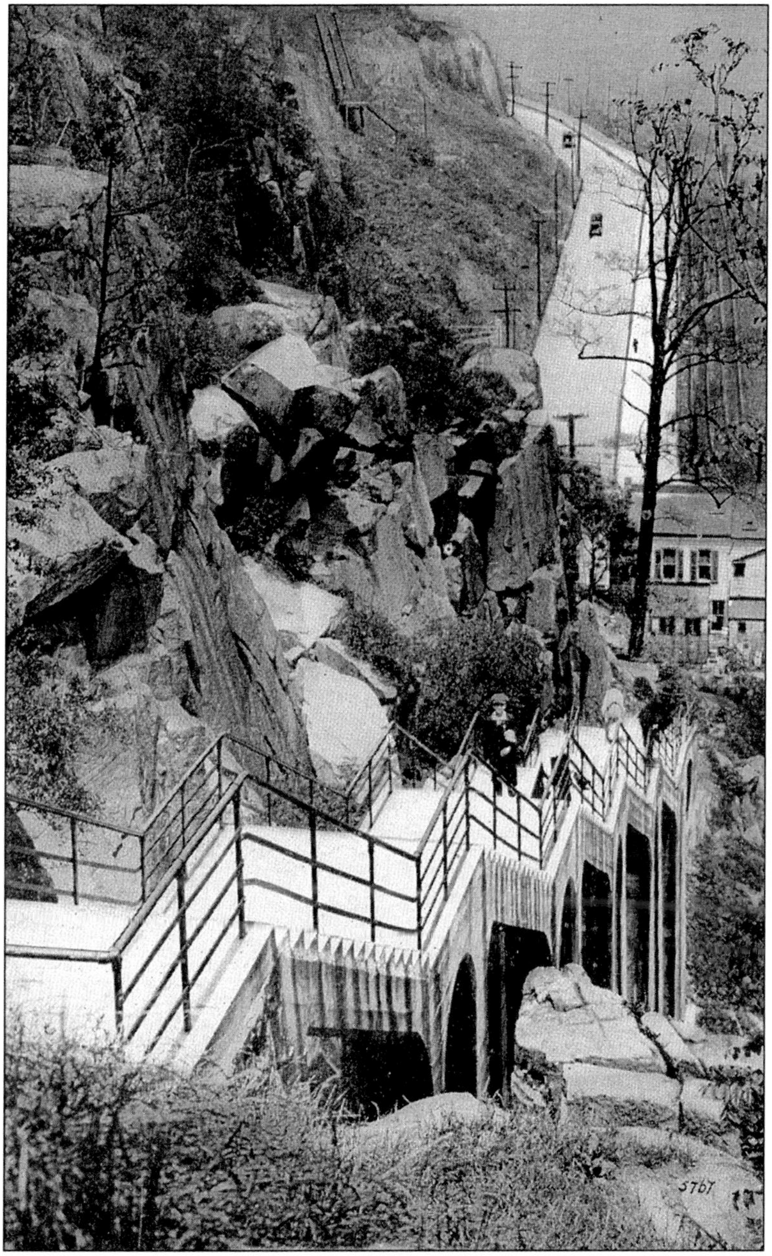

This highly architectural and cleverly engineered set of steps offered a most dramatic descent by foot from Boulevard East to the Weehawken waterfront. Completed in 1915 under the administration of Mayor Emile W. Grauert and known as the Grauert Causeway, it remained in use through the early 1950s. Eventually, the shifting Palisade rock caused the concrete steps and foundation to destabilize, and it was considered too dangerous to use. Grauert, an architect by profession, also presided over the building of the Jefferson Street stairs and had a hand in the design of the new town hall at 400 Park Avenue as well as the soldiers and sailors monument. He died at his home on Bonn Place on April 20, 1931, and his wife finished out his term. Parts of the stairs are still visible and intact when viewed from the soldiers and sailors monument. (Ellen Robb Gaulkin.)

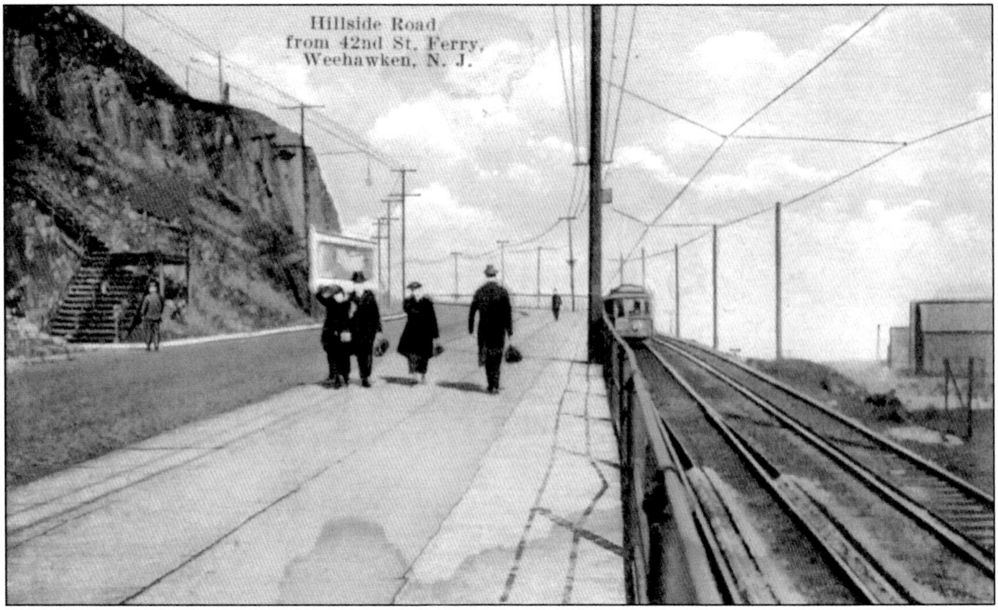

The road from Boulevard East down to the Weehawken ferry has had a history of name changes from Clifton Road (named for Clifton Park) to Hillside Road to Pershing Road (named for Gen. John J. Pershing after World War I) and even as part of the final segment of the Lincoln Highway. Coming down the hill are commuters on their way to the ferry. Advertising billboards were a feature all along Pershing Road from early times. (Al Berg.)

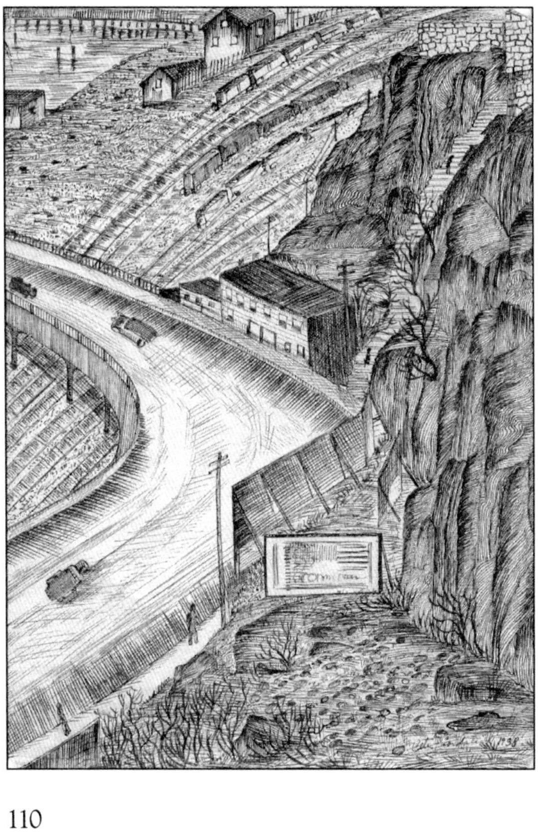

Peter Fiordalisi (1904–1988) was born in Union City, but lived in Weehawken for most of his life. He studied at Mechanic's Institute in New York and received training as a metal engraver in the jewelry trade. Most of his years were spent painting and drawing the rocky cliffs of the Palisades and waterfront in Weehawken and West New York. This 1938 pen-and-ink view looks down from Boulevard East to Pershing Road and the railroad yards below. (Lauren Sherman.)

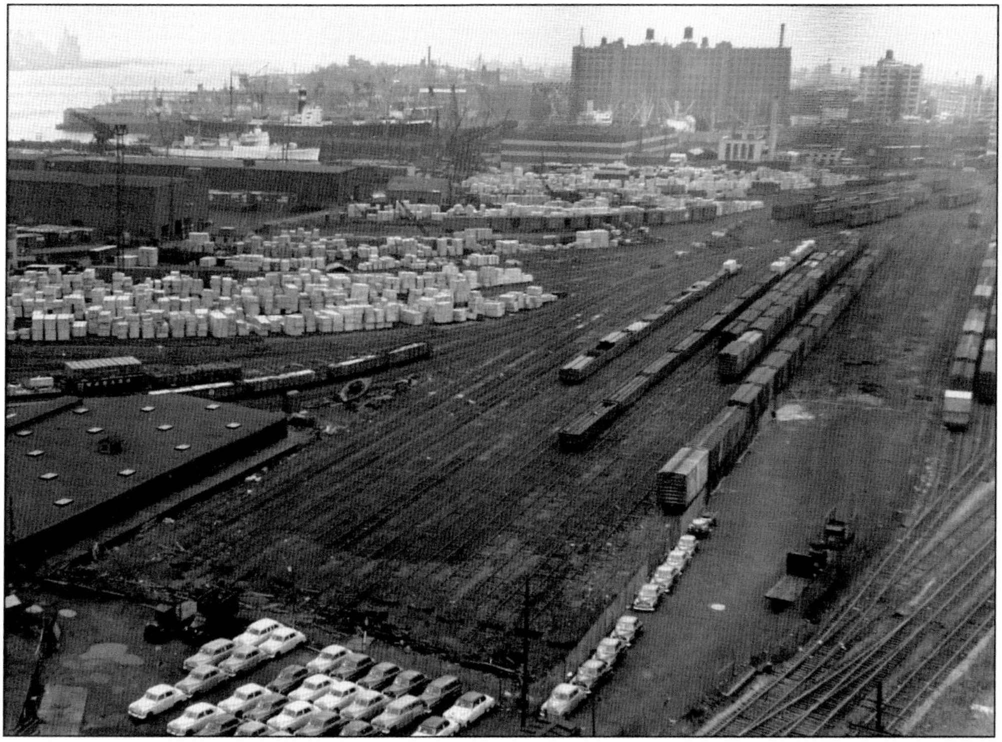

The Erie Railroad facility, with its piers, storage, and railroads, covered the southern end of the Weehawken waterfront. The thousands of pieces of freight indicate the high level of shipping and receiving activity in the Erie yards. The cars in the foreground of this photograph, being readied for delivery, date it to 1950. At top right is the Lipton Tea complex, located in Hoboken just on the other side of the Weehawken cove. (Al Berg.)

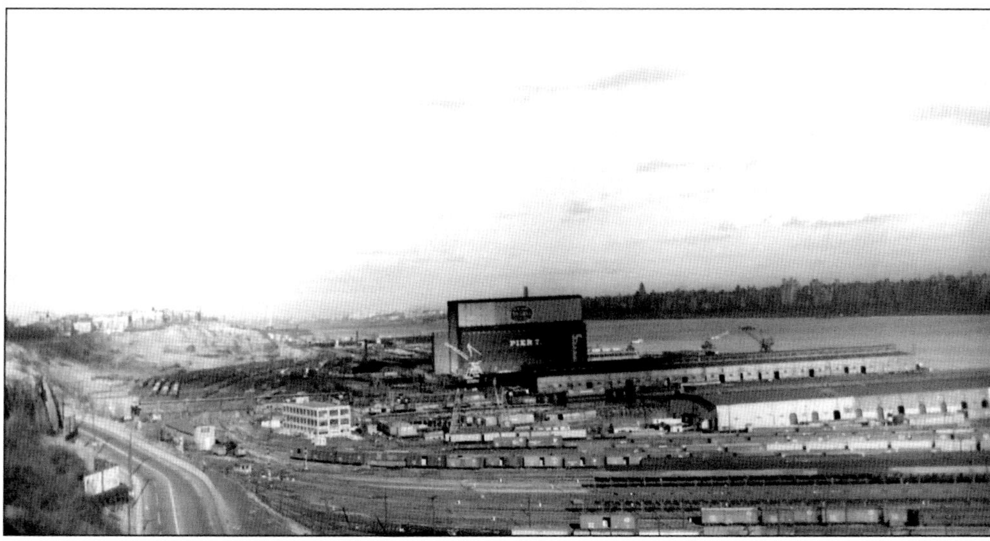

The great Pier 7 grain elevator, with its huge capacity of two million bushels, was completed in 1905 for the West Shore line of the New York Central Railroad. Whole trainloads of grain could be swiftly unloaded, weighed, and immediately reloaded into ocean-bound vessels. The 160-foot-tall structure was located at the border of West New York.

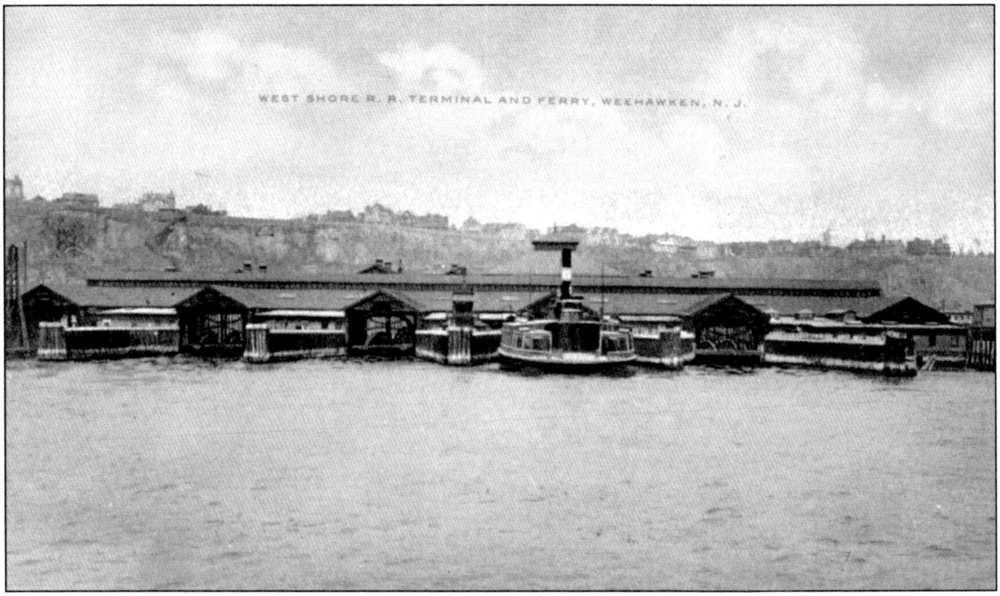

Weehawken's ferry history was one of sporadic service from Weehawken to New York starting in the early 18th century. In 1852, a much-improved Weehawken ferry was incorporated, and the service was regulated and became profitable with its highest ridership during the 1920s. Seen from the vantage point of the Hudson River are the five ferry berths, one with a ferryboat at dock. Behind the slips on the opposite side of the terminal building were the railroad connections. (Al Berg.)

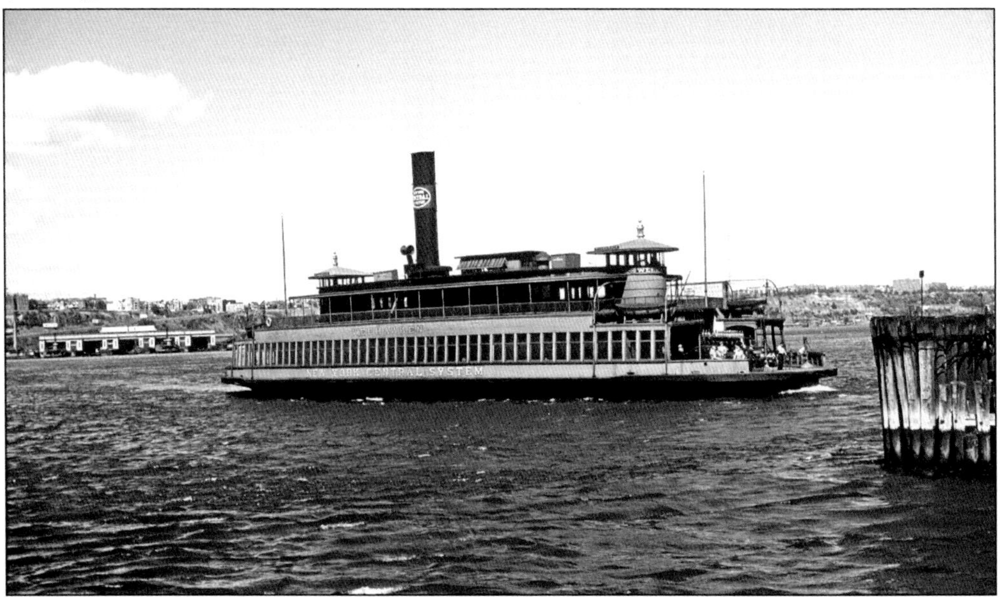

The *Weehawken* was added to New York Central Railroad's West Shore fleet in 1914, its route was to 42nd Street. This 1956 photograph by Conrad Milster shows the ferry about to pull into its Manhattan terminal with the Weehawken terminal visible at left. The *Weehawken* made its final trip on March 25, 1959, when the 42nd Street ferry was discontinued. In 1986, Arthur Imperatore created New York Waterway, reinstituting ferry service between Weehawken and Manhattan with great success. (Conrad Milster.)

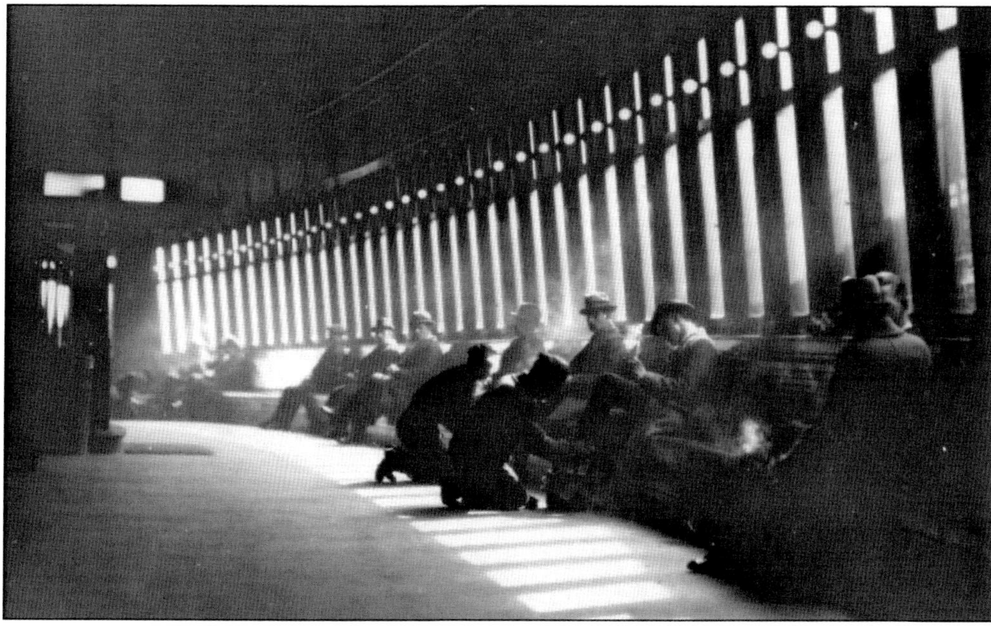

Ferryboats were originally separated by sex, with men on one side, women on the other, and cars and trucks loaded in the center. The decline of the Weehawken ferry was chiefly due to the build up of a car culture and easy trans-Hudson River alternatives like the Holland Tunnel, George Washington Bridge, and Lincoln Tunnel. This smoky 1940s image of commuters having their shoes shined was captured by Charles Schneider, a Weehawken resident and avid photographer.

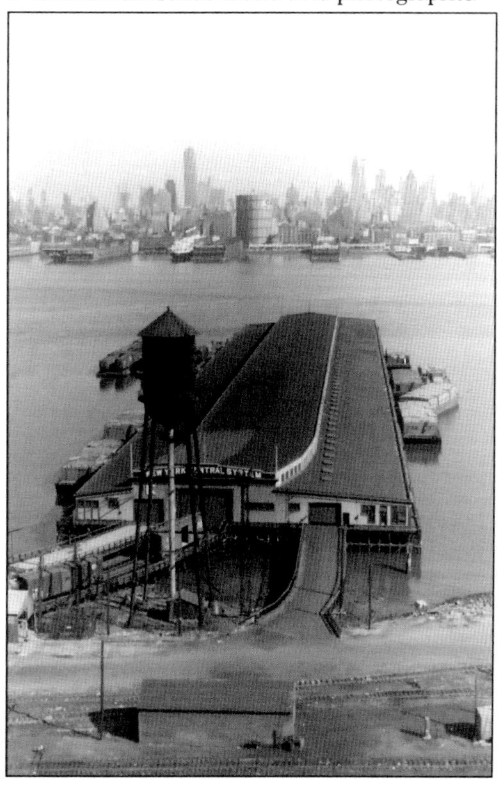

Seen from Hamilton Plaza in the 1950s, Pier K with its distinctive water tower was a longtime fixture on the Weehawken waterfront. Belonging to the New York Central Railroad system, it was located between the banana pier and Union Dry Dock. It was multipurpose, serving trains, trucks, barges, and ships. The pier burned down in an extensive fire on June 10, 1972.

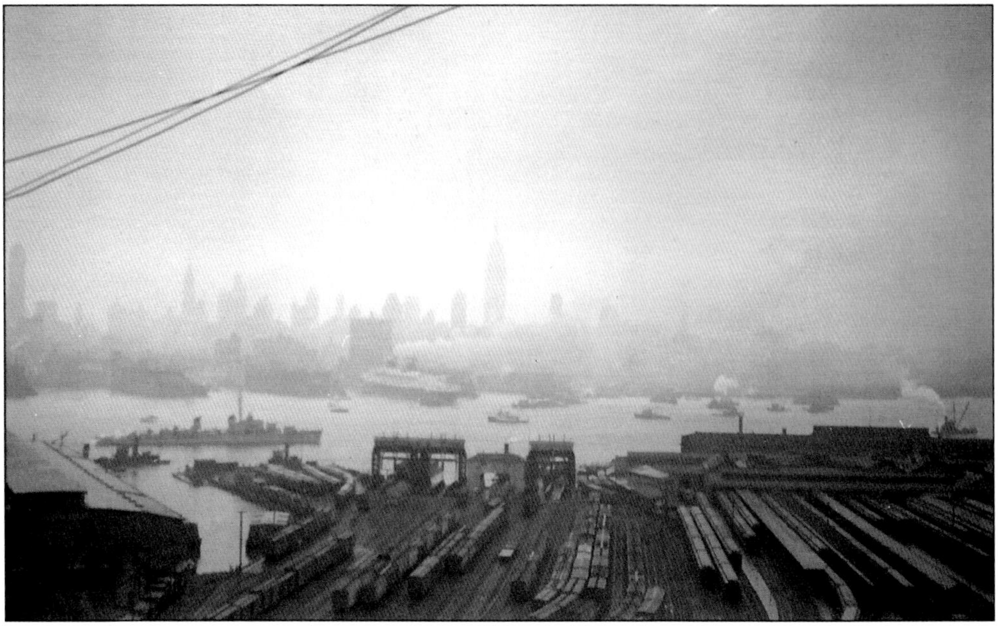

The West Shore Railroad yards are seen from the top of Boulevard East in 1939. At left is the freight train operations with transfer bridges used to load and unload railroad freight cars onto barges. At right is the ferry terminal building that was the connection to the West Shore Railroad and carried trains through the Forty-eighth Street tunnel and to all points north, including Albany and Buffalo.

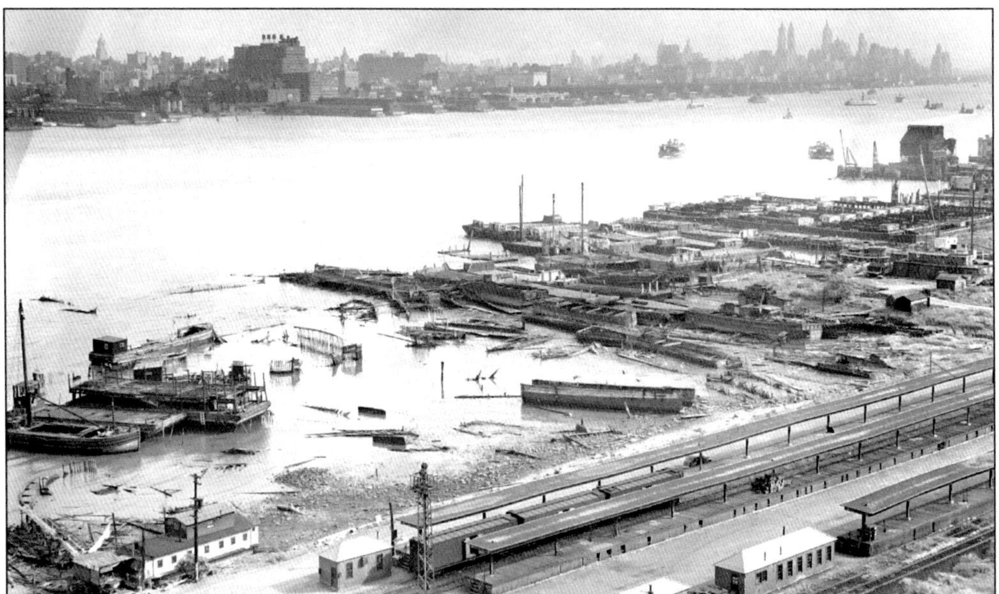

This photograph, taken from the bluff, looks down on the Delaware and Hudson Coal Canal basin and south to some of the burned out Erie Railroad piers that were destroyed by a multimillion-dollar fire in 1921. The waterfront was still active at this time as evidenced by the boxcars at the rail freight terminals and the densely packed coal scows that were used in Erie's oil and coal facilities. (Al Berg.)

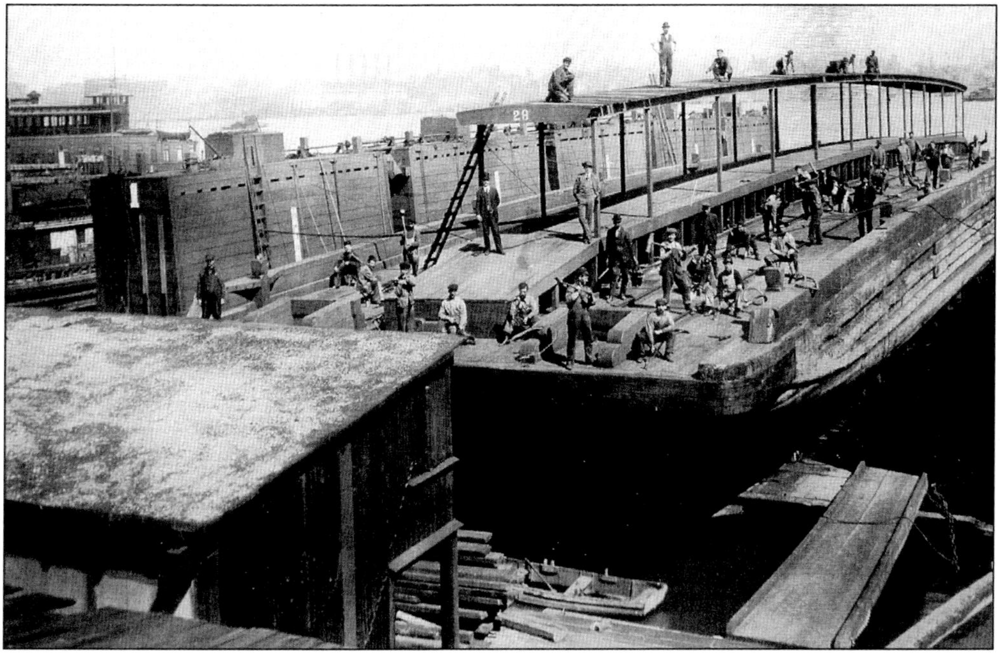

Workers pause to have their picture taken in this 1910 photograph of the Union Dry Dock and Repair Company from the Hudson Waterfront Museum collection. Incorporated in 1908, Union Dry Dock has operated continuously since then, first in Weehawken and now in Hoboken. The apparatus would sink down to allow a vessel to be positioned on the dock and then raised out of the water for the repairs to be made.

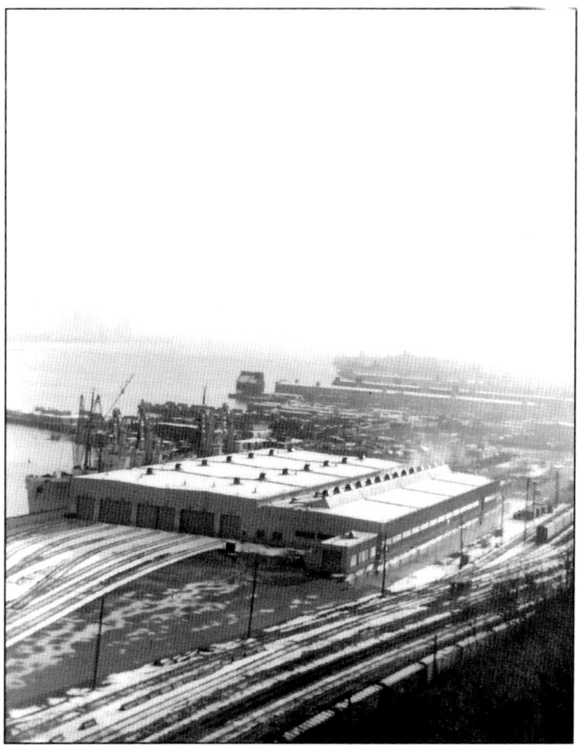

This mid-1950s photograph shows a snow-dusted United Fruit Company facility. Ships loaded with bananas docked beside the 1,000-foot-long terminal, giant gantry cranes dipped into the holds, and the bananas were transferred into the building by a curveyor, a conveyor belt that traveled 200 feet a minute around curves to load the bananas into refrigerated freight cars. The 136,000-square-foot warehouse was for many years the largest banana import facility in the nation.

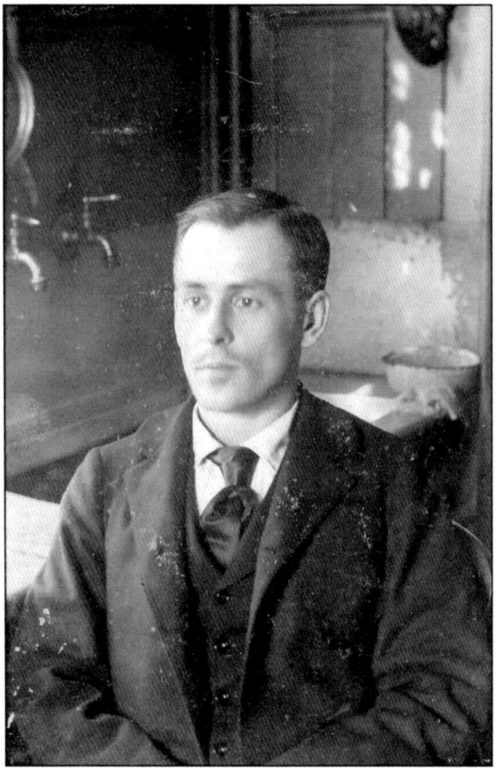

Convicted train bandit Oliver Curtis Perry was captured by railroad detective Edward Clifford of the West Shore Railroad near the depot after escaping from prison in 1895. Questioned by Police Chief Simon Kelly, he was taken to the Hudson County Jail in Jersey City and then sent back to prison. He was eventually moved to the State Hospital for the Criminally Insane at Dannemora, New York, where he died in 1930.

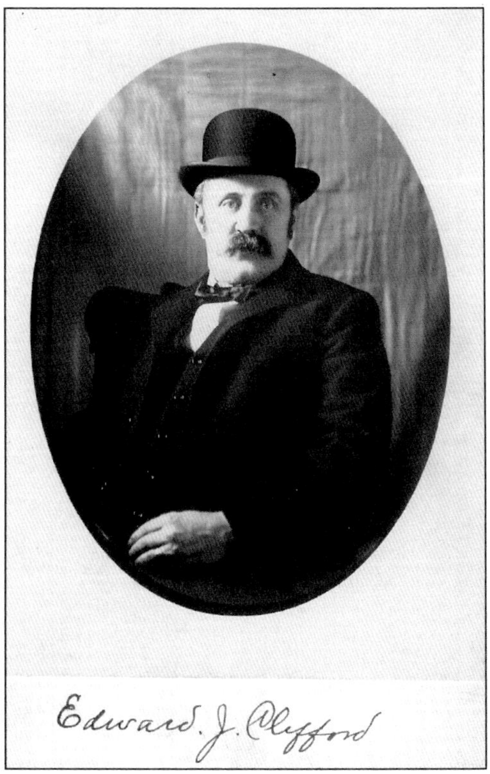

West Shore Railroad detective Cifford's case is an interesting piece of Weehawken history. He received a reward of $1,280 for the apprehension of notorious train robber Perry, after which time he began drinking. In 1896, having been warned about his behavior, he got into an argument with his boss, superintendent William G. Wattson, and was fired. He returned to the office and shot Wattson, who later died. Though the jury convicted him of murder, they recommended mercy; the judge did not agree, and he was sentenced to be hanged. Simon Kelly organized a benefit at the Eldorado casino to help raise money to appeal the case. Appeals and postponements continued until he was finally hanged in Jersey City on May 9, 1900.

Seven

The Lincoln Tunnel

Early in 1931, the Port of New York Authority, with the states of New York and New Jersey, authorized construction of a two-portal tunnel to facilitate vehicular traffic between Manhattan and New Jersey. By the end of 1931, the depressed economic climate of the country could not sustain a project of this size, and planning was suspended.

In September 1933, Public Works Administration funding paved the way for work to begin on the first tube, and official groundbreaking ceremonies took place on May 17, 1934. By August 1935, the tunnel was holed through. By 1936, improved economic conditions permitted work to begin on the second or north tube, and in late 1937, construction commenced on the connecting highway approach and marginal streets and ramps. Initially called the Midtown-Hudson Tunnel, in April 1937, the port authority changed the name to Lincoln Tunnel to avoid confusion with the Queens-Midtown Tunnel also under construction. Dedication ceremonies for the first two-lane tube were held on December 21, 1937, to great fanfare on both sides of the Hudson River.

On May 2, 1938, the north tube was holed through, but shortly thereafter, drilling halted due to insufficient funding. However, on October 15, 1938, the 4,000-foot concrete and steel loop or helix was opened, and on June 30, 1939, the depressed expressway from the tunnel entrance plaza through to the Meadowlands was brought on line. In April 1941, construction resumed on the north tube, and it finally opened on February 1, 1945.

With vehicular traffic increasing, the port authority laid plans for a third tube and began construction on June 2, 1953, without permits, claiming that the tube was an addition to an existing facility and not a new project. Weehawken did not agree. The local police, with Mayor Charles F. Krause Jr. in attendance, stopped work. A series of suits, countersuits, and other legal maneuvers followed, and in 1954, a financial settlement of $300,000 was paid to Weehawken. The third and final tube of the Lincoln Tunnel, built at a cost of $94,129,000, opened on May 25, 1957.

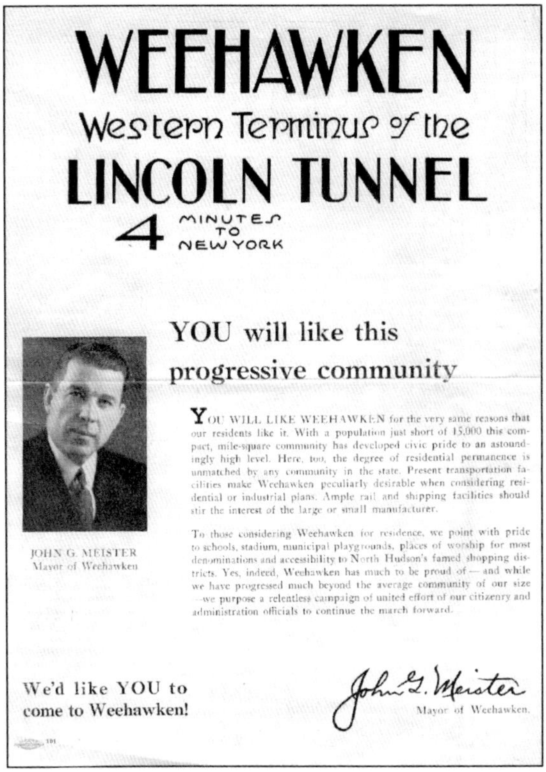

WEEHAWKEN

Western Terminus of the

LINCOLN TUNNEL

4 MINUTES TO NEW YORK

YOU will like this progressive community

JOHN G. MEISTER
Mayor of Weehawken

YOU WILL LIKE WEEHAWKEN for the very same reasons that our residents like it. With a population just short of 15,000 this compact, mile-square community has developed civic pride to an astoundingly high level. Here, too, the degree of residential permanence is unmatched by any community in the state. Present transportation facilities make Weehawken peculiarly desirable when considering residential or industrial plans. Ample rail and shipping facilities should stir the interest of the large or small manufacturer.

To those considering Weehawken for residence, we point with pride to schools, stadium, municipal playgrounds, places of worship for most denominations and accessibility to North Hudson's famed shopping districts. Yes, indeed, Weehawken has much to be proud of — and while we have progressed much beyond the average community of our size —we purpose a relentless campaign of united effort of our citizenry and administration officials to continue the march forward.

We'd like YOU to come to Weehawken!

John G. Meister
Mayor of Weehawken.

This brochure, with Mayor John G. Meister promoting the amenities of the township, was published to entice those looking to relocate in New Jersey to choose Weehawken. The completion of the first tube of the Lincoln Tunnel in 1937 and its convenient, four-minute travel to Manhattan from New Jersey made the area an especially appealing option for disenchanted New Yorkers.

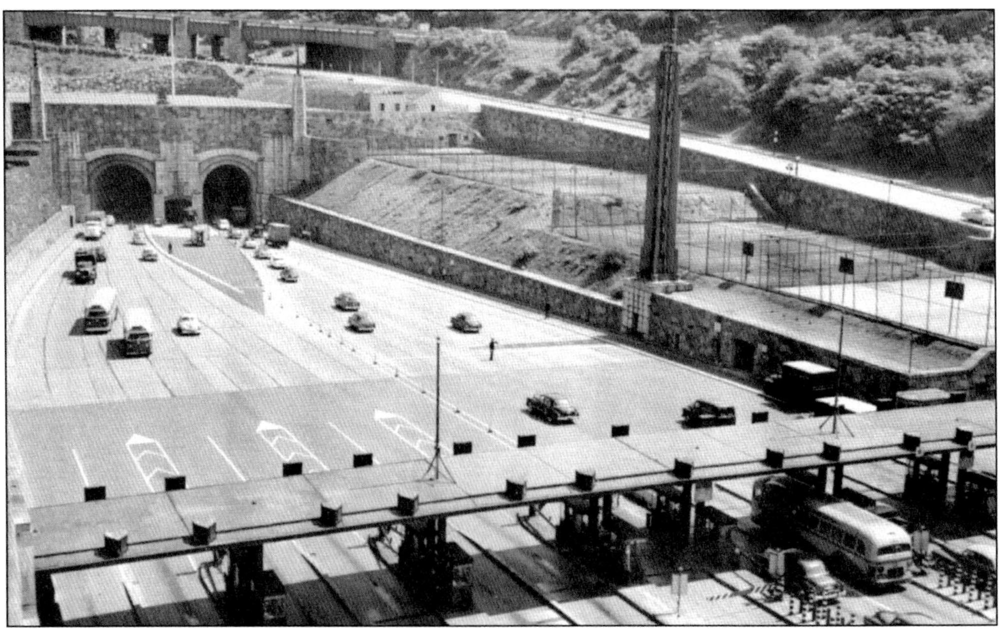

Traffic moved smoothly through the New Jersey tollbooths and the two tunnel tubes in the late 1940s. Work had started on the north tube in 1936 and was ahead of schedule but was stopped for a time due to shortages of metal for the war effort and lack of funding. The tube was sealed over in August 1939 until April 1941, when construction resumed. The second tube was completed at a cost of $80 million and opened on February 1, 1945. (Al Berg.)

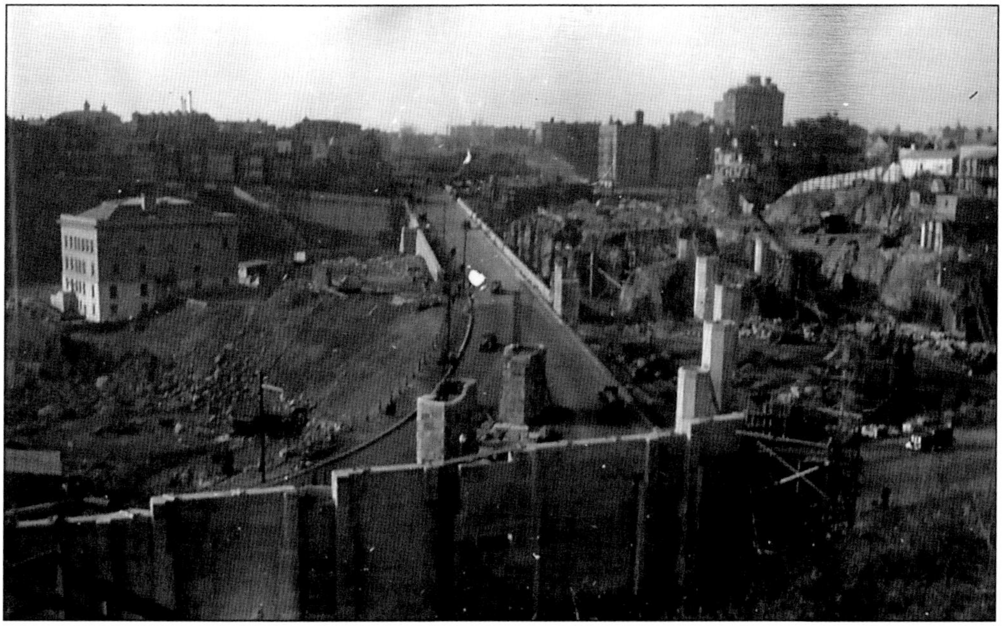

This photograph shows the Park Avenue viaduct fairly complete, which dates it from 1937 or early 1938. North of the viaduct, some of the walls, stanchions, and pylons are in place for the concrete roadway structure that is yet to come. The back of town hall is at left.

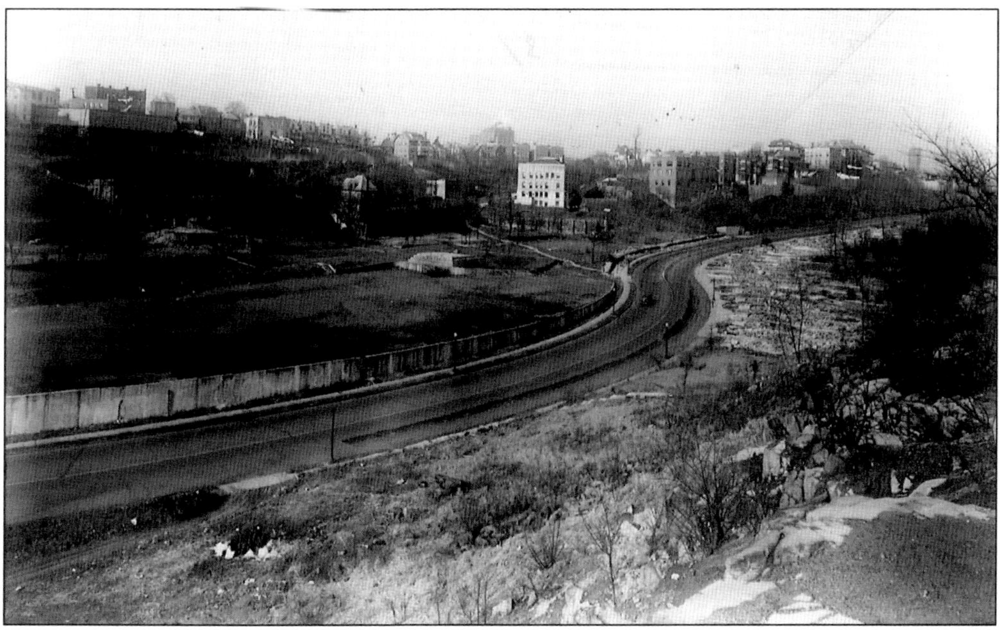

Groundbreaking ceremonies were held on May 17, 1934, for the Midtown-Hudson Tunnel both in New York and at the Weehawken playground, which was later demolished as part of the tunnel construction. There were also 26 homes demolished along Boulevard East in this section of town, as seen here on the right side where the boulevard curves and rises in this 1936 photograph.

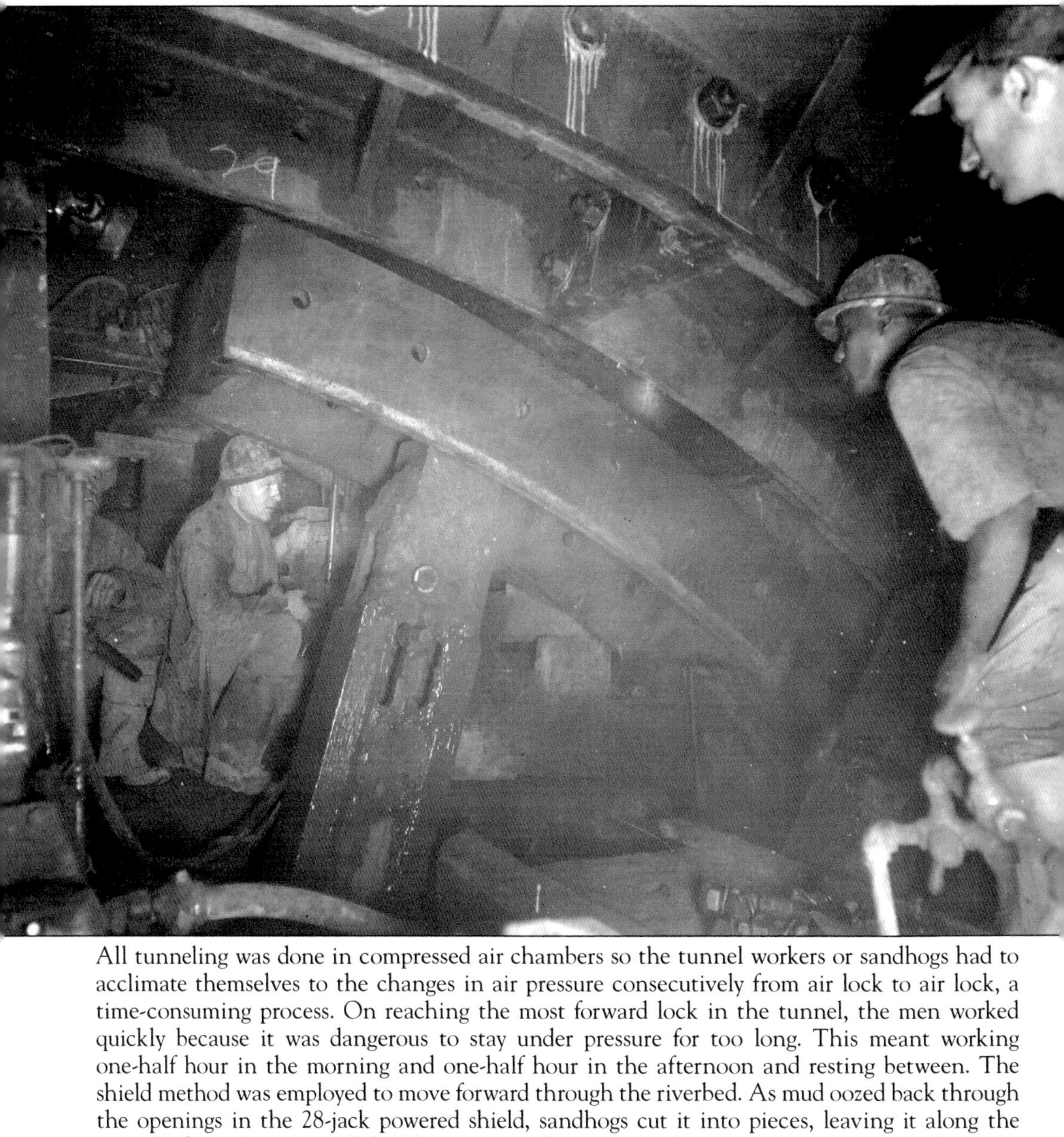

All tunneling was done in compressed air chambers so the tunnel workers or sandhogs had to acclimate themselves to the changes in air pressure consecutively from air lock to air lock, a time-consuming process. On reaching the most forward lock in the tunnel, the men worked quickly because it was dangerous to stay under pressure for too long. This meant working one-half hour in the morning and one-half hour in the afternoon and resting between. The shield method was employed to move forward through the riverbed. As mud oozed back through the openings in the 28-jack powered shield, sandhogs cut it into pieces, leaving it along the tunnel's floor. Segments of the 14-piece tunnel ring plus a key segment were put in place one at a time by an erector arm then sealed by hand. Each segment weighed more than 1.5 tons. Completion of a ring took one and a half hours; the first tube took three years and seven months to complete.

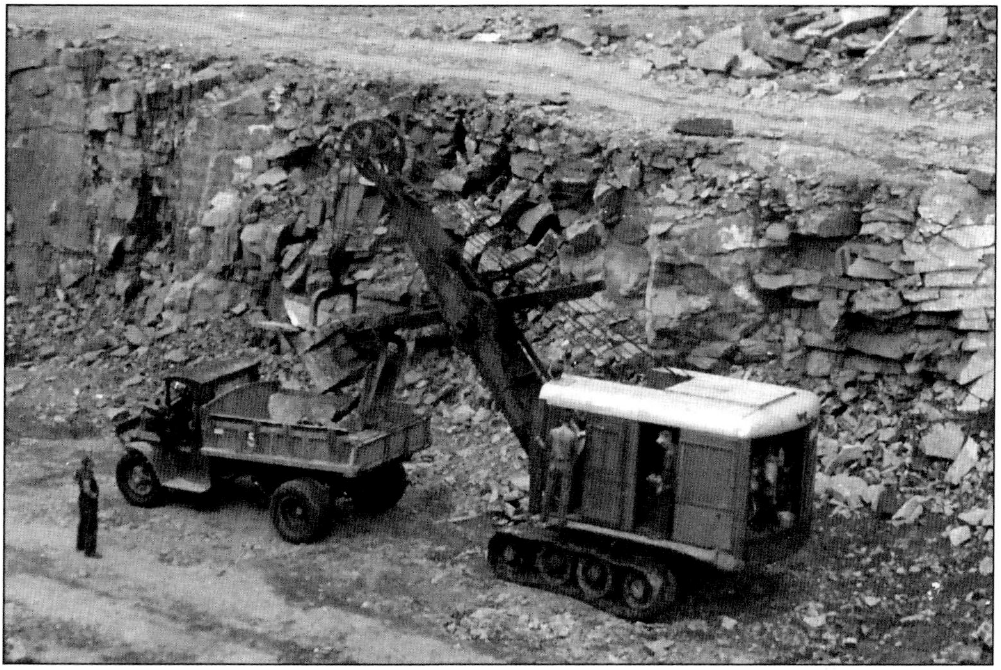

The construction of the marginal streets and ramps that ran along either side of the helix and allowed local traffic access was part of the initial unit of the express roadway structure. The first section of concrete roadway for the tunnel approach was laid on September 18, 1937.

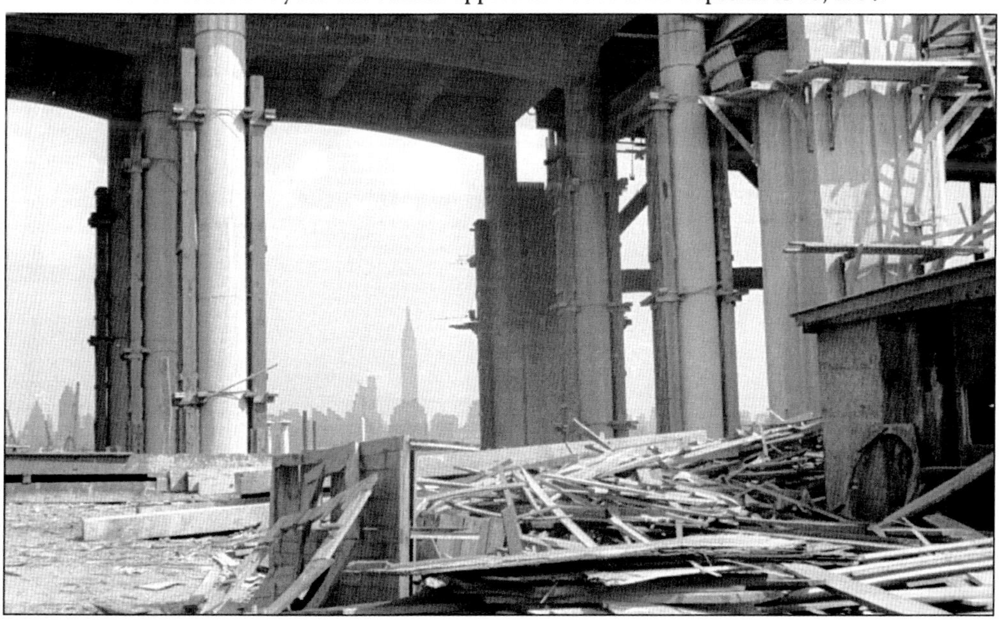

After the first tube opened in December 1937, tunneling continued on the north tube but was halted in 1938. However, all haste was made on the roadway loop to get it completed as quickly as possible. The six-lane loop, or the helix, as locals call it, is seen here still under construction in the early part of 1938. The helix was eventually expanded in 1957 to coincide with the completion of the third tube. A fourth west-bound lane was added, terminating at the Boulevard East exit.

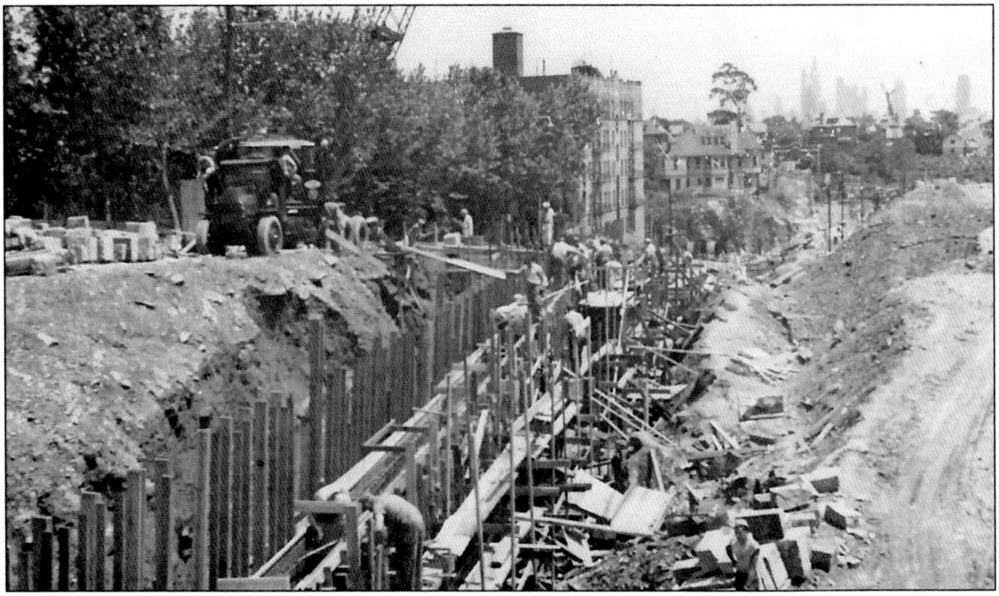

The north side of the marginal highway under construction dates this photograph from 1937 or early 1938, looking towards Park Avenue, the Weehawken Library, and east to New York. The work of the loop and secondary roadways was not completed until October of the following year. The 1939 New York World's Fair that was in planning since 1935 was part of the impetus to get these ancillary roads built quickly to support the expected influx of automobiles traveling into New York.

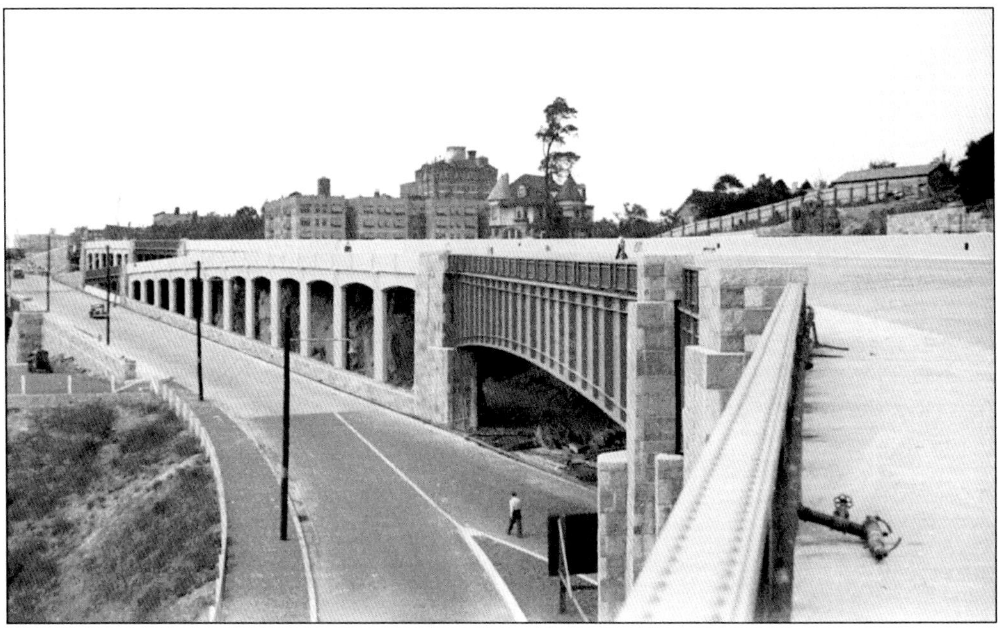

The 4,000-foot concrete and steel loop roadway was finally opened on October 16, 1938, with representatives of the Port of New York Authority and township officials on hand. By increasing the distance from the roadway to the tunnel approach, it allowed for vehicles to adjust to the grade so that the roadway could be negotiated in high gear, similar to roadways designed in the Rocky Mountains.

This pristine view of the first tube was probably taken near its opening on December 22, 1937. According to the *New York Times*, during its first 24 hours of operation, 7,661 motor vehicles passed through the tunnel. Ventilation is provided by the tunnel vent towers that stand on either side of the Hudson River. Exhaust fans remove the depleted air from the tubes, and blower fans carry fresh air from the towers into the tunnels by means of an air duct. The air in the tunnels is changed every one and one-half minutes. (Ellen Robb Gaulkin.)

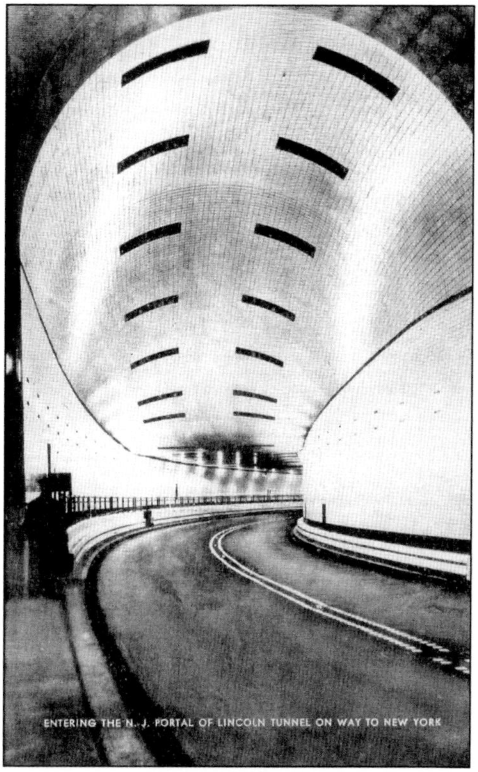

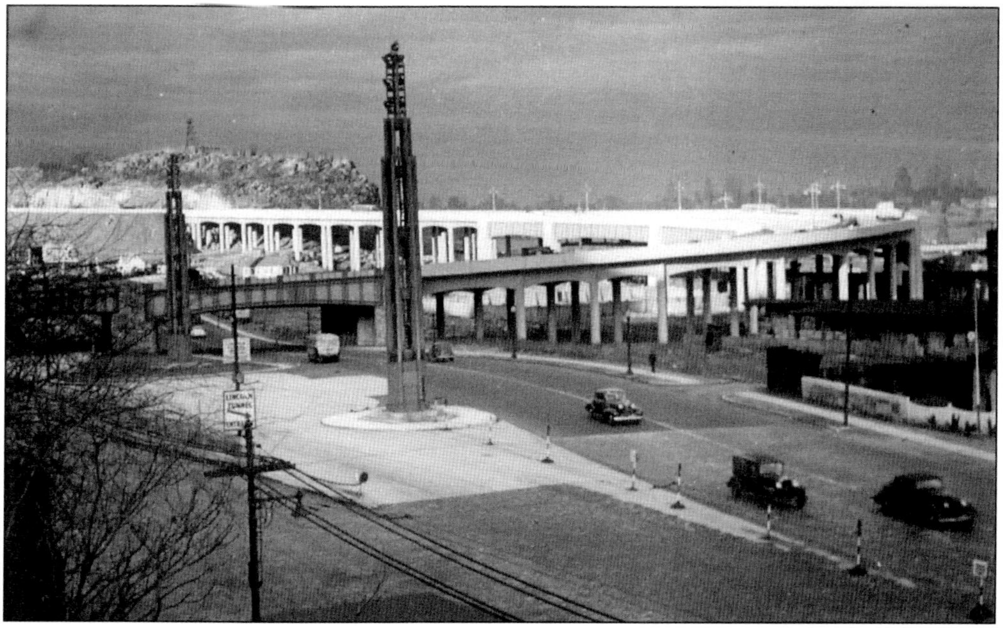

The helix opened in the fall of 1938 and would, with the completion of the depressed roadway to which it was joined, provide a seamless highway approach to the tunnel plaza. Shown here with its gleaming new concrete cladding, it is understandable why it was placed on the New Jersey and National Registers of Historic Places. The beautiful art deco light towers add a further sense of drama to this late-afternoon scene.

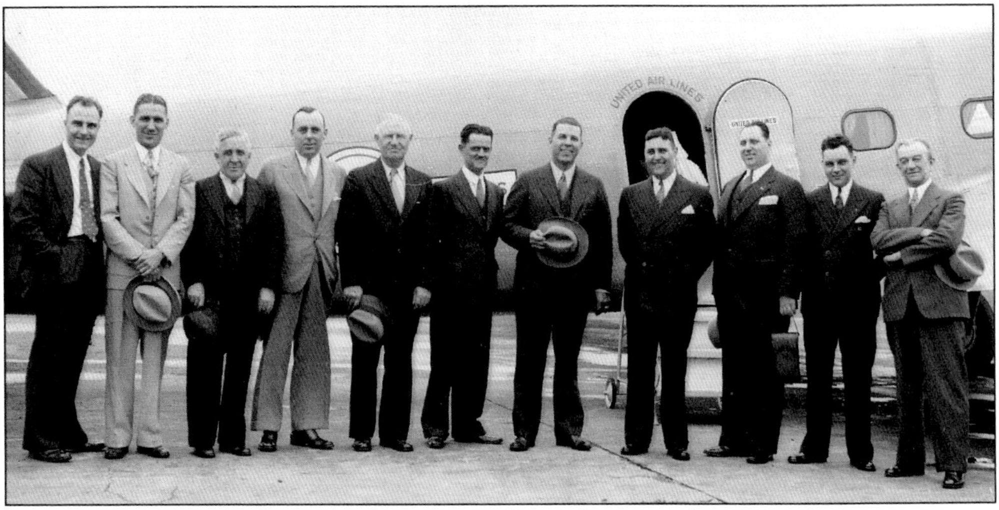

This photograph was taken to commemorate the Midtown-Hudson Tunnel inspection party on May 13, 1936. M. P. Bickley of United Air Lines invited Weehawken township committee members and several guests to view the work on the tunnel from on high despite lightening flashes and low cloud cover. Pictured from left to right are George J. Bergdolt (assistant township clerk), M. P. Bickley, committeeman Thomas A. Donlan, Leo P. Carroll (township clerk), committeeman Henry H. Nagel, W. G. Armbruster of the Packard Motor Car Company of Jersey City, Mayor John G. Meister, Lt. S. D. Sullivan of the Jersey City Police Department, committeeman Fred Bergmann Jr., W. F. Bauer of the Packard Motor Car Company of Jersey City, and committeeman G. H. Hilge.

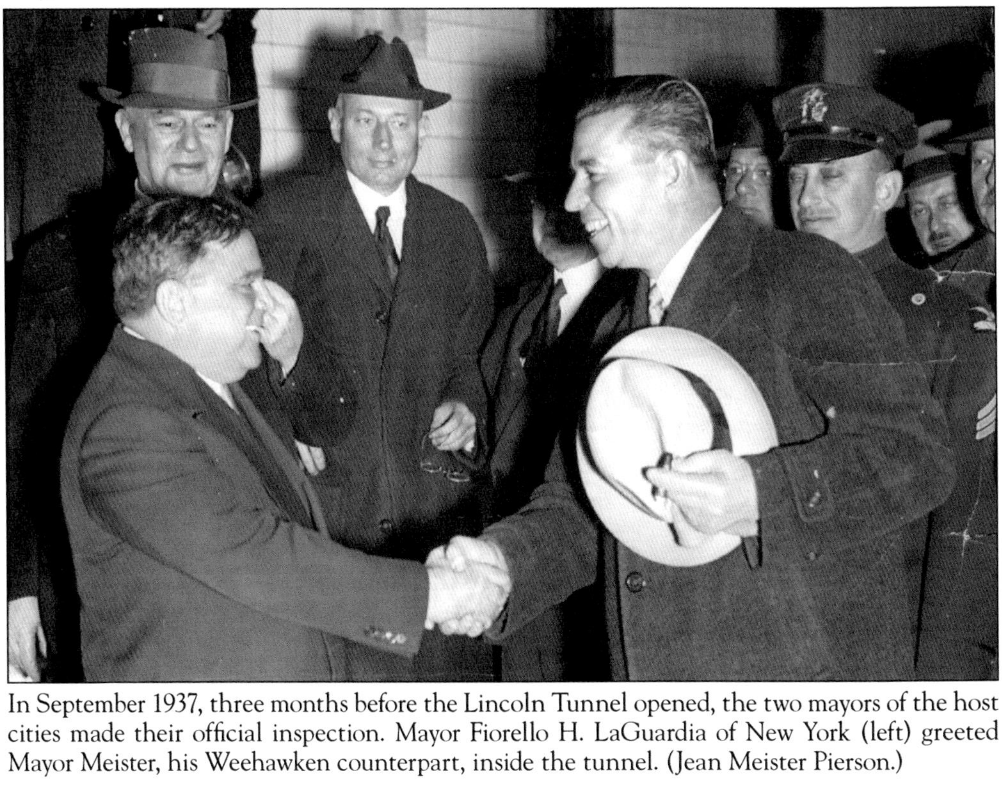

In September 1937, three months before the Lincoln Tunnel opened, the two mayors of the host cities made their official inspection. Mayor Fiorello H. LaGuardia of New York (left) greeted Mayor Meister, his Weehawken counterpart, inside the tunnel. (Jean Meister Pierson.)

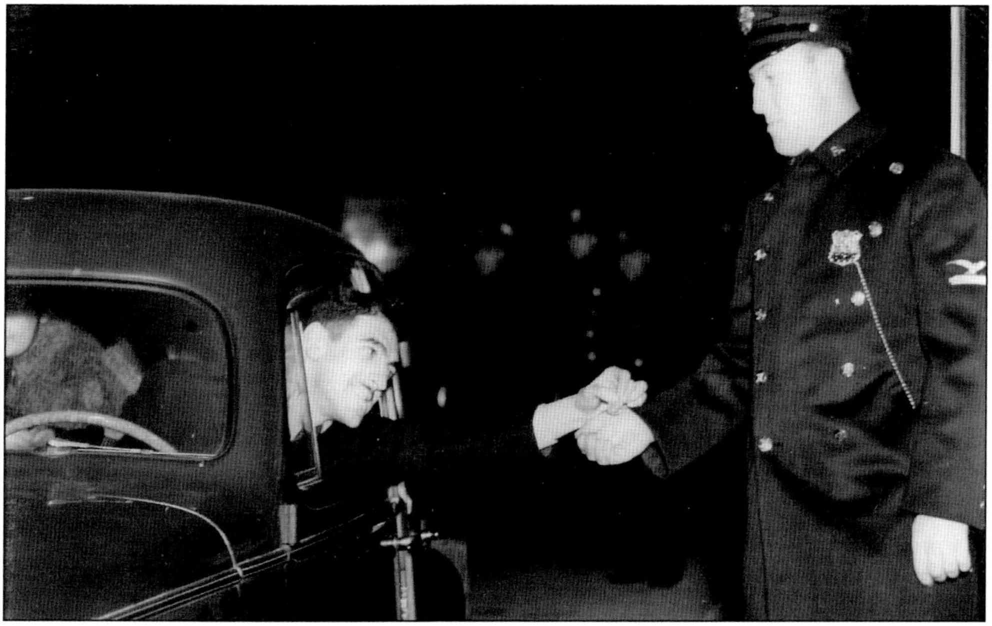

The Lincoln Tunnel opened for business on December 22, 1937. This photograph from the Port Authority of New York and New Jersey captures Omero C. Catan, a 23-year-old salesman from Manhattan, paying the first toll at the New Jersey Plaza at 4:00 a.m., after sleeping all night in his car parked at the entrance. The toll was 50¢. His brother Michael Catan was selected to be the first to lead the public through the second tube opening on February 1, 1945.

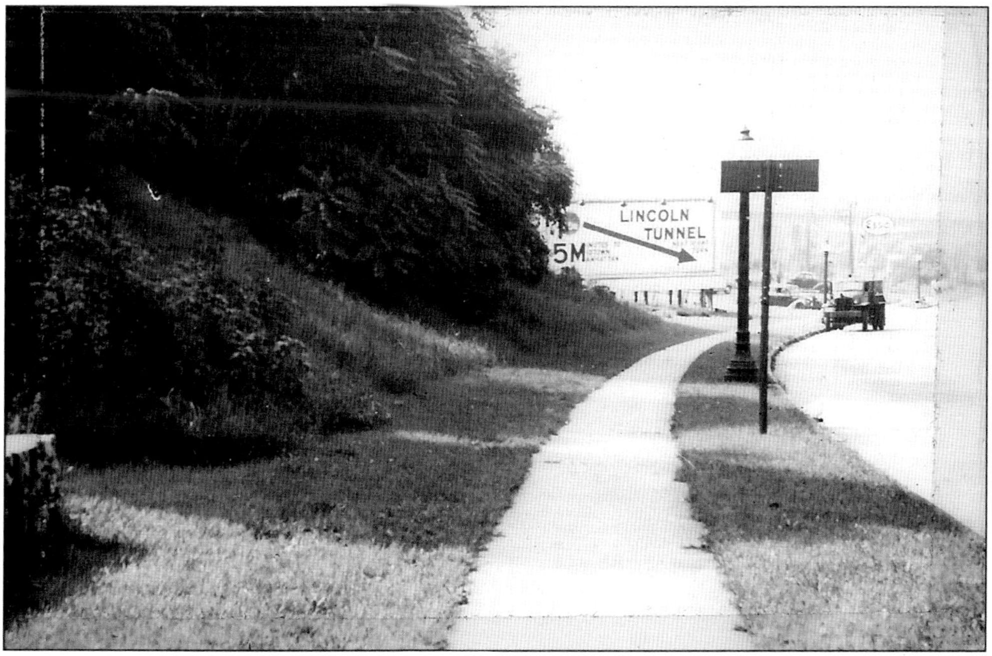

Driving down Boulevard East toward the local Lincoln Tunnel entrance in the 1940s, one would have encountered this sign on the east side of the street. Due to the escalating tunnel traffic, the original "4 minutes to New York" advertised on matchbooks and in the mayor's brochure was revised to "5 minutes to midtown Manhattan."

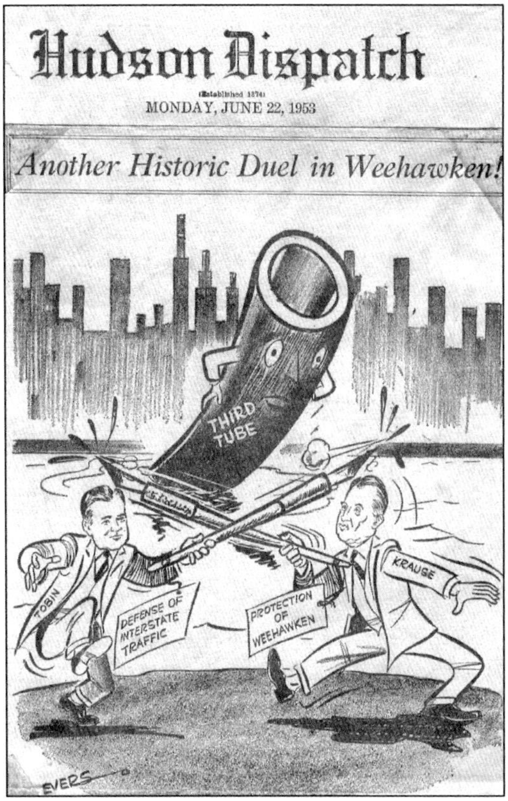

This political cartoon, with its Hamilton-Burr duel reference, depicting Weehawken mayor Charles F. Krause Jr. doing battle by pen with August J. Tobin, executive director of the port authority, was published in the *Hudson Dispatch* on June 22, 1953, and drawn by Frank Evers. In 1953, with two tubes completed and work already begun on the third, a New Jersey legislative committee held hearings to determine how much the Port of New York Authority should pay the Township of Weehawken as remuneration for increased municipal services, loss of property, and increased traffic associated with the new tube. Just prior to these hearings, the township's police department had stopped work by stationing themselves in front of the construction site. (Jersey Journal.)

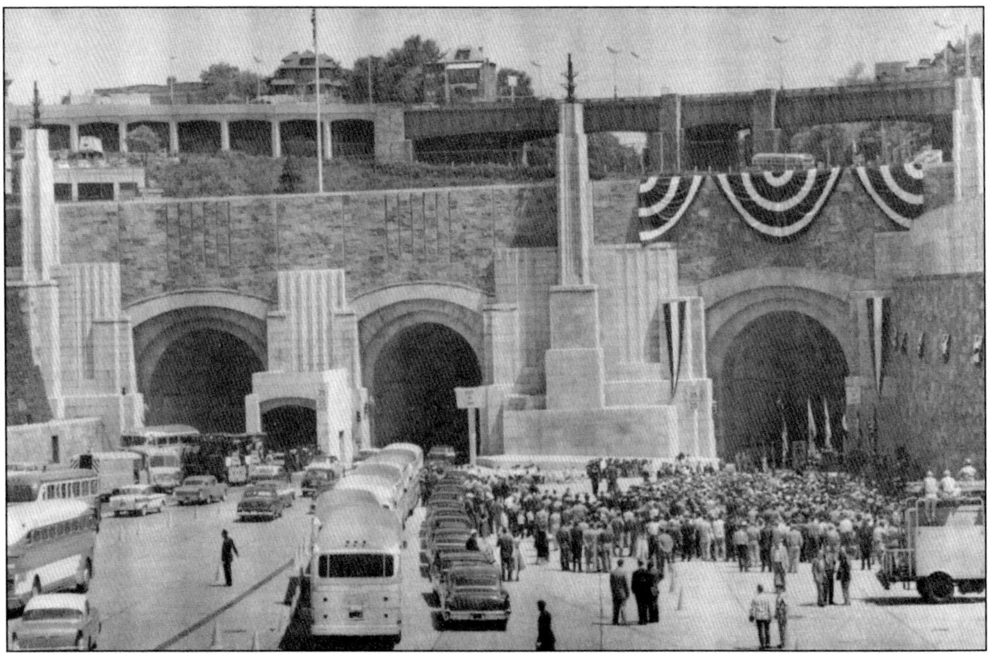

This photograph celebrates the opening of the third or south tube of the Lincoln Tunnel on May 25, 1957. By this time, midtown-bound traffic had increased so much that the two other tubes were occupied with the usual rush hour delays while the third dedication took place. (Al Berg.)

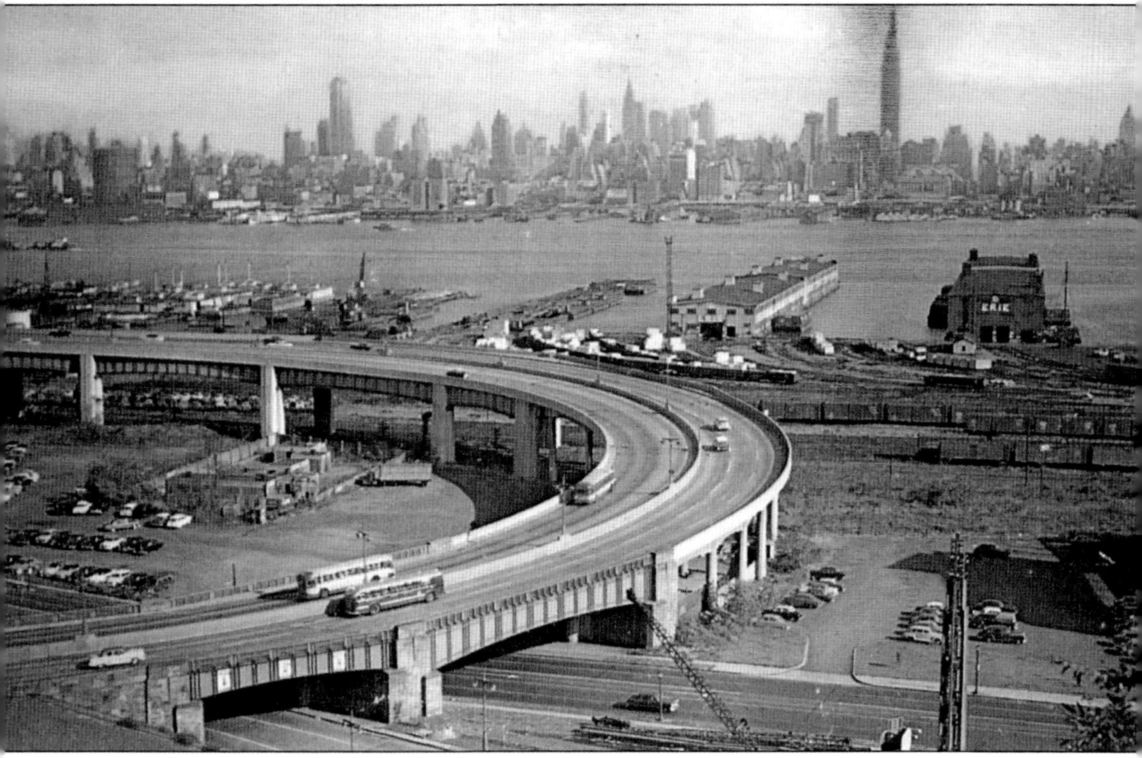

This 1950s view shows an almost empty helix, and encircled by the loop is a commuter parking lot, now the New Jersey Transit bus lot. The Erie Railroad compound, adjacent to the helix and tunnel entrance on the waterfront, had been a presence in Weehawken from the 1860s. By the mid-20th century, there were six Erie piers on the waterfront, three open and three covered, involved in the shipping, storage, and transfer of industrial goods. After the Erie Railroad merged with the Delaware, Lackawanna and Western Railroad in 1960, the property was sold in 1969 to Seatrain Lines, a container shipping company that went bankrupt in 1981. The tract was bought by Hartz Mountain Industries, which started construction of the Lincoln Harbor development in the late 1980s. The site currently encompasses the Chart House pier, 1500 Harbor Boulevard, the Lincoln Harbor Yacht Club directly adjacent, and the Riva Point development. The dazzling New York skyline was and still is a magnificent backdrop to this transportation hub. (Steve Dorio.)

Discover Thousands of Local History Books Featuring Millions of Vintage Images

Arcadia Publishing, the leading local history publisher in the United States, is committed to making history accessible and meaningful through publishing books that celebrate and preserve the heritage of America's people and places.

Find more books like this at
www.arcadiapublishing.com

Search for your hometown history, your old stomping grounds, and even your favorite sports team.

Consistent with our mission to preserve history on a local level, this book was printed in South Carolina on American-made paper and manufactured entirely in the United States. Products carrying the accredited Forest Stewardship Council (FSC) label are printed on 100 percent FSC-certified paper.

MADE IN THE USA